other books by Ronald J. Sider:

Andreas Bodenstein von Karlstadt: The Development of His Thought (1517-1525). *"Studies in Medieval and Reformation Thought," No. 11. Leiden: Brill, 1974.*

The Chicago Declaration. *Carol Stream, Ill.: Creation House, 1974.*

The Graduated Tithe. *Downers Grove, Ill.: InterVarsity Press, 1978.*

Karlstadt's Battle with Luther. *Philadelphia: Fortress Press, 1978.*

Christ and Violence. *Scottdale, Pa.: Herald Press, 1979.*

(Editor) Cry Justice! The Bible Speaks on Hunger and Poverty. *Downers Grove, Ill.: InterVarsity Press, 1980.*

(Editor) Living More Simply: Biblical Principles and Practical Models. *Downers Grove, Ill.: InterVarsity Press, 1980.*

(Editor) A Lifestyle for the Eighties: An Evangelical Commitment to Simple Lifestyle. *Philadelphia, Pa.: Westminster Press, 1982.*

(with Richard K. Taylor) Nuclear Holocaust and Christian Hope. *Downers Grove, Ill.: InterVarsity Press, 1982.*

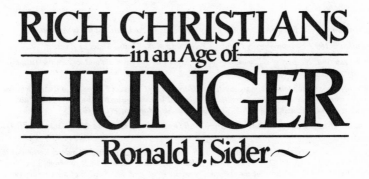

RICH CHRISTIANS
in an Age of
HUNGER
～Ronald J. Sider～

A Biblical Study

REVISED
& EXPANDED

INTER-VARSITY PRESS
DOWNERS GROVE
ILLINOIS 60515

InterVarsity Press is the book-publishing division of Inter-Varsity Christian Fellowship, a student movement active on campus at hundreds of universities, colleges and schools of nursing. For information about local and regional activities, write IVCF, 233 Langdon St., Madison, WI 53703.

Distributed in Canada through InterVarsity Press, 860 Denison St., Unit 3, Markham, Ontario L3R 4H1, Canada.

Cover illustration: Roberta Polfus

ISBN 0-87784-977-3

Printed in the United States of America

Library of Congress Cataloging in Publication Data

Sider, Ronald J.
   Rich Christians in an age of hunger.

   Bibliography: p.
   Includes indexes.
   1. Economics in the Bible. 2. Hunger–Religious
aspects–Christianity. 3. Food supply–Religious aspects
–Christianity. 4. Simplicity–Religious aspects–
Christianity. I. Title.
BS670.S48   1984   261.8'5   84-4549
ISBN 0-87784-977-3

18	17	16	15	14	13	12	11	10	9	8	7	6	5	4	3	2	1
99	98	97	96	95	94	93	92	91	90	89	88	87	86	85	84		

Acknowledgments

I have benefited from the critical comments of many good friends who read parts of the first draft: Judy and John F. Alexander, Arthur Simon, Edgar Stoesz, Richard Taylor, Carol and Merold Westphal. Since I am not an economist, I particularly appreciate the extensive help of two friends who are: Carl Gambs and John Mason. I stubbornly rejected their advice on occasion. Hence they cannot be faulted for the results. But their help and friendship are deeply appreciated.

To Debbie Reumann and Titus Peachy I give special thanks for long hours spent at the typewriter. To Mrs. Anne Allen who typed some of the early chapters, I want to express deep appreciation for her superb secretarial and administrative assistance over several years.

Finally I want to thank HIS magazine for publishing an early version of chapter seven, and Ashland Theological Seminary and Emmanuel School of Religion for the opportunity to present parts of this material as public lectures.

Perhaps all books must be lived before they are written. That is certainly true of books like this one. I must immediately confess that I make no claim to be living out the full implications of this book. But I have begun the pilgrimage. The most important reason I am even a little way down the path is my wife, Arbutus Lichti Sider. Always enthusiastic about a simpler living standard, spontaneously generous and eager to experiment, she has slowly tugged me along. For her critical reading of the manuscript, for our life together without which this book would never have been possible and for her love, I express my deepest appreciation.

Note to the second edition:

In revising chapters one, two, six and nine, I benefited greatly from the extensive assistance of Roland Hoksbergen, now assistant professor of economics at Calvin College. His help and patience are deeply appreciated. In addition, a number of friends who are economists provided critical reaction either to the first edition or to a preliminary draft of the second: Robert Chase, Carl Gambs, Donald Hay, Carl Kreider, John Mason, Henry Rempel and John P. Tiemstra. None of them, I am sure, will be fully satisfied with all my final decisions. Their much appreciated counsel, however, has significantly improved the text.

Helping on this revised edition, Robin Songer was her usual efficient, precise self as she worked with my short deadlines.

PART 3   Implementation

Introduction

Hunger and starvation stalk the land. Famine is alive and well on planet earth. Millions of people die of starvation each year. Even the most conservative statistics reflect a horrifying situation. In his 1982-83 report, the director of the United Nations Children's Fund reported that forty thousand young children die every day of malnutrition and diseases related to malnutrition. He also reported that one quarter of the children in the developing world suffer from malnutrition. One billion of the world's people have an annual income of less than $50 a year.[1]

Can overfed, comfortably clothed and luxuriously housed persons understand poverty? Can we truly feel what it is like to be a nine-year-old boy playing outside a village school which he cannot attend because his father is unable to afford the necessary books? (The books would cost less than my wife and I spent on some entertainment one evening during the writing of this book.) Can we really feel what it means for poverty-stricken parents to watch with helpless grief as their baby daughter dies of a common childhood disease because, like one-third of our global neighbors even today, they lack access to modern medicine? Probably not.

We can, however, make an attempt to understand. We can search for honest answers to questions such as these: How many people are actually hungry today? What are the effects of poverty? Tear-jerking rhetoric aside, how great is the gap between the rich and poor today? And how does our affluence look in comparison with their poverty?

This book develops a biblical response. Part 1 sketches the setting with a brief overview of world poverty and the affluence of the Northern Hemisphere. The heart of our study is Part 2, "A Biblical Perspective on the Poor and Possessions." Part 3 develops concrete suggestions for the individual, the church and society.

Part 1

Poor Lazarus & Rich Christians

1

A Billion Hungry Neighbors

Sometimes I think, "If I die, I won't have to see my children suffering as they are." Sometimes I even think of killing myself. So often I see them crying, hungry; and there I am, without a cent to buy them some bread. I think, "My God, I can't face it! I'll end my life. I don't want to look any more!"[1] [Iracema da Silva, resident of a slum in Brazil]

What does poverty really mean in daily life?

One way to try and answer this question is to list what a typical Western family would need to give up if they were to adopt the lifestyle of a typical family living among our billion hungry neighbors. Economist Robert Heilbroner has itemized the abandoned "luxuries."

We begin by invading the house of our imaginary American family to strip it of its furniture. Everything goes: beds, chairs, tables, television set, lamps. We will leave the family with a few old blankets, a kitchen table, a wooden chair. Along with the bureaus go the clothes. Each member of the family may keep in his "wardrobe" his oldest suit or dress, a shirt or blouse. We will permit a pair of shoes for the head of the family, but none for the wife or children.

We move to the kitchen. The appliances have already been taken out, so we turn to the cupboards. . . . The box of matches may stay, a small bag of flour, some sugar and salt. A few moldy potatoes, already in the garbage can, must be hastily rescued, for they will provide much of tonight's meal. We will leave a handful of onions, and a dish of dried beans. All the rest we take away: the meat, the fresh vegetables, the canned goods, the crackers, the candy.

Now we have stripped the house: the bathroom has been dismantled, the running water shut off, the electric wires taken out. Next we take away the house. The family can move to the toolshed....

Communications must go next. No more newspapers, magazines, books—not that they are missed, since we must take away our family's literacy as well. Instead, in our shantytown we will allow one radio....

Now government services must go. No more postman, no more firemen. There is a school, but it is three miles away and consists of two classrooms.... There are, of course, no hospitals or doctors nearby. The nearest clinic is ten miles away and is tended by a midwife. It can be reached by bicycle, provided that the family has a bicycle, which is unlikely....

Finally, money. We will allow our family a cash hoard of $5.00. This will prevent our breadwinner from experiencing the tragedy of an Iranian peasant who went blind because he could not raise the $3.94 which he mistakenly thought he needed to receive admission to a hospital where he could have been cured.[2]

How many of our brothers and sisters confront that kind of grinding poverty today? Probably at least one billion people are as poor as this, although it is difficult to obtain precise statistics. A Bread for the World (BFW) Background Paper reported in August 1982 that there were one billion people in poor nations who existed on incomes of only $50 per year.[3] Recent World Bank reports refer to more than 800 million who are "destitute."[4] A special supplement to the UN publication *Development Forum* entitled "Facts on Food" (November 1974) estimated that "half the world's population, 2000 million, is badly nourished." We will use a fairly conservative figure of one billion persons who are malnourished in an average year, although this figure rises steeply at times of world food shortage, such as occurred between 1972 and 1974. The figure may, of course, be lower when crops, particularly those in the developing countries, are good; fortunately, the years between 1975 and 1982 saw such crops.

New Economic Divisions in the Third World

Almost all of the billion desperately poor people live in the Third World. Until recently, all countries that were not a part of the developed world (whether capitalist or communist) were lumped together as "Third World" nations. But changes in the last decade, especially since the tripling of oil prices in 1973, require a new division into low income and middle income Third World countries.

India, Bangladesh, Pakistan and many African countries, including Ethiopia, Burundi, Chad, Tanzania and Somalia, belong to the low income countries. Typically, less than one person in four is literate, though in India literacy is 36 per cent and in Tanzania it is 74 per cent.[5] Infant mortality rates are up to ten times higher than in the developed world, and population growth rates are higher (see below, tables 1 and 4). Unless there are major internal and external changes, there is little prospect of a significant improvement in the appalling condition for the people in these low income countries. Hunger will continue to strike down millions.

Some of the Third World countries have a somewhat brighter future. Most Latin American countries and a few other countries in Asia and Africa are known as middle income countries. Some of these nations have experienced significant economic growth. Tragically this has seldom been of any real help to the poor. Brazil and Mexico are classic examples.

In Brazil a military dictatorship strongly supported by the United States fostered real economic growth at the rate of 10 per cent per year from 1968 to 1974. Growth of about 9 per cent per year continued through 1980.[6] But who profited? Even Brazil's own minister of finance admitted in 1972 that only 5 per cent of the people had benefited from the fantastic growth of the Brazilian economy. The Brazilian government did not challenge a 1974 study that showed that the real purchasing power of the poorest two-thirds of the people had declined by more than one-half in the preceding ten years. In 1975, 58 per cent of Brazilian *children* under the age of eighteen were malnourished.[7] In 1980, 40 per cent of the *total population* suffered from malnutrition.[8]

In Brazil in 1972, 60 per cent of the people received only about 16 per cent of the country's total income. The richest 10 per cent, on the other hand, received over 50 per cent of the country's income. From 1960 to 1972 the poorest 40 per cent saw their share of total income decline from 10 to 7 per cent.[9] The infant mortality rate is one of the most sensitive indicators of whether a society is meeting the basic needs of the poorest 50 per cent of its population. In Brazil, the urban infant mortality rate rose between 1961 and 1970 from 103 to 109 per thousand.[10] (Unfortunately, more recent information on the distribution of income and the infant mortality rate, based on the 1980 census, is being withheld by the Brazilian government.)[11]

Things have probably become worse in the last decade for the poor in Brazil, as they have suffered most from the problems experienced by the Brazilian economy since the rise in oil prices in 1973. Tragically, Brazil's rapid economic growth has done little to help the people who need it most.

In Mexico, where average per capita income grew in real terms by 2.7 per cent a year between 1960 and 1978, the richest 20 per cent managed to edge their share of income up from 56.5 per cent to 57.7 per cent. Meanwhile the poor got a smaller share. In 1968 the botton 40 per cent got 12.2 per cent of the income pie; by 1977 it was below 10 per cent. The poorest 20 per cent saw their share cut from 3.6 per cent to below 3 per cent. This is not to say that the poor actually had lower incomes. Figures show that the per capita income of the poorest 20 per cent of the people stayed about the same, rising from $183 to about $187 per year. The wealthy 20 per cent, on the other hand, saw their incomes rise from $2,867 to $3,722. Thus the average poor person saw his meager income rise by $4 over a period of eighteen years, while the average rich person added $850 to his in the same period.[12]

The tears and agony of all these people are captured in the words of Mrs. Alarin from the Philippines. The Alarin family of seven live in an eight-by-ten-foot room. Cooking utensils are their only furniture. Mr. Alarin makes 70¢ on good days as an ice vendor. Several times a month Mrs. Alarin stays up all night to make a coconut sweet which she sells on the street. Total income for her midnight toil: 40¢. The family had not tasted meat for a month when Stanley Mooneyham of World Vision visited Mrs. Alarin:

> Tears washed her dark, sunken eye-sockets as she spoke: "I feel so sad when my children cry at night because they have no food. I know my life will never change. What can I do to solve my problems? I am so worried about the future of my children. I want

them to go to school but how can we afford it? I am sick most of the time, but I can't go to the doctor because each visit costs two pesos [28¢] and the medicine is extra. What can I do?" She broke down into quiet sobbing. I admit without shame that I wept with her.[13]

World poverty is a hundred million mothers weeping, like Mrs. Alarin, because they cannot feed their children.

What has led to our tragic situation?

The Background

In the late 1960s the Green Revolution created widespread optimism. Agricultural specialists produced new strains of rice and wheat. As a result, poor countries like Mexico and India were almost self-sufficient in cereals by the early 1970s. However, population growth had matched increased agricultural productivity,[14] so when there was a bad crop in 1972, as a result of bad weather conditions, starvation increased. Total world food production per capita declined substantially in 1972 for the first time since World War 2.

When oil prices tripled in 1973, farmers in the developing world could not afford the oil needed to run the irrigation pumps for the new strains of grain. Nor could they afford the necessary fertilizer which had increased in price by 150 per cent between 1972 and 1974.[15]

Tragically, poor harvests in North America, Europe, the U.S.S.R. and Japan combined with unexpectedly large U.S. sales of grain to the U.S.S.R. to almost triple the cost of grain for export in the same short period. When poor nations searched desperately for grain to feed their hungry masses in 1974, they had to pay two and a half times as much as two years earlier for every ton they needed. For some of the millions of people who were already spending 80 per cent of their budget on food, there was only one possible outcome—starvation. Millions died.

In 1975 good harvests returned, and through 1983 there were no worldwide problems like those of the early seventies. That is not to ignore *local* emergencies, such as Africa saw in 1984. But the long-term problems remain. John Sewell, of the Washington-based Overseas Development Council, notes that "even though total production has continued to increase in all regions (since 1970), per capita food production has barely increased in the developing countries." Sewell goes on to predict that "because 90% of the world population growth expected by 1990 will occur in the developing countries, these nations will at least have to double their imports in order to meet the increased demand forecast for 1990 *unless there is a fundamental improvement in their capacity to produce more food.*"[16] Rising imports of food by the poor countries will be a severe drain on their foreign exchange accounts if they are not able to increase exports enough to pay for the increasing quantities of imported food. And currently there is no compelling reason to believe their export industries will boom in the next decade.

Sewell is right. Unless there is a major international effort aimed specifically at improving the lot of the rural agricultural masses in the hungry nations, the lot of perhaps a billion persons will be the same in 1990 as it is today.

Famine Redefined
Lester Brown, one of the specialists on the hunger crisis, points out that we must redefine famine.

> One reason it is possible for the world's affluent to ignore such tragedies is that changes have occurred in the way that famine manifests itself. In earlier historical periods, ... whole nations ... experienced widespread starvation and death. Today the advancement in both national and international distribution systems has concentrated the effects of food scarcity among the world's poor, wherever they are.[17]

People with money can always buy food; famine affects only the poor.

When food scarcity triples the price of grain imports, as it did in 1972 to 1974, middle and upper income persons in developing countries continue to eat. But people who are already devoting 60 to 80 per cent of their income to food simply eat less and die sooner. Death usually results from a disease their underfed bodies could not resist.

Children are the first victims. In developing countries one child in four dies before the age of five. The infant mortality rate there is ten times higher than in developed countries. And half of these deaths are related to inadequate diets. In 1974 UNICEF estimated that 210 million children under five in the world were malnourished —one for every U.S. citizen.[18] In 1982-83, UNICEF reported the even more ghastly statistic that more than one of every four children in the developing world suffer from malnutrition.[19] Studies in Latin America, the World Bank reports, "show malnutrition to be either the primary cause of—or a major contributing factor in—50 to 75 per cent of the deaths of children under five years."[20]

Carolina Maria de Jesus helps one feel the terror and anguish endured by the poor in a land where they could have enough food. The feelings faithfully recorded daily on scraps of paper by this uneducated, brilliant woman who struggled to survive in the slums of Brazil's second largest city, Sâo Paulo, were published in a gripping diary called *Child of the Dark.*

Today I'm sad. I'm nervous. I don't know if I should start crying or start running until I fall unconscious. At dawn it was raining. I couldn't go out to get any money [she gathered junk each day to earn money for food]. . . . I have a few tin cans and a little scrap that I'm going to sell to Senhor Manuel. When Joâo came home from school, I sent him to sell the scrap. He got 13 cruzeiros. He bought a glass of mineral water: two cruzeiros. I was furious with him. . . .

The children eat a lot of bread. They like soft bread but when they don't have it, they eat hard bread. . . .

Oh Sâo Paulo! A queen that vainly shows her skyscrapers that are her crown of gold. All dressed up in velvet and silk but with cheap stockings underneath—the *favela* [the slum].

The money didn't stretch far enough to buy meat, so I cooked macaroni with a carrot. I didn't have any grease, it was horrible. Vera was the only one who complained yet asked for more.

"Mama, sell me to Dona Julita, because she has delicious food."[21]

Stan Mooneyham tells of a heart-rending visit to the home of Sebastian and Maria Nascimento, a poor Brazilian couple. The one-room, thatched lean-to had a sand floor. One stool, a charcoal hibachi and four cots covered with sacks partly filled with a bit of straw were the only furniture.

My emotions could scarcely take in what I saw and heard. The three-year-old twins, lying naked and unmoving on a small cot, were in the last act of their personal drama. Mercifully, the curtain was coming down on their brief appearance. Malnutrition was the villain. The two-year-old played a silent role, his brain already vegetating from marasmus, a severe form of malnourishment.

The father is without work. Both he and Maria are anguished over their existence, but they are too proud to beg. He tries to shine shoes. Maria cannot talk about their condition. She tries, but words just will not come. Her mother's love is deep and tender, and the daily deterioration of her children is more than she can bear. Tears must be the vocabulary of the anguished soul.[22]

Carolina's little girl need not have begged to be sold to a rich neighbor. While Sebastian and Maria's twins lay dying, there was an abundance of food in the world. But it was not divided fairly. The well-to-do in Brazil had plenty to eat. Two hundred and ten million U.S. citizens were consuming enough food (partly because of high consumption of grain-fed livestock) to feed over one billion people in the poor countries.

This is how famine has been redefined, or rather, redistributed! It no longer inconveniences the rich and powerful. It strikes only the poor and powerless. Since the poor usually die quietly in relative obscurity, the rich of all nations comfortably ignore this kind of famine. But famine—redefined and redistributed—is alive and well. Even in good times, millions and millions of persons go to bed hungry. Their children's brains vegetate and their bodies succumb prematurely to disease.

Poverty means illiteracy, inadequate medical care, disease, brain damage. Only 36 per cent of India's 688 million people could read in 1981. Indeed, in 1981 only about one-half (54 per cent) of all the 3.4 billion people in the developing world were literate.[23]

People in the West have enjoyed the security offered by modern medicine for so long that we assume it must now be available for all. In 1982, however, 40 per cent of all people in Latin America had no access to health care whatever.[24] In Africa and Asia the situation was probably worse.

Infants, Brain Damage and Protein

Lacking both food and medicine, Third World nations have high infant mortality rates. As shown in table 1, the rate of infant mortality is much higher in the less developed countries than it is in the developed world.

Permanent brain damage caused by protein deficiency is one of

Infant Mortality Per 1000 Live Births

Sweden	—7
Australia	———12
United States	———13
U.K.	———13
West Germany	————19
U.S.S.R.	——————36
Chile	——————38
Guatemala	————————69
Egypt	——————————90
Rwanda	————————————127
India	————————————134
Malawi	—————————————142

Source: *Roger D. Hanson, ed.,* U.S. Foreign Policy and the Third World: Agenda 1982 *(New York: Praeger, 1982), pp. 161-69.*

Table 1

the most devastating aspects of world poverty. Eighty per cent of total brain development takes place between the moment of conception and the age of two. Adequate protein intake—precisely what at least 210 million malnourished children do not have—is necessary for proper brain development. A recent study in Mexico found that a group of severely malnourished children under five had an IQ thirteen points lower than a scientifically selected, adequately fed control group.[25] Medical science now agrees that severe malnutrition produces irreversible brain damage.

When a poor family runs out of food, the children suffer most. For the present, an inactive child is not as serious a problem as an inactive wage earner. But malnutrition produces millions of retarded children.

Little Marli, a happy six-year-old girl from Rio de Janeiro is just one of these. Little Marli looked normal in every way. Healthy.

Happy. There was just one thing wrong with her. She couldn't learn. At first the teachers thought perhaps her difficulty was psychological, the result of neglect in a family of eleven children. Her younger sister had the same problem. But after careful observation and testing, it was evident that Marli, a child of Brazil's poor and wretched *favelas* [slums], was unable to learn because as an infant her malnourished body could not produce a healthy brain.[26]

No one knows how many poor children have suffered irreversible brain damage because of insufficient protein during childhood. But there were 210 million malnourished children in 1974 and more by 1983. So the number of mental cripples like Marli must number millions.

Hunger, illiteracy, disease, brain damage, death. That's what world poverty means. Perhaps a billion people experience its daily anguish.

Population

The population explosion is another fundamental problem. Not until 1830 did the world have one billion people. But then it took only a hundred years (1930) to add another billion. Within a mere thirty years another billion human beings appeared. The fourth billion arrived in only fifteen years (1975). By about the year 2000

Years Required to Add One Billion People

	Years required	Year reached
First billion	10,000 plus	1830
Second billion	100	1930
Third billion	30	1960
Fourth billion	15	1975
Fifth billion	11	1986
Sixth billion	9	1995

Source: Lester Brown, The Twenty-Ninth Day *(New York: Norton, 1978), p. 74.*

Table 2

the world's population will have climbed to approximately six billion people.[27]

The population explosion prompts some people to despair completely. The Environmental Fund ran an advertisement in 1976 in many newspapers including the *New York Times* and the *Wall Street Journal*. Drafted by William Paddock and Garrett Hardin, among others, the statement declared, "The world as we know it will likely be ruined before the year 2000. . . . The momentum toward tragedy is at this moment so great that there is probably no way of halting it."[28]

Such views, of course, are clearly too pessimistic. Population trends in the last twenty years offer some hope. Whereas the overall population growth rate in the world was about 2 per cent in 1960, the Population Reference Bureau's *1983 World Population Data Sheet* indicates that it has dropped to 1.8 per cent.

The present rate of population growth, however, cannot continue indefinitely. A population growing at the rate of 2.3 per cent per year (the 1983 rate for all of Latin America) grows to nearly 10 times its current size in 100 years. If Latin America's population of 390 million were to increase at present rates for one hundred years, there would be almost as many people in Latin America in 2083 as in the entire world today (see table 3).

Population Increase over 25, 50 and 100 years

Population growth rate per cent per year	Ratio of projected population to current population		
	25 years	50 years	100 years
0.5	1.13	1.28	1.65
1.0	1.28	1.65	2.70
1.5	1.45	2.11	4.43
2.0	1.64	2.69	7.24
2.5	1.85	3.44	11.81
3.0	2.09	4.38	19.22
3.5	2.36	5.58	31.19

Table 3

Population Growth Rate Per Year for Selected Countries (mid 1983)

	Growth rate	Population mid 1983 (in millions)		Growth rate	Population mid 1983 (in millions)
West Germany	−0.2%	61.5	India	2.1%	730.0
U.K.	0.1%	56.1	Brazil	2.3%	131.3
United States	0.7%	234.2	Ethiopia	2.5%	31.3
Japan	0.7%	119.2	Mexico	2.6%	75.5
Canada	0.8%	24.9	Mozambique	2.7%	13.1
U.S.S.R.	0.8%	272.0	Philippines	2.7%	52.8
Australia	0.9%	15.3	Pakistan	2.8%	95.7
China	1.5%	1023.3	Nigeria	3.3%	84.2
World	1.8%	4677.0			

Source: Population Reference Bureau, 1983 World Population Data Sheet.

Table 4

Mexico's present growth rate of 2.6 per cent, if continued for one hundred years, would produce a total population of over 900 million people. Fortunately, Mexico's growth is slowing down (from about 3.5 per cent in 1968 to 2.6 per cent in 1983).

In considering the issue of population growth, it is important to remember that although Western developed nations have now much lower population growth rates than developing nations (see table 4), the number of children per family in West Europe and North America was much higher in the latter half of the last century than the two or three children per family common now. Infant mortality rates were of course higher. Despite this, however, family size and population growth in the West at that time were quite close to size and growth rates in many developing countries since the war. Affluence and decline in population growth seem to go together, in the long term anyway.

Limits to Growth?

Along with the food crisis and the population explosion, a third set of complex, interrelated issues makes our dilemma even more desperate. How long can the earth sustain the present rate of industrialization? What will be the effect of the resulting pollution? When will we run out of natural resources (especially fossil fuels such as coal and oil)? In 1972 the Club of Rome (a group of elite, international corporation executives, technocrats and scholars) shocked the world with an answer based on a sophisticated, computerized analysis.

In their book *Limits to Growth,* the Club of Rome concluded, "If the present growth trends in world population, industrialization, pollution, food production, and resource depletion continue unchanged, the limits to growth will be reached sometime within the next one hundred years. The most probable result will be a rather sudden and uncontrollable decline in both population and industrial capacity."[29]

Many valid objections have been raised against the computer model used in the *Limits to Growth* study, and both the Club of Rome and the United Nations (UN) have since published less pessimistic projections.[30] But the issues which it spotlighted are still alive. In chapter six we will take a look at some of these.

Although growth rates in industrial production and population have been lower since the oil crisis, the growth in Western and even less developed countries' industrial production may still place intolerable strains on the world's resources in the future. Many people agree with the world-famous economist Robert Heilbroner: "Ultimately, there is an absolute limit to the ability of the earth to support or tolerate the process of industrial activity, and there is reason to believe that we are now moving toward that limit very rapidly."[31]

The Future and Our Response

The population explosion and the possible necessity of slowing industrialization (at least in the affluent nations) compound the difficulties involved in trying to share the world's resources more justly. Not surprisingly, predictions of doomsday are legion. What are our future prospects?

No one can predict with any certainty what will happen in the next decades. Vast, mushrooming famines in the poorer nations may tempt their leaders to unleash wars of redistribution in a demand for a fairer share of the earth's resources. Such a prospect is not sheer fantasy. Professor Heilbroner has predicted nuclear terrorism and wars of redistribution. He suggests that the world is like "an immense train, in which a few passengers, mainly in the advanced capitalist world, ride in first-class coaches, in conditions of comfort unimaginable to the enormously greater numbers crammed into the cattle cars that make up the bulk of the train's carriages."[32] As millions die and imminent starvation stares even more in the face, a country like India will have to seek some way out.

> There seems little doubt that some nuclear capability will be in the hands of the major underdeveloped nations certainly within the next few decades and perhaps much sooner.... I will suggest that it may be used as an instrument of blackmail to force the developed world to undertake a massive transfer of wealth to the poverty-stricken world.... "Wars of redistribution" may be the only way by which the poor nations can hope to remedy their condition.[33]

Less than a year after Heilbroner's book appeared, India exploded her first nuclear bomb.

The result of such a confrontation could only be ghastly bloodshed on a scale never before seen in human history. We would undoubtedly use our vast military might to defend our unfair share of the world's goods. Tens of millions would die. Such an outcome seems too horrible to contemplate. But realism demands that we honestly face the fact that unless the affluent quarter of the world makes fundamental changes quickly, wars of unprecedented size and ferocity are quite possible.

Stanley Mooneyham, former president of World Vision, a large evangelical relief and development agency, helps us understand why: "They have suffered long with 'aid' that isn't, with discriminatory trade policies, with the rape of their resources."[34] U.S. Senator Mark Hatfield concurs. He has warned, "The greatest threat to this nation [the United States] and the stability of the entire world is hunger. It's more explosive than all the atomic weaponry possessed by the big powers. Desperate people do desperate things, and remember that nuclear fission is now in the hands of even the developing nations."[35]

In 1980, the Presidential Commission on World Hunger (composed of Democrats and Republicans, conservatives and liberals) repeated this warning:

The most potentially explosive force in the world today is the frustrated desire of poor people to attain a decent standard of living. . . . The Commission believes that promoting economic development in general, and overcoming hunger in particular, are tasks far more critical to U.S. national security than most policy makers acknowledge or even believe. Since the advent of nuclear weapons, most Americans have been conditioned to equate national security with the strength of strategic military forces. The Commission considers this prevailing belief to be a simplistic illusion.[36]

As the *Global 2000 Report to the President* (1980) suggested, global cooperation to reduce hunger and injustice is the only path to peace.[37]

Professor Georg Borgstrom, world-renowned specialist in food science and nutrition, fears that "the rich world is on a direct collision course with the poor of the world. . . . We cannot survive behind our Maginot Line of missiles and bombs."[38] But the probability is that we would try. And the result could only be war and carnage, repression and totalitarianism.

What will Christians do in such a time? Will we dare to insist that the God revealed in Scripture is always at work seeking to "set at liberty those who are oppressed" (Lk 4:18)? Will Christians have the courage to seek justice for the poor, even if that means prison? Where will you and I stand? With the starving or the overfed? With poor Lazarus or the rich man? Most of the rich countries are White and at least nominally Christian. What an ironic tragedy if the White, affluent, "Christian" minority in the world continue to amass wealth while hundreds of millions of people hover on the edge of starvation!

One popular fundamentalist newsletter (with a circulation of over 60,000) has called on Christians to stockpile new dried foods. In a most ingenious combination of apocalyptic piety and slick salesmanship, the newsletter quoted several "Bible scholars" to prove that some Christians will live through the tribulation. And the conclusion? Since we cannot be absolutely certain where we will be during the tribulation, we ought to purchase a seven-year supply of reserve foods for a couple of thousand dollars![39]

In an Age of Hunger most Christians, regardless of theological label, will be severely tempted to succumb to the liberal heresy of following current cultural and societal values rather than biblical truth.[40] Society will offer demonically convincing justification for enjoying our affluence and forgetting about a billion hungry neighbors.

But if the Christ of Scripture is our Lord, then we will refuse to be squeezed into the mold of our affluent, sinful culture. In an Age of Hunger Christians of necessity must be radical nonconformists. But nonconformity is painful. Only if we are thoroughly grounded in the scriptural view of possessions, wealth and poverty will we be capable of living an obedient lifestyle.

2

The Affluent Minority

I used to think when I was a child, that Christ might have been exaggerating when he warned about the dangers of wealth. Today I know better. I know how very hard it is to be rich and still keep the milk of human kindness. Money has a dangerous way of putting scales on one's eyes, a dangerous way of freezing people's hands, eyes, lips, and hearts. [1] *[Dom Helder Camara]*

The North-South division is one of the most dangerous divisions in the world today. With one or two exceptions, the rich countries are in the Northern Hemisphere, and the poor countries are in the south. North America, Europe, Russia and Japan are an affluent northern aristocracy. Our standard of living is at least as luxurious in comparison with that of a billion poor neighbors as was the lifestyle of the medieval aristocracy in comparison with their serfs.

And the chasm widens every year. Between 1960 and 1980 the gap between the richest one-fifth and the poorest one-fifth in the world more than doubled. [2]

A Widening Chasm

The Gross National Product (GNP) provides one standard of comparison. A country's GNP is the sum of all goods and services produced in a year, minus the profit and interest payments that leave the country to pay foreign owners of capital, and plus similar payments that are made to local businessfolk who own capital in foreign countries. If you divide a country's GNP by the number of persons in

Per Capita GNP in 1981 (in U.S. dollars)

Sweden	14,500
United States	12,530
Japan	9,890
Brazil	2,214
Nigeria	873
Kenya	432
India	253
Bangladesh	144

Source: Adapted from John P. Lewis and Valeriana Kallab, eds., U.S. Foreign Policy and the Third World: Agenda 1983 (New York: Praeger, 1983), pp. 210-18.

Table 5

the country, you arrive at a per capita GNP which can be compared with that of other nations.[3] As table 5 shows, the per capita GNP in the United States was $12,530 in 1981. In India it was a mere $253.

Virtually all authorities agree that the chasm will widen still more by the year 2000. The *Global 2000 Report to the President* (1980) predicted:

The present income disparities between the wealthiest and poorest nations are projected to widen. Assuming that present trends continue, the group of industrialized countries will have a per capita GNP of nearly $8,500 (in 1975 dollars) in 2000, and North America, Western Europe, Australia, New Zealand, and Japan will average more than $11,000. By contrast, per capita GNP in the LDCs [less developed countries] will average less than $600. For every $1 increase in GNP per capita in the LDCs, a $20 increase is projected for the industrialized countries.[4]

Recognizing that per capita GNP comparisons are open to several criticisms (see note 3), some development specialists have tried to improve on the GNP comparisons. A frequently quoted conclusion is that "differences in income per head between the poor and rich countries were around 1:2 at the beginning of the 19th century; they are . . . today . . . around 1:20."[5]

In 1975 Professor Irving Kravis, a specialist in income comparisons at the University of Pennsylvania, published a massive, painstaking comparison of total output and real purchasing power in different countries. He concluded that the real income per person in the United States is fourteen times that of India and seventeen times that of Kenya.[6] Thus, according to the careful calculations of economist Kravis, the average American was fourteen times as rich as the average Indian.

A comparison of energy usage simply underscores our affluence. Because of a lengthening list of luxuries—numerous electrical gadgets and toys, large air-conditioned cars, skyscrapers and so on—North Americans consume more than twice as much energy per person as their counterparts in industrialized countries like France and England. And we use 150 times as much as the average person in Zaire.[7]

There are many ways of showing our incredible affluence in the West relative to that of the LDCs, but undoubtedly the most striking measure of the gap between rich and poor is our consumption of the most basic commodity of all—food. As table 6 indicates, U.S. citizens consume more than four times as much grain per person as do people in LDCs.

Average Annual Per Capita Cereal Consumption
(in pounds, direct and indirect)

	1969-71 average	1973-75 average
United States	1818	1649
U.S.S.R.	1462	1754
European Community	952	976
Japan	590	604
China	485	489
Less Developed Countries (excluding China)	414	401

Source: *Adapted from* Global 2000 *(1980), pp. 20-21.*

Table 6

The major reason for this glaring difference is that we eat much of our grain indirectly—via grain-fed livestock and fowl. Why is this important? Because it takes many pounds of grain to produce just one pound of beef.

In July, 1983, I talked with George Allen, an agricultural economist in the Economic Research Service of the U.S. Department of Agriculture.[8] Allen reported that a steer in a feedlot gains one pound of edible meat for every thirteen pounds of grain equivalents consumed. (In a typical feedlot, a steer would consume about 8-1/2 pounds of grain and 4-1/2 pounds of silage, hay and protein for every pound of weight gained.) But the animal also spends time on the range eating grass. It does not, however, spend as much time on the range as in the past. On November 28, 1974, the *New York Times* reported that in the 1940s only one-third of all beef was grain-fed. By 1970, 82 per cent of all cattle slaughtered came in from feedlots where they had been fed grain.) USDA economist Allen said that when the total life of the animal is considered, each pound of edible beef represents seven pounds of grain. That means that, in addition to all the grass, hay and other food involved, it also took seven

Grain Consumption by Main Uses 1982-83

	Total population (millions)	Total grain consumption (in million metric tons)	Grain consumed directly (in million metric tons)	Grain fed to livestock (in million metric tons)	Portion fed to livestock
World	4,436	1,485	948	537	36%
Centrally planned economies	1,413	582	399	183	31%
Less developed nations	2,248	475	400	75	16%
Developed nations	775	428	149	279	65%

Source: U.S. Department of Agriculture, Economic Research Service; information from Brad Karmen, grain analyst, 21 July 1983.

Note: Grain consumed directly (column 3) includes grain used for industrial purposes and alcohol as well as that used as food.

Table 7

pounds of grain to produce a typical pound of beef purchased in the supermarket. Fortunately, the conversion rates for chicken and pork are lower: slightly more than 2 to 1 for chicken and 4 or 4-1/4 to 1 for pork. Beef is the cadillac of meat products.[9] Should we move to compacts?

It is because of this high level of meat consumption that the rich minority of the world devours such an unequal share of the world's available food. Table 7 shows that, in 1982, 775 million people in the developed nations consumed almost as much grain (428 million tons) as the 2.248 billion people (475 million tons) in the less developed nations. Whereas we eat much of our grain indirectly via meat, people in the poor countries eat almost all of their grain directly. The United Nations reported in 1974 that livestock in the rich countries ate as much grain as did all the people of India and China.[10]

Table 7 shows that the less developed nations feed only 16 per cent of their grain to livestock. In the developed nations we feed 65 per cent of our grain to cattle. That is why we consume so much more grain than poor nations.

The final irony is that our high meat consumption is harmful to our health. According to Harvard nutritionist Jean Mayer, a diet high in saturated fats contributes to heart disease.[11] (Beef, especially choice and prime cuts, pork, eggs and whole milk all contain large amounts of saturated fats.) Diets high in meat and low in roughage are also harmful for the bowel. The National Cancer Institute has indicated that diets high in meat may contribute to colon cancer, the second most common cancer in North America.[12] Mark Hegsted of the Harvard School of Public Health says that "meat consumption in this country is preposterously high, relative to need, and cannot be justified on a nutritional basis."[13] Fortunately, national trends have moved in the right direction recently. From 1940 to 1972, the annual per-person consumption of beef jumped from 55 to 116 pounds. In 1973, however, it dropped to 109 pounds, and by 1982 it was down to 79 pounds.[14]

The percentage of income spent on food in different countries provides another stark comparison. In the United States it is a mere 12.7 per cent. In India it is 55.5 per cent, and in Niger, 63.6 per cent.

Agony and anguish are concealed in the simple statistics of table 8. If you are spending 13 per cent of your disposable income on food, a 50-per-cent increase in food costs is a minor irritation. But if

Share of Expenditures on Food out of Total Private Domestic Expenditures (1979)

	Per capita income after taxes (in U.S. dollars)	Per cent spent on food
United States	9,595	12.7
Canada	8,323	14.5
United Kingdom	6,297	17.3
West Germany	10,837	19.5
Japan	7,414	21.5
Venezuela	3,332	31.8
U.S.S.R.	4,040	33.7
Honduras	340	44.1
Panama	1,119	48.6
Ghana	873	53.6
India	195	55.5
Philippines	343	56.9
Tanzania	159	57.9
Niger	80	63.6

Source: UN Yearbook of National Accounts Statistics, 1980, Volumes 1, 2, 3; supplemented with OECD National Accounts.

Table 8

you are already spending 64 per cent of your income on food, a 50-per-cent increase means starvation.

Table 9, on available calories, tells the same story. Whereas people in many poor nations have less than the daily minimal requirements, people in North America and Western Europe have more calories than they need. While lack of food destroys millions in poor lands, too much food devastates millions in affluent countries. According to a 1980 survey by the National Center for Health Statistics, 32 per cent of American men and 36 per cent of American women between the ages of 20 and 74 are overweight.[15]

Calorie Supply Per Capita, 1978-80

	Calories available	Calories as per cent of requirements
United States	3624	138
U.S.S.R.	3460	135
France	3390	134
Canada	3358	126
Japan	2916	125
China	2472	105
Pakistan	2300	100
Guatemala	2064	94
Brazil	2121	89
Zambia	1992	86
Bangladesh	1877	85
Haiti	1882	83
Afghanistan	1833	75
Chad	1808	76

Source: FAO statistics cited in World Military and Social Expenditures 1982 by Ruth Leger Sivard, © World Priorities, Leesburg, VA 22075 USA, pp. 31-35. Calorie requirements are FAO estimates (January 1980) of intake necessary for moderate activity, taking into account differences of age, sex, climate and so on.

Table 9

The facts are clear. North Americans, Europeans, Russians and Japanese devour an incredibly unequal share of the world's available food. Whether measured in terms of GNP or energy and food consumption, we are many, many times more affluent than the poor majority of our sisters and brothers. And the chasm widens every year.

Poverty at $30,000 a Year?
It was late 1974. Millions were literally dying from starvation. But

that was not the concern of Judd Arnett, a syndicated columnist with Knight Newspapers. In a column read (and probably believed) by millions of North Americans, Arnett lamented the fact that people earning $15,000 a year were on the edge of poverty. (Remember that $15,000 in 1974 is the same as $30,435 in 1983.)[16] "One of the great mysteries of life to me is how a family in the $15,000 [= $30,435] bracket, before taxes, or even $18,000 [= $36,522], can meet all its obligations and still educate its children."[17] A few years later *Newsweek* did a story on "The Middle Class Poor," calmly reporting that U.S. citizens earning $25,000, $30,000 or even $40,000 a year (in 1983 dollars) felt they were at the edge of poverty.[18]

To the vast majority of the world's people, such statements would be unintelligible—or dishonest. To be sure, we do need $30,000, $40,000 or even more each year if we insist on two cars, an expensively furnished, sprawling suburban home, a $100,000 life insurance policy, new clothes every time fashions change, the most recent "labor-saving devices" for home and garden, an annual three-week vacation to travel and so on. Many North Americans have come to expect precisely that. But that is hardly life at the edge of poverty.

By any objective criterion, the five per cent of the world's people who live in the United States are an incredibly rich aristocracy living in the midst of impoverished masses. Surely one of the most astounding things, therefore, about this affluent minority is that we honestly think we barely have enough to survive in modest comfort.

Constant, seductive advertising helps to create this destructive delusion. Advertisers regularly con us into believing that we genuinely need one luxury after another. We are convinced that we must keep up with or even go one better than our neighbors. So we buy another dress, sports jacket or sports car and thereby force up the standard of living. The ever more affluent standard of living is the god of twentieth-century North America and the adman is its prophet.

The purpose of advertising is no longer primarily to inform. It is to create desire. "CREATE MORE DESIRE" shrieked an inch-high headline for an unusually honest ad in the *New York Times*. It continued: "Now, as always, profit and growth stem directly from the ability of salesmanship to create more desire."[19] Luxurious houses in *Better Homes and Gardens* make our perfectly adequate houses shrink by comparison into a dilapidated, tiny cottage in need of immediate renovation. The advertisements for the new fall fashions make our almost new dresses and suits from previous years look shabby and positively old-fashioned.

We are bombarded by costly, manipulative advertising at every turn. The average American teen-ager has watched 350,000 TV commercials before he or she leaves high school![20] We spend more money on advertising than on all our public institutions of higher education. In 1981, $61.3 billion went into advertising "to convince us that Jesus was wrong about the abundance of possessions."[21]

Luxuries are renamed necessities by advertising. Our postman recently delivered an elegant brochure complete with glossy photographs of exceedingly expensive homes. The brochure announced the seductive lie that *Architectural Digest* would help one quench "man's passionate *need* for beauty and *luxury*" (my emphasis). Evidently we "need" luxury!

Sometimes advertising overkill is hilarious. An evangelical book discount house once created this promotional gem: "Your mouth is going to water, and your soul is going to glow, when you feast your eyes on the bargains we have been providentially provided for your benefit this month." (I promptly ordered books worth twenty-four dollars.)

Promises, Promises
Perhaps the most devastating, demonic part of advertising is that it attempts to persuade us that material possessions will bring joy and fulfillment. "That happiness is to be attained through limitless material acquisition is denied by every religion and philosophy known to man, but is preached incessantly by every American television set."[22] Advertisers promise that their products will satisfy our deepest needs and inner longings for love, acceptance, security and sexual fulfillment. The right deodorant, they promise, will bring acceptance and friendship. The newest toothpaste or shampoo will make one irresistible. A comment by New York jewelry designer Barry Kieselstein shows how people search for meaning and friendship in things: "A nice piece of *jewelry you can relate to is like having a friend* who's always there."[23]

Examples are everywhere. A bank in Washington, D.C., advertised for new savings accounts with the question "Who's gonna love you when you're old and grey?" For a decade, our savings bank used a particularly enticing ad: "Put a little love away. Everybody needs a penny for a rainy day. Put a little love away." Those words are unbiblical, heretical, demonic. They teach the Big Lie of our secular, materialistic society. But the words and music are so seductive that they have danced through my head hundreds of times.

If no one paid any attention to these lies, they would be harmless. But that is impossible. Advertising has a powerful affect on all of us. It shapes the values of our children.

In a sense we pay too little attention to advertisements. Most of us think we ignore them. But in fact they seep into our unconscious minds. We experience them instead of analyzing them. We should examine their blatant lies and then laugh hilariously at their preposterous promises. John V. Taylor has suggested that Christian families ought to adopt the slogan "Who are you kidding?" and shout it in unison every time a commercial appears on the screen.[24]

Perhaps the "TV Victim's Lament" could be the theme song of our lighthearted (yet deadly serious) crusade against advertising. Sing it to the tune of "Blowin' in the Wind."

> How many times must a guy spray with Ban
>   Before he doesn't offend?
> And how many times must he gargle each day
>   Before he can talk to a friend?
> How many tubes of shampoo must he buy
>   Before his dandruff will end?
> The sponsors, my friend, will sell you all they can.
>   The sponsors will sell you all they can.
>
> How many times must a man use Gillette
>   Before shaving won't make him bleed?
> And how many cartons of Kent must he smoke
>   Before the girls all pay him heed?
> How many products must one person buy
>   Before he has all that he'll need?
> The sponsors, my friend, will sell you all they can.
>   The sponsors will sell you all they can.
>
> How many times must a girl clean her sink
>   Before Ajax scours that stain?

And how many times must she rub in Ben Gay
   Before she can rub out the pain?
How many ads on TV must we watch
   Before we are driven insane?
The sponsors, my friend, will broadcast all they can.
   The sponsors will broadcast all they can.[25]

Theologian Patrick Kerans has argued that our society's commitment to a growth economy and an ever-increasing standard of living promoted by constant advertising is really a sell-out to the Enlightenment. During the eighteenth century, Western society decided that the scientific method would shape our relationship to reality. Since only quantitative criteria of truth and value were acceptable, more intangible values such as community, trust and friendship became less important. Unlike friendship and justice, GNP can be measured. The result is our competitive growth economy where winning and economic success (and they are usually the same) are all-important.[26]

The result, if Kerans is correct, can only be social disintegration. If our basic social structures are built on the heretical supposition of the Enlightenment that the scientific method is the only way to truth and value, and if Christianity is true, then our society must eventually collapse.

Advertising itself contains a fundamental inner contradiction.[27] We all long for those qualities of life that satisfy our deepest needs; we long for significance and joy. Marketing recognizes our needs and hooks into them. Now Christians know that affluence does not guarantee love, acceptance and joy. But advertising promises them to those who strive for more gadgets and bigger bank accounts. Our inherent bent for idolatry gives advertising the power to be convincing; so people persist in the fruitless effort to quench their thirst for meaning and fulfillment with an ever-rising river of possessions.

The result within the person is agonizing distress and undefined dissatisfaction; the broader, external result is structural injustice. Our affluence fails to satisfy our restless hearts. And it also helps deprive one billion hungry neighbors of badly needed food and resources. Will we affluent Christians have the courage and faithfulness to learn how to be unconformed to this world's seductive, Satanic advertising?

Estimated Official Development Assistance from Industrialized Countries as a Percentage of GNP (1981)

Netherlands	————————————————————1.08
Sweden	———————————————————.83
Norway	———————————————————.82
Denmark	————————————————.73
France	———————————————.71
Belgium	—————————————.59
Austria	——————————.48
Germany	——————————.46
Canada	—————————.43
U.K.	—————————.43
Australia	————————.41
New Zealand	——————.29
Japan	—————.28
Finland	—————.28
Switzerland	—————.24
United States	————.20
Italy	———.19

Source: The World Bank, World Development Report 1982 *(New York: Oxford Univ. Press), pp. 140-41.*

Table 10

How Generous Are We?

The United States is one of the richest nations in the world. But the data in table 10 reveal that the U.S. government ranks second from the bottom (in percentage of GNP given) among major Western donors of foreign aid.

Popular opinion does not reflect this reality. One survey discovered that more than two-thirds (69 per cent) of all Americans think that the United States is more generous in foreign aid than other developed nations.[28] Perhaps our illusion of generosity is a necessary protective device. In order to justify our affluence, we foster an image of a generous nation dispensing foreign aid on a grand scale.

The United States did display national generosity at the end of World War 2. At the height of the Marshall Plan (begun in 1947 to rebuild war-torn Europe) we actually gave annually 2.79 per cent of our total GNP.[29] But in 1960 the figure for foreign aid had dropped to .53 per cent of GNP, and by 1981 it had plummeted to a mere .2 per cent of GNP (see table 10). From 1960 to 1981 our per capita income had risen from $4,087 to $6,537 (calculated in terms of constant prices and wages based on the year 1972). But our aid to LDCs did not follow the same trend. In 1960 the average person in the United States contributed $21.7 a year to foreign aid. In 1981 the average person contributed a paltry $13.10.[30] The richer we have become, the less we care to share with others.

In 1975 the Organization for Economic Cooperation and Development (an organization of rich nations) underlined the contrast between growing wealth and declining foreign aid. In 1961 and 1962 developed countries as a whole gave .52 per cent of total GNP. By 1974 it had declined to a mere .33 per cent (one-third of one per cent).[31] By 1981 the figure stood just slightly higher at .35 per cent. Ironically, the economies of developed countries had grown at an annual rate of 3.6 per cent during these same twenty years.[32] Although vastly richer, we shared a smaller per cent.

Table 11 sets out the flows of official development assistance (ODA) in more detail. Although the volume of aid is obviously important (as reflected in percentage of GNP in column one), its effectiveness in helping the poorest people is the crucial issue.

Effectiveness is significantly determined by how it is given (multilaterally or bilaterally), the terms of the aid (grants or loans), the countries to which it is given, and how the aid is used in those countries. ODA can be given either bilaterally, country to country, or multilaterally through international institutions such as the United Nations, the World Bank and regional development banks. It is generally agreed that multilateral aid is usually more effective in reducing poverty. Since a donor country has more control over bi-

Official Development Assistance (ODA) Net from Selected Developed Countries (1981)

	1 Total ODA as % of GNP	2 % of ODA given as bilateral aid	3 Grant aid as % of bilateral aid	4 % of bilateral aid given low income countries
Netherlands	1.08	76	72	43
Sweden	.83	65	100	69
Norway	.82	56	99	61
Denmark	.73	50	67	74
France	.71	85	81	15
Belgium	.59	64	80	61
West Germany	.46	71	60	28
Canada	.43	63	66	41
U.K.	.43	61	101	42
Australia	.41	84	101	23
New Zealand	.29	75	100	14
Japan	.28	71	36	55
United States	.20	75	73	20
Italy	.19	26	110	20

Sources: Development Co-operation, 1982 Review, *Development Assistance Committee (OECD), table 2.A.8, pp. 206-7, for columns 1 to 3. Column 4 adapted from* World Development Report 1982, *pp. 140-41.*

Note: Australia, Italy and the United Kingdom all have in column 3 figures greater than 100% either because they receive some development loans and in return distribute those as bilateral grants or, more likely, because they are receiving payment on old loans faster than they are issuing new development loans. As a result, the net ODA is less than total grants.

Table 11

lateral than multilateral aid, an analysis of its bilateral program will reveal whether its first concern is foreign policy goals or reducing poverty. Column two of table 11 shows the proportion of bilateral aid in each country's aid program; in eleven out of the fourteen countries it is above 60 per cent. This reflects the desire of these countries to use foreign aid to promote their own national foreign policy goals.

One of the problems of postwar "aid" from rich countries was that so much of it was in the form of loans—often with interest. The result has been the growth of a huge burden of debt which many LDCs can repay only with great economic difficulty. Now, however, some rich countries are giving their new aid, at least to the poorer countries, on grant (that is, gift) terms. For the United States, 73 per cent of bilateral aid was given as outright grants in 1981, up from 59 per cent in 1978. Column three shows the percentages of bilateral aid given as grants for the countries listed.

The final issue the table deals with is whether bilateral ODA goes to the poorest countries. The World Bank defined low income countries as those which had per capita incomes of less than $410 in 1980.

Military Expenditures and Foreign Economic Aid of the Developed Countries

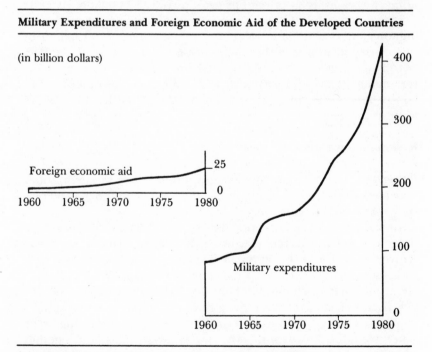

Source: World Military and Social Expenditures 1981 *by Ruth Leger Sivard,* © *World Priorities, Leesburg, VA 22075 USA.*

Table 12

There are thirty-three of these countries. Column four shows, unfortunately, that not enough of the ODA goes to these poorest countries. Only 20 per cent of the bilateral aid given by the United States goes there. The rest of it goes to less needy nations who are, however, more strategic to U.S. foreign policy objectives. (In 1979, for instance, 40 per cent of all U.S. bilateral aid went to Israel and Egypt to further the peace treaty between those two countries.)[33] When all this is taken into account, it is easy to see not only that the developed world is not very generous, but also that our aid is often given in ways that prevent maximum impact.

A comparison of Western expenditures on foreign aid and the military is startling. Table 12 shows that all developed nations (including Communist nations) increased their military expenditures by $320 billion from 1960 to 1980. In that same period their economic assistance to poor nations grew by only $23 billion. By 1982 world military expenditures had reached $600 billion per year—one million dollars a minute. (Nuclear weapons take $100 billion of this.)[34] As the author of the widely respected annual *World Military and Social Expenditures* pointed out, "In dollar equivalent terms, [current military expenditures] exceed the annual income of the two billion people in the world's poorest countries."[35] Is that the way we want to use our abundance?

Rationalizing Our Affluence

It would be impossible for the rich minority to live with themselves if they did not invent plausible justifications. These rationalizations take many forms. Analyzing a few of the most common may help us spot each year's new models.

In the last decade concepts like "triage"[36] and "lifeboat ethics" became popular. Garrett Hardin, a distinguished biologist at the University of California at Santa Barbara, provoked impassioned, widespread debate with his provocative articles on lifeboat ethics.[37] He argues that we should not help the poor countries with food or aid. Each rich country is a lifeboat that will survive only if it refuses to waste its limited resources on the hungry masses swimming in the water around it. If we eat together today, we will all starve together tomorrow. Furthermore, since poor countries "irresponsibly" permit unrestrained population growth, starvation is the only way to check the ever-growing number of hungry mouths. Hence, increased aid merely postpones the day of reckoning. When it comes, our aid will only have preserved even more persons for ultimate starvation. Therefore it is ethically correct to help them learn the hard way—by letting them starve now.

There are, however, fatal flaws in Hardin's argument.

Hardin ignores data which show that poor countries can (and have) cut population growth fairly rapidly if, instead of investing in advanced technology and industrial development, they concentrate on improving the lot of the poor masses. If the poor masses have a secure food supply, access to some (relatively inexpensive) health services and modest educational opportunities, population growth tends to decline quickly. Lester Brown summarizes these findings:

> There is new striking evidence that in an increasing number of poor countries . . . birth rates have dropped sharply *despite relatively low per capita income.* . . . Examination of societies as different as China, Barbados, Sri Lanka, Uruguay, Taiwan, The Indian Punjab, Cuba and South Korea suggests a common factor. In all these countries, a large portion of the population has gained access to modern social and economic services—such as education, employment, and credit systems. . . . There is increasing evidence that the very strategies which cause the greatest improvement in the welfare of the entire population also have the greatest effect on reducing population growth.[38]

The right kind of aid—focused especially on promoting labor-intensive, agricultural development using intermediate technology—will help check population growth.[39] Hardin's thesis suggests doing nothing at a time when the right kind of action could probably avoid disaster.

Another omission in Hardin's thesis is even more astonishing. He totally ignores the fact that the ever-increasing affluence among the rich minority is one of the fundamental causes of the present crisis. It is simply false to suggest that there is not enough food to feed everyone. There is enough—if it is more evenly distributed. In 1970 the United Nations estimated that it would take only 12 million additional tons of grain per year to provide 260 extra calories per day to everyone suffering from malnutrition. That is only 30 per cent of what the United States feeds its livestock.[40] In a world where the rich minority feed more grain to their livestock than is eaten by one

quarter of all the world's people, it is absurd and immoral to talk of
the necessity of letting selected hungry nations starve. The boat in
which the rich sail is not an austerely equipped lifeboat. It is a lavishly stocked luxury liner.

Hardin's proposal, of course, is also unrealistic. Hungry nations
left to starve would not disappear in submissive silence. India is one
of the nations frequently nominated for this dubious honor. As indicated before, a nation with nuclear weapons would certainly not
tolerate such a decision.[41]

A second rationalization has a pious ring to it. Some evangelical
Christians argue that they must adopt an affluent lifestyle in order
to evangelize wealthy persons. Rationalization is dreadfully easy.
Garden Grove Community Church in California has a lavish, multi-
million-dollar plant complete with a series of water fountains that
begin spraying when the minister touches a button in the pulpit. The
pastor, Robert Schuller, defends his luxurious facilities:

> We are trying to make a big, beautiful impression upon the afflu-
> ent non-religious American who is riding by on this busy freeway.
> It's obvious that we are not trying to impress the Christians! . . .
> Nor are we trying to impress the social workers in the County
> Welfare Department. They would tell us that we ought to be con-
> tent to remain in the Orange Drive-In Theater and give the
> money to feed the poor. But suppose we *had* given this money to
> feed the poor? What would we have today? We would still have
> hungry, poor people and God would not have this tremendous
> base of operations which He is using to inspire people to become
> more successful, more affluent, more generous, more genuinely
> unselfish in their giving of themselves.[42]

Where does valid justification end and rationalization begin? We
must avoid simplistic legalism. Christians certainly ought to live in
the suburbs as well as the inner city. But those who defend an affluent lifestyle on the basis of a call to witness to the rich must ask themselves hard questions: How much of my affluent lifestyle is directly
related to my witnessing to rich neighbors? How much of it could I
abandon for the sake of Christ's poor and still be able to witness
effectively? Indeed how much of it *must* I abandon in order to faithfully proclaim the biblical Christ who taught that failure to feed the
poor entails eternal damnation (Mt 25:45-46)?

The response of top U.S. leaders to proposals by the developing nations shows how rationalization can degenerate into double talk. In 1974 there was a historic meeting at the United Nations. The developing nations adopted a document calling for a new international economic order. They insisted on higher prices for their raw materials and other changes in trade patterns and international monetary arrangements that they believed would facilitate their development. U.S. Secretary of State Henry Kissinger and other U.S. leaders charged the large coalition of poor countries with "using" the United Nations. Some highly placed U.S. officials suggested that this "tyranny of the majority" warranted U.S. withdrawal from the UN. Is not the democratic principle of majority rule *our* principle? Is it not dishonest double talk to speak of tyranny when the majority use their numbers to demand justice? It would surely be ironic if we were to belittle democratic principles in order to defend our affluence!

In the coming decades rationalizations for our affluence will be legion. They will be popular and persuasive. "Truly, I say to you, it will be hard for a rich man to enter the kingdom of heaven" (Mt 19:23). But all things are possible with God—if we will hear and obey his Word. If there is any ray of hope for the future, it is in the possibility that growing numbers of affluent Christians will dare to allow the Bible to shape their relationship to a billion sons and daughters of poor Lazarus. The next four chapters will develop a biblical perspective on poverty and possessions.

Part 2

A Biblical Perspective on the Poor & Possessions

Martin Luther once said that "if you preach the Gospel in all aspects with the exception of the issues which deal specifically with your time you are not preaching the Gospel at all."[1]

Luther's comment relates directly to the findings of a recent scholarly study. Social scientists examined the factors that shape American attitudes on matters related to the development of the poor nations. They discovered that religion plays no significant role at all! Those with deep religious beliefs are no more concerned about assistance and development for the poor than are persons with little or no religious commitment.[2]

American Christians have failed to declare God's perspective on the plight of our billion hungry neighbors—surely one of the most pressing issues of our time.

But I refuse to believe that this failure must inevitably continue. I believe there are millions of Christians in affluent lands who care more about Jesus than anything else in the world. There are millions of Christians who will take any risk, make any sacrifice, forsake any treasure, if they see clearly that God's Word demands it. That is why Part 2, "A Biblical Perspective on the Poor and Possessions," is the most important section of our study.

Part 2 is full of Scripture. But even so it is only a small selection of the vast volume of biblical material. *Cry Justice* contains almost two hundred pages of biblical texts that relate directly to the theme of this section.[3]

3

God & the Poor

He who is kind to the poor lends to the LORD. [Proverbs 19:17]
I know that the LORD maintains the cause of the afflicted, and executes justice for the needy. [Psalm 140:12]

What is God's attitude toward the poor and oppressed?

Is God biased in favor of the poor? Some theologians have said yes.[1] The question, however, is ambiguous. Does it mean that God desires the salvation of poor people more than the salvation of the rich? Does it mean that God and his people treat the poor so conspicuously differently from the way the rich and powerful normally treat them that we can only say that God seems to have a special concern for the poor and oppressed? Is God on the side of the poor in a way that he is not on the side of the rich? Just who are "the poor" in the Bible?

The Hebrew words for the poor are *'anî, 'anāw, 'ebyôn, dal* and *rāš*. *'Anî* (and *'anāw*, which originally had approximately the same meaning) denotes one who is "wrongfully impoverished or dispossessed."[2] *'Ebyôn* refers to a beggar imploring charity. *Dal* connotes a thin, weakly person, that is, an impoverished, deprived peasant.[3] Unlike the others, *rāš* is an essentially neutral term. In their persistent polemic against the oppression of the poor, the prophets used the terms *'ebyôn, 'anî* and *dal*. Thus the primary connotation of "the poor" in the Scriptures is economic. Usually, too, calamity or some form of oppression is the assumed cause of the poverty.

The Scriptures also teach that some folk are poor because they are lazy and slothful (for example, Prov 6:6-11; 19:15; 20:13; 21:25; 24:30-34). And the Bible knows of voluntary poverty for the sake of the kingdom. The most common biblical connotation of "the poor," however, is of those who are economically impoverished because of calamity or exploitation.[4] In this chapter, we use this last meaning of "the poor."

We can only answer the questions about God's bias toward the poor after we have searched for biblical answers to five related questions: (1) What concern for the poor did God disclose at those pivotal points (especially the exodus, the destruction of Israel and Judah, and the Incarnation) where he acted in history to reveal himself? (2) In what sense does God identify with the poor? (3) How significant is the fact that God frequently chooses to work through the poor and oppressed? (4) What does the Bible mean by the recurring teaching that God destroys the rich and exalts the poor? (5) Does God command his people to have a special concern for the poor?

Pivotal Points of Revelation History
The Bible clearly and repeatedly teaches a fundamental point that we have often overlooked. At the crucial moments when God displayed his mighty acts in history to reveal his nature and will, God *also* intervened to liberate the poor and oppressed.

1. The Exodus. God displayed his power at the exodus in order to free oppressed slaves. When he called Moses at the burning bush, God's intent was to end suffering and injustice: "I have seen the affliction of my people who are in Egypt, and have heard their cry because of their taskmasters; I know their sufferings, and I have come down to deliver them out of the hand of the Egyptians" (Ex 3:7-8). This text does not reflect an isolated perspective on the great event of the exodus. Each year at the harvest festival the Israelites repeated a liturgical confession celebrating the way God had acted to free a poor, oppressed people.

A wandering Aramean was my father; and he went down into Egypt and sojourned there.... And the Egyptians treated us harshly, and afflicted us, and laid upon us hard bondage. Then we cried to the LORD the God of our fathers, and the LORD heard our voice, and saw our affliction, our toil, and our oppression;

and the LORD brought us out of Egypt with a mighty hand. (Deut 26:5-8)

The God of the Bible cares when people enslave and oppress others. At the exodus he acted to end economic oppression and bring freedom to slaves.

Now of course the liberation of oppressed slaves was not God's only purpose in the exodus. God also acted because of his covenant with Abraham, Isaac and Jacob. In addition, he wanted to create a special people to whom he could reveal himself.[5] Both of these concerns were clearly central to God's activity at the exodus. The liberation of a poor, oppressed people, however, was also right at the heart of God's design. The following passage discloses God's multifaceted purpose in the exodus:

Moreover I have heard the groaning of the people of Israel whom the Egyptians hold in bondage and I have remembered my covenant [with Abraham, Isaac and Jacob]. . . . I will bring you out from under the burdens of the Egyptians, and I will deliver you from their bondage, and I will redeem you with an outstretched arm and with great acts of judgment, and I will take you for my people, and I will be your God; and you shall know that I am the LORD your God, who has brought you out from under the burdens of the Egyptians. (Ex 6:5-7)

Yahweh wanted his people to know him as the One who freed them from slavery and oppression.

The preamble to the Ten Commandments, probably the most important portion of the entire law for Israel, begins with this same revolutionary truth. Before he gives the two tables of the law, Yahweh identifies himself: "I am the LORD your God, who brought you out of the land of Egypt, out of the house of bondage" (Deut 5:6; Ex 20:2). Yahweh is the one who frees from bondage. The God of the Bible wants to be known as the liberator of the oppressed.

The exodus was certainly the decisive event in the creation of the chosen people. We distort the biblical interpretation of this momentous occasion unless we see that at this pivotal point the Lord of the universe was at work correcting oppression and liberating the poor.

2. Destruction and Captivity. When they settled in the Promised Land, the Israelites soon discovered that Yahweh's passion for justice was a two-edged sword. When they were oppressed, it led to their freedom. But when they became the oppressors, it led to their destruction.

When God called Israel out of Egypt and made his covenant with them, he gave them his law so that they could live together in peace and justice. But Israel failed to obey the law of the covenant. As a result, God destroyed Israel and sent his chosen people into captivity.

Why?

The explosive message of the prophets is that God destroyed Israel because of mistreatment of the poor. Idolatry, of course, was an equally prominent reason. Too often, however, we remember only Israel's "spiritual" problem of idolatry and overlook the clear, startling biblical teaching that economic exploitation also sent the chosen people into captivity.

The middle of the eighth century B.C. was a time of political success and economic prosperity unknown since the days of Solomon.[6] But it was precisely at this moment that God sent his prophet Amos to announce the unwelcome news that the northern kingdom of Israel would be destroyed. Penetrating beneath the façade of current prosperity and fantastic economic growth, Amos saw oppression of the poor. He saw the rich "trample the head of the poor into the dust of the earth" (2:7). He saw that the affluent lifestyle of the rich was built on oppression of the poor (6:1-7). He denounced the rich women ("cows" was his word!) "who oppress the poor, who crush the needy, who say to their husbands, 'Bring, that we may drink!' " (4:1). Even in the courts the poor had no hope because the rich bribed the judges (5:10-15).

Archaeologists have confirmed Amos's picture of shocking extremes of wealth and poverty.[7] In the early days of settlement in Canaan, the land was distributed equally among the families and tribes. All Israelites enjoyed a similar standard of living. In fact, as late as the tenth century B.C., archaeologists have found that houses were all approximately the same size. But by Amos's day, two centuries later, everything is different. Archaeologists have uncovered bigger, better-built houses in one area and poorer houses huddled together in another section.[8] No wonder Amos warned the rich, "You have built houses of hewn stone, but you shall not dwell in them" (5:11)!

God's word through Amos was that the northern kingdom would

be destroyed and the people taken into exile (7:11, 17).

Woe to those who lie upon beds of ivory,
    and stretch themselves upon their couches,
and eat lambs from the flock,
    and calves from the midst of the stall. . . .
Therefore they shall now be the first of those
    to go into exile,
and the revelry of those who stretch themselves
    shall pass away. (6:4, 7)

Only a few years after Amos spoke it happened just as God had said. The Assyrians conquered the northern kingdom and took thousands into captivity. Because of their mistreatment of the poor, God destroyed the northern kingdom—forever.

As in the case of the exodus, we must not ignore another important factor. The prophet Hosea, a contemporary of Amos, disclosed that the nation's idolatry was another cause of impending destruction. Because they had forsaken Yahweh for idols, the nation would be destroyed (Hos 8:1-6; 9:1-3).[9] According to the prophets, then, the northern kingdom fell because of both idolatry and economic exploitation of the poor.

God sent other prophets to announce the same fate for the southern kingdom of Judah. Isaiah warned that destruction from afar would befall Judah because of its mistreatment of the poor:

Woe to those who decree iniquitous decrees. . . .
to turn aside the needy from justice
    and to rob the poor of my people of their right. . . .
What will you do on the day of punishment,
    in the storm which will come from afar? (Is 10:1-3)

Micah denounced those in Judah who "covet fields, and seize them; and houses, and take them away; they oppress a man and his house, a man and his inheritance" (2:2). As a result, he warned, Jerusalem would one day become "a heap of ruins" (3:12).

Fortunately Judah was more open to the prophetic word, and the nation was spared for a time. But oppression of the poor continued. A hundred years after the time of Isaiah, the prophet Jeremiah again condemned the wealthy who had amassed riches by oppressing the poor:

Wicked men are found among my people;
    they lurk like fowlers lying in wait.

> They set a trap;
>   they catch men.
> Like a basket full of birds,
>   their houses are full of treachery;
> therefore, they have become great and rich,
>   they have grown fat and sleek.
> They know no bounds in deeds of wickedness;
>   they judge not with justice
> the cause of the fatherless, to make it prosper,
>   and they do not defend the rights of the needy.
> Shall I not punish them for these things?
>   says the LORD,
>   and shall I not avenge myself
>   on a nation such as this? (Jer 5:26-29)

Even at that late date Jeremiah could promise hope if the people would forsake *both* injustice *and* idolatry. "If you truly execute justice one with another, if you do not oppress the alien, the fatherless or the widow . . . and if you do not go after other gods to your own hurt, then I will let you dwell in this place, in the land that I gave of old to your fathers for ever" (Jer 7:5-7).

But they continued to oppress the poor and helpless (Jer 34:3-17). As a result Jeremiah persisted in saying God would use the Babylonians to destroy Judah. In 587 B.C. Jerusalem fell and the Babylonian captivity began.

The destruction of Israel and Judah, however, was not mere punishment. God wanted to use the Assyrians and Babylonians to purge his people of oppression and injustice. In a remarkable passage Isaiah showed how God would attack his foes and enemies (that is, his chosen people!) in order to purify them and restore justice.

> How the faithful city [Jerusalem]
>   has become a harlot,
>   she that was full of justice!
> Righteousness lodged in her,
>   but now murderers.
> Your silver has become dross,
>   your wine mixed with water. . . .
> Every one loves a bribe
>   and runs after gifts.
> They do not defend the fatherless,

and the widow's cause does not come to them.
Therefore the Lord says,
   the LORD of hosts,
   the Mighty One of Israel:
"Ah, I will vent my wrath on my enemies,
   and avenge myself on my foes.
I will turn my hand against you
   and will smelt away your dross as with lye
   and remove all your alloy.
And I will restore your judges as at the first,
   and your counselors as at the beginning.
Afterward you shall be called the city of righteousness,
   the faithful city." (Is 1:21-26)

The catastrophe of national destruction and captivity reveals the God of the exodus still at work correcting the oppression of the poor.

3. The Incarnation. Christians believe that God revealed himself most completely in Jesus of Nazareth. How did the Incarnate One define his mission?

Jesus' words in the synagogue at Nazareth, spoken near the beginning of his public ministry, throb with hope for the poor. He read from the prophet Isaiah:

The Spirit of the Lord is upon me,
because he has anointed me to preach good news to the poor.
He has sent me to proclaim release to the captives
and recovering of sight to the blind,
to set at liberty those who are oppressed,
to proclaim the acceptable year of the Lord. (Lk 4:18-19)

After reading these words, Jesus informed his audience that this Scripture was now fulfilled in himself. The mission of the Incarnate One was to free the oppressed and heal the blind. (It was also to preach the gospel. And this is *equally* important, although the focus of this book precludes further discussion of it.)[10] The poor are the only group specifically singled out as recipients of Jesus' gospel. Certainly the gospel he proclaimed was for all, but he was particularly concerned that the poor realize that his good news was for them.

Some try to avoid the clear meaning of Jesus' statement by spiritualizing his words. Certainly, as other texts show, he came to open our blinded hearts, to die for our sins and to free us from the oppression of guilt. But that is not what he means here. The words about releasing captives and liberating the oppressed are from Isaiah. In their original Old Testament setting they unquestionably referred to physical oppression and captivity. In Luke 7:18-23, which contains a list similar to that in Luke 4:18-19, it is clear that Jesus is referring to material, physical problems.[11]

Jesus' actual ministry corresponded precisely to the words of Luke 4. He spent most of his time not among the rich and powerful in Jerusalem, but among the poor in the cultural and economic backwater of Galilee. He healed the sick and blind. He fed the hungry. And he warned his followers in the strongest possible words that those who do not feed the hungry, clothe the naked and visit the prisoners will experience eternal damnation (Mt 25:31-46).

At the supreme moment of history when God took on human flesh, the God of Israel was still liberating the poor and oppressed and summoning his people to do the same. That is the central reason for Christian concern for the poor.

It is not just at the exodus, captivity and Incarnation, however, that we learn of God's concern for the poor, the weak and the oppressed. The Bible is full of passages which speak of this. Two illustrations from the Psalms are typical of a host of other texts.

Psalm 10 begins with despair. God seems to have hidden himself far away while the wicked prosper by oppressing the poor (vv. 2, 9). But the psalmist concludes with hope:

The hapless commits himself to thee;
      thou hast been the helper of the fatherless. . . .
O LORD, thou wilt hear the desire of the meek . . .
      thou wilt incline thy ear
to do justice to the fatherless and the oppressed. (vv. 14, 17-18)

Psalm 146 is a ringing declaration that to care for the poor is central to the very nature of God. The psalmist exults in the God of Jacob because he is both the creator of the universe and the defender of the oppressed.

Praise the LORD!
Praise the LORD, O my soul! . . .
Happy is he whose help is the God of Jacob,
      whose hope is in the LORD his God,
who made heaven and earth,

the sea, and all that is in them;
who keeps faith for ever;
   who executes justice for the oppressed;
   who gives food to the hungry.
the LORD sets the prisoners free;
   the LORD opens the eyes of the blind.
The LORD lifts up those who are bowed down;
   the LORD loves the righteous.
The LORD watches over the sojourners,
   he upholds the widow and the fatherless;
   but the way of the wicked he brings to ruin. (vv. 1, 5-9)

According to Scripture it is just as much a part of God's essence to defend the weak, the stranger and the oppressed as to create the universe. Because of who he is, Yahweh lifts up the mistreated.[12] The foundation of Christian concern for the hungry and oppressed is that God cares especially for them.

God Identifies with the Poor

God not only acts in history to liberate the poor, but in a mysterious way that we can only half fathom the Sovereign of the universe identifies with the weak and destitute. Two proverbs state this beautiful truth. Proverbs 14:31 puts it negatively: "He who oppresses a poor man insults his Maker." Even more moving is the positive formulation: "He who is kind to the poor lends to the LORD" (19:17). What a statement! Helping a poor person is like helping the Creator of all things with a loan.

Only in the Incarnation can we begin to perceive what God's identification with the weak, oppressed and poor really means. "Though he was rich," Paul says of our Lord Jesus, "yet for your sake he became poor" (2 Cor 8:9).

He was born in a small, insignificant province of the Roman Empire. His first visitors, the shepherds, were persons viewed by Jewish society as thieves. His parents were too poor to bring the normal offering for purification. Instead of a lamb, they brought two pigeons to the Temple (Lk 2:24; compare Lev 12:6-8). Jesus was a refugee and then an immigrant in Galilee (Mt 2:13-15, 19-23). Since Jewish rabbis received no fees for their teaching, Jesus had no regular income during his public ministry. (Scholars belonged to the poorer classes in Judaism.)[13] Nor did he have a home of his own.

Jesus warned an eager follower who promised to follow him everywhere, "Foxes have holes, and birds of the air have nests; but the
Son of man has nowhere to lay his head" (Mt 8:20). He sent out his
disciples in extreme poverty (Lk 9:3; 10:4).

His identification with the poor and unfortunate was, Jesus said, a
sign that he was the Messiah. When John the Baptist sent messengers to ask him if he were the long-expected Messiah, Jesus simply
pointed to his deeds: he was healing the sick and preaching to the
poor (Mt 11:2-6). Jesus also preached to the rich. But apparently it
was his particular concern to preach to the poor that validated his
claim to messiahship. His preoccupation with the poor and disadvantaged contrasted sharply with the style of his contemporaries.
Was that perhaps why he added a final word to take back to John:
"Blessed is he who takes no offense at me" (Mt 11:6)?

Only as we feel the presence of the incarnate God in the form of a
poor Galilean can we begin to understand his words: "I was hungry
and you gave me food, I was thirsty and you gave me drink. . . . I was
naked and you clothed me. . . . Truly, I say to you, as you did it to
one of the least of these my brethren, you did it to me" (Mt 25:35-36,
40). What does it mean to feed and clothe the Creator of all things?
We cannot know. We can only look on the poor and oppressed with
new eyes and resolve to heal their hurts and help end their oppression.

If Jesus' saying in Matthew 25:40 is awesome, its parallel is terrifying: "Truly, I say to you, as you did it not to one of the least of
these, you did it not to me" (v. 45). What does that mean in a world
where millions die each year while rich Christians live in affluence?
What does it mean to see the Lord of the universe lying by the road-
side starving and walk by on the other side? We cannot know. We
can only pledge, in fear and trembling, not to kill him again.

God's Special Instruments
When God selected a chosen people, he picked poor slaves in Egypt.
When God called the early church, most of the members were poor
folk. When God became flesh, he came as a poor Galilean. Are these
facts isolated phenomena or part of a significant pattern? This is our
third question in discerning God's special concern for the poor.

God might have selected a rich, powerful nation as his chosen
people. Instead he chose oppressed slaves. God picked an im-

poverished, enslaved people to be his special instrument of revelation and salvation for all people. (See also Gideon in Judges 6:15-16; 7:2.)

In the early church most members were poor. In a recent book sketching the social history of early Christianity, Martin Hengel points out that the early gentile Christian communities "were predominantly poor."[14] St. Paul marveled at the kind of people God called into the church: "Not many of you were wise according to worldly standards, not many were powerful, not many were of noble birth; but God chose what is foolish in the world to shame the wise, God chose what is weak in the world to shame the strong, God chose what is low and despised in the world, even things that are not, to bring to nothing things that are, so that no human being might boast in the presence of God" (1 Cor 1:26-29).

Likewise James:

My brethren, show no partiality as you hold the faith of our Lord Jesus Christ, the Lord of glory. For if a man with gold rings and in fine clothing comes into your assembly, and a poor man in shabby clothing also comes in, and you pay attention to the one who wears the fine clothing and say, "Have a seat here, please," while you say to the poor man, "Stand there," or, "Sit at my feet," have you not made distinctions among yourselves, and become judges with evil thoughts? Listen, my beloved brethren. Has not God chosen those who are poor in the world to be rich in faith and heirs of the kingdom which he has promised to those who love him? But you have dishonored the poor man. Is it not the rich who oppress you, is it not they who drag you into court? Is it not they who blaspheme the honorable name which was invoked over you? (Jas 2:1-7)

The rhetorical question in verse five indicates that the Jerusalem church too was far from rich. But the entire passage illustrates the way the church so often forsakes God's way and opts instead for the way of the world. At both the exodus and the emergence of the early church, God chose poor folk as his special instruments.

Of course one must not overstate the case. Abraham seems to have been well off. Moses lived at Pharaoh's court for forty years. Paul and Luke were neither poor nor uneducated. God does not work exclusively through impoverished, oppressed people. There is a sharp contrast, nonetheless, between God's procedure and ours.

When we want to effect change, we almost always contact people with influence, prestige and power. When God wanted to save the world, he selected slaves, prostitutes and sundry other disadvantaged folk.

Again the Incarnation is the most important example. Nowhere is the contrast between God's ways and ours clearer than here. God might have entered history as a powerful Roman emperor or at least as an influential Sadducee with a prominent place in the Sanhedrin. Instead he came and lived as a poor carpenter in Nazareth, a humble hamlet too insignificant to be mentioned either in the Old Testament or the writings of Josephus, the first-century Jewish historian.[15] Yet this is how God chose to effect our salvation.

When Jesus chose his disciples, the persons who were to carry on his mission, all except Matthew were fishermen and other common folk. Those who think that only the rich and powerful change history continue to take offense at Jesus' preoccupation with the poor and weak.

Again we must oppose the view that God never uses rich, powerful people as his chosen instruments. He has and does. But we *always* choose such people. God, on the other hand, frequently selects the poor to carry out his most important tasks. He sees potential that we do not. And when the task is done, the poor and weak are less likely to boast that they deserve the credit. God's selection of the lowly to be his special messengers of salvation to the world is striking evidence of his special concern for them. And his incarnation as a poor Galilean suggests that the frequent use of the poor as his special instruments is not insignificant historical trivia. It points to something significant about the very nature of God.

Is God a Marxist?

Jesus' story of the rich man and Lazarus echoes and illustrates a fourth teaching prominent throughout Scripture: The rich may prosper for a time, but eventually God will destroy them; the poor on the other hand, God will exalt. Mary's Magnificat puts it simply and bluntly:

My soul magnifies the Lord....
He has put down the mighty from their thrones,
    and exalted those of low degree;
he has filled the hungry with good things,

and the rich he has sent empty away. (Lk 1:46, 52-53)
Centuries earlier Hannah's song had proclaimed the same truth:
> There is none holy like the LORD,
> > there is none besides thee. . . .
> Talk no more so very proudly,
> > let not arrogance come from your mouth. . . .
> The bows of the mighty are broken,
> > but the feeble gird on strength.
> Those who were full have hired themselves out for bread,
> > but those who were hungry have ceased to hunger. . . .
> The LORD makes poor and makes rich. . . .
> He raises up the poor from the dust;
> > he lifts the needy from the ash heap. (1 Sam 2:2-8)

Jesus pronounced a blessing on the poor and a curse on the rich:
> Blessed are you poor, for yours is the kingdom of God.
> Blessed are you that hunger now, for you shall be satisfied. . . .
> Woe to you that are rich, for you have received your consolation.
> Woe to you that are full now, for you shall hunger. (Lk 6:20-25)[16]

"Come now, you rich, weep and howl for the miseries that are coming upon you" (Jas 5:1) is a constant theme of biblical revelation.

Why does Scripture declare that God regularly reverses the good fortunes of the rich? Is God engaged in class warfare? Our texts never say that God loves the poor more than the rich. But they do constantly assert that God lifts up the poor and disadvantaged. They persistently insist that God casts down the wealthy and powerful—precisely because they became wealthy by oppressing the poor or because they failed to feed the hungry.

Why did James warn the rich to weep and howl because of impending misery? Because they had cheated their workers: "You have laid up treasure for the last days. Behold, the wages of the laborers who mowed your fields, which you kept back by fraud, cry out; and the cries of the harvesters have reached the ears of the Lord of hosts. You have lived on the earth in luxury and in pleasure; you have fattened your hearts in a day of slaughter" (Jas 5:3-5). God does not have class enemies. But he hates and punishes injustice and neglect of the poor. And the rich, if we accept the repeated warnings of Scripture, are frequently guilty of both.[17]

Long before the days of James, the psalmist knew that the rich were often rich because of oppression. He took comfort in the faith that God would punish such evildoers.

> In arrogance the wicked hotly pursue the poor. . . .
> His ways prosper at all times. . . .
> He thinks in his heart, "I shall not be moved;
>> throughout all generations I shall not meet adversity. . . ."
> he lurks in secret like a lion in his covert;
> he lurks that he may seize the poor,
>> he seizes the poor when he draws him into his net. . . .
> Arise, O LORD; O God, lift up thy hand;
>> forget not the afflicted. . . .
> Break thou the arm of the wicked and evildoer. . . .
> O LORD, thou wilt hear the desire of the meek;
>> thou wilt strengthen their heart,
>> thou wilt incline thy ear
> to do justice to the fatherless and the oppressed. (Ps 10)

God announced the same message through the prophet Jeremiah:

> Wicked men are found among my people;
>> they lurk like fowlers lying in wait.
> They set a trap;
>> they catch men.
> Like a basket full of birds
>> their houses are full of treachery;
> *therefore they have become great and rich,*
>> *they have grown fat and sleek.*
> They know no bounds in deeds of wickedness;
>> they judge not with justice
> the cause of the fatherless, to make it prosper,
>> and they do not defend the rights of the needy.
> Shall I not punish them for these things?
>> says the LORD. (Jer 5:26-29)

Nor was the faith of Jeremiah and the psalmist mere wishful thinking. Through the prophets God announced devastation and destruction for both rich individuals and rich nations who oppressed the poor. And it happened as they predicted. Jeremiah pronounced one of the most biting, satirical diatribes in all of Scripture against the unjust King Jehoiakim of Judah:

> "Woe to him who builds his house by unrighteousness,
>> and his upper rooms by injustice;
> who makes his neighbor serve him for nothing,

and does not give him his wages;
who says, 'I will build myself a great house
    with spacious upper rooms,'
and cuts out windows for it,
    paneling it with cedar,
    and painting it with vermilion.
Do you think you are a king
    because you compete in cedar?
Did not your father eat and drink
    and do justice and righteousness?
Then it was well with him.
He judged the cause of the poor and needy;
    then it was well.
Is not this to know me?
    says the LORD.
But you have eyes and heart
    only for your dishonest gain,
for shedding innocent blood,
    and for practicing oppression and violence."
    Therefore thus says the LORD concerning Jehoiakim: . . .
"With the burial of an ass he shall be buried,
    dragged and cast forth beyond the gates of Jerusalem."
    (Jer 22:13-19)
Jehoiakim, historians think, was assassinated.[18]

God destroys whole nations as well as rich individuals because of
oppression of the poor. We have already examined a few of the pertinent texts.[19] One more is important. Through Isaiah God declared
that the rulers of Judah were rich because they had cheated the
poor. Surfeited with affluence, the wealthy women had indulged in
self-centered wantonness, oblivious to the suffering of the oppressed. The result, God said, would be destruction.

The LORD enters into judgment
    with the elders and princes of his people:
"It is you who have devoured the vineyard,
    the spoil of the poor is in your houses.
What do you mean by crushing my people,
    by grinding the face of the poor?"
        says the Lord GOD of hosts.
The LORD said:

Because the daughters of Zion are haughty
and walk with outstretched necks,
glancing wantonly with their eyes,
mincing along as they go,
tinkling with their feet;
the Lord will smite with a scab
the heads of the daughters of Zion. . . .
In that day the Lord will take away the finery
of the anklets, the headbands, and the crescents. . . .
Instead of perfume there will be rottenness;
and instead of a girdle, a rope;
and instead of well-set hair, baldness;
and instead of a rich robe, a girding of sackcloth;
instead of beauty, shame.
Your men shall fall by the sword
and your mighty men in battle. (Is 3:14-25)

Because the rich oppress the poor and weak, the Lord of history is at work pulling down their houses and kingdoms.

Sometimes Scripture does not charge the rich with direct oppression of the poor. It simply accuses them of failure to share with the needy. But the result is the same.

In the story of the rich man and Lazarus, Jesus does not say that the rich man exploited Lazarus (Lk 16). He merely shows that he had no concern for the sick beggar lying outside his gate. "Clothed in purple and fine linen [the rich man] feasted sumptuously every day" (Lk 16:19). Lazarus, on the other hand, "desired to be fed with what fell from the rich man's table" (Lk 16:21). Did the rich man deny hungry Lazarus even the scraps? Perhaps not. But obviously he had no real concern for him.

Such sinful neglect of the needy infuriates the God of the poor. When Lazarus died, God comforted him in Abraham's bosom. When the rich man died, torment confronted him.[20] The meaning of the name *Lazarus,* "one whom God has helped," underlines the basic point.[21] God aids the poor, but the rich he sends empty away.

Clark Pinnock is surely correct when he notes that "a story like that of Dives and Lazarus ought to explode in our hands when we read it sitting at our well-covered tables while the third world stands outside."[22] Not only the Law and the Prophets declare the terrifying word that God destroys the rich when they fail to assist the poor; our Lord himself declares it.

The biblical explanation of Sodom's destruction provides another illustration of this terrible truth. If asked why Sodom was destroyed, virtually all Christians would point to the city's gross sexual perversity. But that is a one-sided recollection of what Scripture actually teaches. Ezekiel shows that one important reason God destroyed Sodom was that it stubbornly refused to share with the poor!

> Behold, this was the guilt of your sister Sodom: she and her daughters had pride, *surfeit of food, and prosperous ease, but did not aid the poor and needy.* They were haughty, and did abominable things before me; therefore I removed them, when I saw it. (Ezek 16:49-50; see also Is 1:10-17)

The text does not say that they oppressed the poor, although they probably did. It simply accuses them of failing to assist the needy.

Affluent Christians remember Sodom's sexual misconduct and forget its sinful unconcern for the poor. Is it because the former is less upsetting? Have we allowed our economic self-interest to distort our interpretation of Scripture? Undoubtedly we have. But precisely to the extent that our affirmation of scriptural authority is sincere, we will permit painful texts to correct our thinking. As we do, we will acknowledge in fear and trembling that the God of the Bible wreaks horrendous havoc on the rich. But it is not because he does not love rich persons. It is because the rich regularly oppress the poor or neglect the needy.

God's Concern and Ours

Since God cares so much for the poor, it is hardly surprising that he wants his people to do the same. God's command to believers to have a special regard for the poor, weak and disadvantaged is the fifth theme of biblical literature we shall follow.

Equal justice for the poor in court is a constant concern of Scripture. The law commanded it (Ex 23:6). The psalmist invoked divine assistance for the king so that he could provide it (Ps 72:1-4). And the prophets announced destruction because the rulers stubbornly subverted it (Amos 5:10-15).

Widows, orphans and strangers also receive particularly frequent attention. "You shall not wrong a stranger or oppress him, for you were strangers in the land of Egypt. You shall not afflict any widow or orphan. If you do afflict them, and they cry out to me, I will surely hear their cry; and my wrath will burn, and I will kill you with the sword, and your wives shall become widows and your children fatherless" (Ex 22:21-24).

"The fatherless, widows, and foreigners," John F. Alexander observes, "each have about forty verses that command justice for them. God wants to make it very clear that in a special sense he is the protector of these weak ones. Strangers are to be treated nearly the same as Jews, and woe to people who take advantage of orphans or widows."[23]

Rare indeed are the Christians who pay any attention to Jesus' command to show bias toward the poor in their dinner invitations. "When you give a dinner or a banquet, do not invite your friends or your brothers or your kinsmen or rich neighbors. . . . But when you give a feast, invite the poor, the maimed, the lame, the blind, and you will be blessed, because they cannot repay you" (Lk 14:12-14; see also Heb 13:1-3).

Obviously Jesus was employing hyperbole, a typical technique of Hebrew literature to emphasize his point. He did not mean to forbid parties with friends and relatives. But he certainly did mean that we ought to entertain the poor and disadvantaged (who cannot reciprocate) at least as often—and perhaps a lot more often than we entertain friends, relatives and "successful" folk. Have you ever known a Christian who took Jesus that seriously?

The Bible specifically commands believers to imitate God's special concern for the poor and oppressed. In the Old Testament, Yahweh frequently reminded the Israelites of their former oppression in Egypt when he commanded them to care for the poor. God's unmerited concern for the Hebrew slaves in Egyptian bondage is the model to imitate (Ex 22:21-24; Deut 15:13-15).

Jesus taught his followers to imitate God's mercy in their lending as well. "If you do good to those who do good to you, what credit is that to you? . . . And if you lend to those from whom you hope to receive, what credit is that to you? . . . Lend, expecting nothing in return; and your reward will be great, and you will be sons of the Most High; for he is kind to the ungrateful and the selfish. Be merciful, even as your Father is merciful" (Lk 6:33-36). Why lend without expecting return? Because that is the way our Father acts. Jesus' followers are to reverse normal human patterns precisely because they are sons and daughters of God and want to reflect his nature.

When Paul took up the collection for the poor in Jerusalem, he pointedly reminded the Corinthians that the Lord Jesus became poor so that they might become rich (2 Cor 8:9). When the author of 1 John called on Christians to share with the needy, he first mentioned the example of Christ: "By this we know love, that he laid down his life for us; and we ought to lay down our lives for the brethren" (1 Jn 3:16). Then, in the very next verse, he urged Christians to give generously to the needy. It is the amazing self-sacrifice of Christ which Christians are to imitate as they relate to the poor and oppressed.

We have seen that God's Word commands believers to care for the poor. In fact the Bible underlines the command by teaching that when God's people care for the poor, they imitate God himself. But that is not all. God's Word teaches that those who neglect the poor and oppressed are really not God's people at all—no matter how frequent their religious rituals or how orthodox their creeds and confessions.

God thundered again and again through the prophets that worship in the context of mistreatment of the poor and disadvantaged is an outrage. Isaiah denounced Israel (he called it Sodom and Gomorrah!) because it tried to worship Yahweh and oppress the weak at the same time:

Hear the word of the LORD,
　　you rulers of Sodom!
Give ear to the teaching of our God,
　　you people of Gomorrah!
"What to me is the multitude of your sacrifices? . . .
Bring no more vain offerings;
　　incense is an abomination to me.
New moon and sabbath and the calling of assemblies—
　　I cannot endure iniquity and solemn assembly.
Your new moons and your appointed feasts
　　my soul hates; . . .
even though you make many prayers,
　　I will not listen;
　　your hands are full of blood." (Is 1:10-15)

What does God want? "Cease to do evil, learn to do good; seek justice, correct oppression; defend the fatherless, plead for the widow" (Is 1:16-17).

Equally powerful are Isaiah's words against mixing fasting and injustice:
"Why have we fasted, and thou seest it not?
    Why have we humbled ourselves,
    and thou takest no knowledge of it?"
Behold, in the day of your fast you seek your own pleasure,
    and oppress all your workers. . . .
Is not this the fast that I choose:
    to loose the bonds of wickedness,
    to undo the thongs of the yoke,
to let the oppressed go free,
    and to break every yoke?
Is it not to share your bread with the hungry,
    and bring the homeless poor into your house? (Is 58:3-7)
God's words through the prophet Amos are also harsh:
I hate, I despise your feasts,
    and I take no delight in your solemn assemblies.
Even though you offer me your burnt offerings and cereal offer-
        ings,
    I will not accept them. . . .
But let justice roll down like waters,
    and righteousness like an ever-flowing stream. (Amos 5:21-24)[24]
Earlier in Amos 5 the prophet had condemned the rich and power-
ful for oppressing the poor. They even bribed judges to prevent
redress in the courts. God wants justice, not mere religious rituals,
from such people.[25] Their worship is a mockery and abomination
to the God of the poor.

God has not changed. Jesus repeated the same theme. He warned
the people about the scribes "who devour widows' houses and for a
pretense make long prayers" (Mk 12:40). Their pious-looking garments and frequent visits to the synagogue were a sham. Jesus was a
Hebrew prophet in the tradition of Amos and Isaiah. Like them he
announced God's outrage against those who try to mix pious practices and mistreatment of the poor.

The prophetic word against religious hypocrites raises a difficult
question. Are the people of God truly God's people if they oppress
the poor? Is the church really the church if it does not work to free
the oppressed?

We have seen how God declared that the people of Israel were really Sodom and Gomorrah rather than the people of God (Is 1:10). God simply could not tolerate their exploitation of the poor and disadvantaged any longer. Hosea solemnly announced that, because of their sins, Israel was no longer God's people and he was no longer their God (Hos 1:8-9). In fact God destroyed them. Jesus was even more blunt and sharp. To those who do not feed the hungry, clothe the naked and visit the prisoners, he will speak a terrifying word at the final judgment: "Depart from me, you cursed, into the eternal fire prepared for the devil and his angels" (Mt 25:41). The meaning is clear and unambiguous. Jesus intends that his disciples imitate his own special concern for the poor and needy. Those who disobey will experience eternal damnation.

But perhaps we have misinterpreted Matthew 25. Some people think that "the least of these" (v. 45) and "the least of these my brethren" (v. 40) refer only to Christians. This exegesis is not certain. But even if the primary reference of these words is to poor believers, other aspects of Jesus' teaching not only permit but require us to extend the meaning of Matthew 25 to both believers and unbelievers who are poor and oppressed. The story of the good Samaritan teaches that anybody in need is our neighbor (Lk 10:29-37). Matthew 5:43-45 is even more explicit: "You have heard that it was said, 'You shall love your neighbor and hate your enemy.' But I say to you, Love your enemies and pray for those who persecute you, so that you may be sons of your Father who is in heaven; for he makes his sun rise on the evil and on the good, and sends rain on the just and on the unjust."

The ideal in the Qumran community (known to us through the Dead Sea Scrolls) was indeed to "love all the sons of light" and "hate all the sons of darkness" (1 QS 1:9-10, the Essenes' Community Rule). Even in the Old Testament, Israelites were commanded to love the neighbor who was the son of their own people and ordered not to seek the prosperity of Ammonites and Moabites (Lev 19:17-18; Deut 23:3-6). But Jesus explicitly forbids his followers to limit their loving concern to the neighbor who is a member of their own ethnic or religious group. He explicitly commands his followers to imitate God who does good for all people everywhere.

As George Ladd has said, "Jesus redefines the meaning of love for neighbor; it means love for any man in need."[26] In light of the parable of the good Samaritan and the clear teaching of Matthew

5:43-48, one is compelled to say that part of the full teaching of Matthew 25 is that those who fail to aid the poor and oppressed (whether they are believers or not) are simply not the people of God.

In 1 John 3:17-18 we find the same message: "If any one has the world's goods and sees his brother in need, yet closes his heart against him, how does God's love abide in him? Little children, let us not love in word or speech but in deed and in truth." (See also James 2:14-17.) Again the words are plain. What do they mean for Western Christians who demand increasing affluence each year while Christians in the Third World suffer from malnutrition, deformed bodies and brains—even starvation? The text clearly says that if we fail to aid the needy, we do not have God's love—no matter what we may say. It is deeds that count, not pious phrases and saintly speeches. Regardless of what we do or say at 11:00 A.M. Sunday morning, affluent people who neglect the poor are not the people of God.

But still the question persists. Are professing believers no longer Christians because of continuing sin? Obviously not. The Christian knows that sinful selfishness continues to plague even the most saintly. Salvation is by grace alone, not works-righteousness. We are members of the people of God not because of our own righteousness but solely because of Christ's death for us.

That response is true—but inadequate by itself. Matthew 25 and 1 John 3 surely mean more than that the people of God are disobedient (but still justified all the same) when they neglect the poor. These verses pointedly assert that some people so disobey God that they are not his people at all in spite of their pious profession. Neglect of the poor is one of the oft-repeated biblical signs of such disobedience. Certainly none of us would claim that we fulfill Matthew 25 perfectly. And we cling to the hope of forgiveness. But there comes a point (and, thank God, he alone knows where!) when neglect of the poor is not forgiven. It is punished. Eternally.

Is it not possible that many Western "Christians" have reached that point? North Americans earn fourteen times as much as the people in India, but we give only a small amount to the church. Most churches spend much of that pittance on themselves. Can we claim we are obeying the biblical command to have a special concern for the poor? Can we honestly say we are imitating God's concern for the poor and oppressed? Can we seriously hope to experience eternal love rather than eternal separation from the God of the poor?

The biblical teaching that Yahweh has a special concern for the poor and oppressed is unambiguous. But does that mean, as some assert today, that God is biased in favor of the poor? Not really. Scripture explicitly forbids being partial. "You shall do no injustice in judgment; you shall not be partial to the poor or defer to the great, but in righteousness shall you judge your neighbor" (Lev 19:15; also Deut 1:17). Exodus 23:3 contains precisely the same injunction: "Nor shall you be partial to a poor man in his suit." God instructs his people to be impartial because he himself is not biased.

The most crucial point for us, however, is not God's impartiality, but rather the result of his freedom from bias. The text declares Yahweh's impartiality and then immediately portrays God's tender care for the weak and disadvantaged. "For the LORD your God is God of gods and LORD of lords, the great, the mighty, and the terrible God, *who is not partial* and takes no bribe. He executes justice for the fatherless and the widow, and loves the sojourner, giving him food and clothing" (Deut 10:17-18).

God is not partial. He has the same loving concern for each person he has created.[27] Precisely for that reason he cares as much for the weak and disadvantaged as he does for the strong and fortunate. By contrast with the way you and I, as well as the comfortable and powerful of every age and society, always act toward the poor, God seems to have an overwhelming bias in favor of the poor. But it is biased only in contrast with our sinful unconcern. It is only when we take our perverse preference for the successful and wealthy as natural and normative that God's concern appears biased.

On the Side of the Poor

When I say that God is on the side of the poor, there are several important things I do not mean. First, God is not biased. Second, material poverty is not a biblical ideal. Third, the poor and oppressed, just because they are poor and oppressed, are not thereby members of the church. (The poor sinfully disobey God just as do middle class sinners, and they too need to repent and be saved by God's justifying grace.) Fourth, God does not care more about the salvation of the poor than the salvation of the rich. Fifth, we dare not start with some ideologically interpreted context of oppression (for example, Marxist analysis) and then reinterpret Scripture from that ideological bias. Sixth, God does not overlook the sin of those who are poor because of sloth or alcoholism. God punishes such sinners.[28]

God, however, is not neutral. His freedom from bias does not mean that he maintains neutrality in the struggle for justice. He is indeed on the side of the poor! The Bible clearly and repeatedly teaches that God is at work in history casting down the rich and exalting the poor because frequently the rich are wealthy precisely because they have oppressed the poor or have neglected to aid the needy. As we shall see in the next chapter, God also sides with the poor because he disapproves of extremes of wealth and poverty. The God of the Bible is on the side of the poor just because he is *not* biased, for he is a God of impartial justice.

The rich neglect or oppose justice because justice demands that they end their oppression and share with the poor. Therefore God actively opposes the rich. But that does not in any way mean that he loves the rich less than the poor. God longs for the salvation of the rich as much as for the salvation of the poor. He desires fulfillment, joy and happiness for all his creatures. But that does not contradict the fact that he is on the side of the poor. Genuine biblical repentance and conversion lead people to turn away from all sin—including economic oppression.[29] Salvation for the rich will include liberation from their injustice. Thus God's desire for the salvation and fulfillment of the rich is in complete harmony with the scriptural teaching that God is on the side of the poor.

God's concern for the poor is astonishing and boundless. At the pivotal points of revelation history, Yahweh was at work liberating the oppressed. We can only begin to fathom the depth of his identification with the poor disclosed in the Incarnation. Frequently the poor are his specially chosen instruments of revelation and salvation. His passion for justice compels him to obliterate rich societies and individuals that oppress the poor and neglect the needy. Consequently, God's people—if they are indeed his people—follow in the footsteps of the God of the poor.

In light of this clear biblical teaching, how biblical is our theology? I think we must confess that Christians in North America are largely on the side of the rich oppressors rather than the oppressed poor. Imagine what would happen if all our church institutions—our youth organizations, our publications, our colleges and seminaries, our congregations and denominational headquarters—would all dare to undertake a comprehensive two-year examination of their total program and activity to answer this question: Is there the same balance and emphasis on justice for the poor and oppressed in our programs as there is in Scripture? I am willing to predict that, if we did that with an unconditional readiness to change whatever did not correspond with the scriptural revelation of God's special concern for the poor and oppressed, we would unleash a new movement of biblical social concern that would change the course of modern history.

But our problem is not primarily one of ethics. It is not that we have failed to live what our teachers have taught. Our theology itself has been unbiblical. By largely ignoring the central biblical teaching that God is on the side of the poor, our theology has been profoundly unorthodox. The Bible has just as much to say about this doctrine as it does about Jesus' resurrection. And yet we insist on the resurrection as a criterion of orthodoxy and largely ignore the equally prominent biblical teaching that God is on the side of the poor and the oppressed.

Now please do not misunderstand me at this point. I am not saying that the resurrection is unimportant. The bodily resurrection of Jesus of Nazareth is absolutely central to Christian faith and anyone who denies it or says it is unimportant has fallen into heresy.[30] But if centrality in Scripture is any criterion of doctrinal importance, then the biblical teaching that God is on the side of the poor ought to be an extremely important doctrine for Christians.

I am afraid those who have thought themselves most orthodox, however, have fallen into theological liberalism. Of course, we usually think of theological liberalism in terms of classical nineteenth-century liberals who denied the deity, the atonement and the bodily resurrection of Jesus our Lord. And that is correct. People who abandon those central biblical doctrines have fallen into terrible heresy. But notice what the essence of theological liberalism is—it is allowing our thinking and living to be shaped by the surrounding society's views and values rather than by biblical revelation. Liberal theologians thought that belief in the deity of Jesus Christ and his bodily resurrection was incompatible with a modern scientific world view. So they followed surrounding scientific society rather than Scripture.

Orthodox Christians rightly called attention to this heresy—and then tragically made exactly the same move in another area. We have allowed the values of our affluent materialistic society to shape our thinking and acting toward the poor. It is much easier in theologically conservative circles today to insist on an orthodox Christology than to insist on the biblical teaching that God is on the side of the poor. We have allowed our theology to be shaped by the economic preferences of our materialistic contemporaries rather than by Scripture. And that is to fall into theological liberalism. We have not been nearly as orthodox as we have claimed.

Past failure, however, is no reason for despair. I think we mean it when we sing, "I'd rather have Jesus than houses or lands." I think we mean it when we write and affirm doctrinal statements that boldly declare that we will not only believe but also live whatever Scripture teaches. But if we do mean it, then we must teach and live, in a world full of injustice and starvation, the important biblical doctrine that God and his faithful people are on the side of the poor and oppressed. Unless we drastically reshape both our theology and our entire institutional church life so that the fact that God is on the side of the poor and oppressed becomes as central to our theology and institutional programs as it is in Scripture, we will demonstrate to the world that our verbal commitment to *sola scriptura* is a dishonest ideological support for an unjust, materialistic status quo.

I hope and believe that in the next decade millions of Christians will allow the biblical teaching that God is on the side of the poor and oppressed to fundamentally reshape our culturally conditioned theology and our unbiblically one-sided programs and institutions. If that happens, we will forge a new, truly biblical theology of liberation that will change the course of modern history.

4

Economic Relationships among the People of God

I do not mean that others should be eased and you burdened, but that as a matter of equality your abundance at the present time should supply their want, so that their abundance may supply your want, that there may be equality. As it is written, "He who gathered much had nothing over, and he who gathered little had no lack." [2 Corinthians 8:13-15]

God requires radically transformed economic relationships among his people. Sin has alienated us from God and from each other. The result has been personal selfishness, structural injustice and economic oppression. Among the people of God, however, the power of sin is broken. The new community of the redeemed begins to display an entirely new set of personal, social and economic relationships. The present quality of life among the people of God is to be a sign of that coming perfection and justice which will be revealed when the kingdoms of this world finally and completely become the kingdom of our Lord at his second coming.

In this chapter we will look at some central biblical models of transformed economic relationships. We discover in the Scriptures that God created mechanisms and structures to prevent great economic inequality among his people. As economic relationships are redeemed in the body of Christ, the church's common life of mutual availability is to point convincingly to the coming kingdom. And —as if that were not enough—the loving oneness among Christians is to become so visible and concrete that it convinces the world that Jesus came from the Father (Jn 17:20-23).

The Jubilee Principle

Leviticus 25 is one of the most radical texts in all of Scripture. At least it seems that way for people born in countries committed to either laissez-faire economics or communism. Every fifty years, God said, all land was to return to the original owners—without compensation! Physical handicaps, death of a breadwinner or lack of natural ability may lead some people to become poorer than others. But God does not want such disadvantages to lead to greater and greater divergence of wealth and poverty. God therefore gave his people a law which would equalize land ownership every fifty years (Lev 25:10-24).

In an agricultural society, land is capital. Land was the basic means of producing wealth in Israel. At the beginning, of course, the land had been divided more or less equally among the tribes and families (Num 26:52-56).[1] Apparently God wanted that basic economic equality to continue. Hence his command to return all land to the original owners every fifty years. Private property was not abolished. But the means of producing wealth were to be equalized regularly.

What is the theological basis for this startling command? Yahweh's ownership of everything is the presupposition. The land cannot be sold permanently because Yahweh owns it: "The land shall not be sold in perpetuity, *for the land is mine;* for you are strangers and sojourners with me" (Lev 25:23). God owns the land. For a time he permits his people to sojourn on his good earth, cultivate it, eat its produce and enjoy its beauty. But we are only stewards. Stewardship is one of the central theological categories of any biblical understanding of our relationship to the land and economic resources generally.[2]

Before and after the year of jubilee, land could be bought or sold. But the buyer actually purchased a specific number of harvests, not the land itself (Lev 25:16). And woe betide the person who tried to make a killing by demanding what the market would bear rather than a just price for the intervening harvests from the date of purchase to the next jubilee! "If the years are many you shall increase the price, and if the years are few you shall diminish the price, for it is the number of the crops that he is selling to you. You shall not wrong one another, but you shall fear your God; for I am the LORD your God" (Lev 25:16-17). Yahweh is Lord—even of economics.

There is no hint here of some sacred law of supply and demand totally independent of biblical ethics and the lordship of Yahweh. The people of God submit to him, and he demands economic justice among his people.

That this passage prescribes justice rather than haphazard handouts by wealthy philanthropists is extremely significant. The year of jubilee envisaged an institutionalized structure that affected all Israelites automatically. It was to be the poor person's *right* to receive back his inheritance at the time of jubilee. Returning the land was not a charitable courtesy that the wealthy might extend if they pleased.[3]

The jubilee principle also provided for self-help and self-development. With his land returned, the poor person could again earn his own living. The biblical concept of jubilee underlines the importance of institutionalized mechanisms and structures that promote justice.

It is striking that this jubilee passage challenges both capitalism and communism in an equally fundamental way. Only God is an absolute owner. Furthermore, the right of each person to have the means to earn his own way takes priority over a purchaser's "property rights" or a totally free market economy. At the same time, this text clearly affirms not only the right but the importance of private property managed by families who understand that they are stewards responsible to God. God wants each family to have the resources to produce their own livelihood—in order to strengthen the family, in order to give people the freedom to be co-creators of history, and in order to prevent the centralization of power and totalitarianism that almost always accompanies centralized ownership of land or capital by either the state or small elites.

One final aspect of Leviticus 25 is striking. It is surely more than coincidental that the trumpet blast announcing the jubilee sounded forth on the Day of Atonement (Lev 25:9). Reconciliation with God is the precondition for reconciliation with brothers and sisters.[4] Conversely, genuine reconciliation with God leads inevitably to a transformation of all other relationships. Reconciled with God by the sacrifice on the Day of Atonement, the more prosperous Israelites were to liberate the poor by freeing Hebrew slaves as well as returning all land to the original owners.[5]

Unfortunately, we do not know whether the people of Israel ever practiced the year of jubilee. The absence of references to jubilee in the historical books suggests that it may never have been implemented.[6] Regardless of its antiquity or implementation, Leviticus 25 remains a part of God's authoritative Word. Because he disapproves of extremes of wealth among his people, God ordains equalizing mechanisms like the year of jubilee.

The Sabbatical Year

The law also provides for liberation of soil, slaves and debtors every seven years. Again the concern is justice for the poor and disadvantaged.

Every seven years the land is to lie fallow (Ex 23:10-11; Lev 25:2-7).[7] The purpose, apparently, is both ecological and humanitarian. Not planting any crops every seventh year certainly helps preserve the fertility of the soil. God, however, is particularly concerned with the poor: "For six years you shall sow your land and gather in its yield; but the seventh year you shall let it rest and lie fallow, *that the poor of your people may eat*" (Ex 23:10-11). In the seventh year the poor are free to gather for themselves whatever grows spontaneously in the fields and vineyards.

Hebrew slaves also receive their freedom in the sabbatical year (Deut 15:12-18). Poverty sometimes forced Israelites to sell themselves as slaves to more prosperous neighbors (Lev 25:39-40).[8] But this inequality, God decrees, is not to be permanent. At the end of six years the Hebrew slaves are to be set free. And masters are to share the proceeds of their joint labors with the departing brothers: "And when you let him go free from you, you shall not let him go empty-handed; you shall furnish him liberally out of your flock, out of your threshing floor, and out of your wine press; as the LORD your God has blessed you, you shall give to him" (Deut 15:13-14; see also Ex 21:2-6). The freed slave would thereby have the means to earn his own way.[9]

The sabbatical provision on loans is even more revolutionary (Deut 15:1-6). Every seven years all debts are to be canceled! Yahweh even adds a footnote for those with a sharp eye for loopholes: It is sinful to refuse a loan to a poor man just because it is the sixth year and the money will be lost in twelve months.

Take heed lest there be a base thought in your heart, and you say, "The seventh year, the year of release is near," and your eye be hostile to your poor brother, and you give him nothing, and he cry to the LORD against you, and it be sin in you. You shall give to him freely, and your heart shall not be grudging when you give to him; because for this the LORD your God will bless you. (Deut 15:9-10)[10]

As in the case of the year of jubilee, it is crucial to note that Scripture prescribes justice rather than mere charity. The sabbatical release of debts was an institutionalized mechanism for preventing an ever-growing gap between rich and poor.

Deuteronomy 15 is both an idealistic statement of God's perfect demand and also a realistic reference to Israel's probable performance concerning debts. Verse 4 promises that there will be no poor in Israel—if they obey all the commands God provides! But God knew they would not attain that standard. Hence the recognition in verse 11 that poor people will always exist in Israel. But the conclusion is not that one can therefore ignore the needy because hordes of paupers will always far exceed one's resources. It is precisely the opposite. "For the poor will never cease out of the land; *therefore* I command you, You shall open wide your hand to your brother, to the needy and to the poor, in the land."

Jesus knew and Deuteronomy implies that sinful persons and societies will always produce poor people (Mt 26:11). Rather than justifying negligence, however, God intends this insight to lead to renewed concern for the needy and to the creation of structural mechanisms for promoting justice.

The sabbatical year, unfortunately, was practiced only sporadically. In fact, some texts suggest that failure to obey this law was one reason for the Babylonian exile (2 Chron 36:20-21; Lev 26:34-36).[11] Israel's disobedience, however, does not weaken God's demand. Institutionalized structures to reduce poverty and great economic inequality are God's will for his people.

Laws on Tithing and Gleaning

Other legal provisions extend the concern of the year of jubilee and the sabbatical year. The law calls for one-tenth of all farm produce, whether animal, grain or wine, to be set aside as a tithe. "At the end of every three years you shall bring forth all the tithe of your produce in the same year; . . . and the Levite . . . and the sojourner, the fatherless, and the widow, who are within your towns, shall come and eat and be filled; that the LORD your God may bless you" (Deut 14:28-29; see also Lev 27:30-32; Deut 26:12-15; Num 18:21-32).[12]

The poor widow Ruth was able to survive because of this law of gleaning. When she and Naomi returned to Bethlehem penniless, the grandmother of King David went into the fields at harvest time and gathered the stalks of grain dropped by the gleaners (Ruth 2). She could do that because God's law decreed that farmers should leave some of the harvest, including the corners of grain fields, for the poor. Grapes that had been dropped accidentally were to be left. "You shall leave them for the poor and for the sojourner: I am the LORD your God" (Lev 19:10).

The memory of their own poverty and oppression in Egypt was to prompt them to leave generous gleanings for the poor sojourner, the widow and the fatherless. "You shall remember that you were a slave in the land of Egypt; therefore I command you to do this" (Deut 24:22). The law of gleaning was an established method for preventing debilitating poverty among the people of God and sojourners in the land.

Models to Follow and Avoid
How do we apply biblical revelation on the year of jubilee, the sabbatical year, tithes and gleaning today? Should we attempt to implement these mechanisms? Are these laws, even the basic principles, applicable to the church at all?

God gave Israel the law so that his people would know how to live together in peace and justice. The church is now the new people of God (Gal 3:6-9; 6:16; 1 Pet 2:9-10). Certainly, as Paul and other New Testament writers indicate, parts of the Mosaic law (the ceremonial law, for instance) no longer apply to the church. But there is no indication that the moral law has ceased to be normative for Christians (Mt 5:17-20; Rom 8:4).[13] The Old Testament's revelation about the kind of economic relationships that promote love and harmony among God's people should still guide the church today. (Whether these laws have any relevance for society as a whole will be discussed in chapter nine.)

How then do we apply the actual laws we have discussed? Should we attempt to revive the specific mechanisms proposed in Leviticus 25 and Deuteronomy 15?

Certainly not. The specific provisions of the year of jubilee are not binding today. Modern technological society is vastly different from rural Palestine. If Kansas farmers left grain standing in the corners of their fields, it would not help the hungry in inner-city New York or rural India. We need methods appropriate to our own civilization. It is the basic principles, not the specific details, which are important and normative for Christians today.

The history of the prohibition against charging interest is instructive at this point. The annual rate of interest in the ancient Near East was incredibly high—often as much as 25 per cent or more.[14] It is not hard, therefore, to see why the law includes prohibitions against charging interest to fellow Israelites (Ex 22:25; Deut 23:19-20; Lev 25:35-38).[15] The *International Critical Commentary* suggests that this legislation reflects a time when most loans were charitable loans rather than commercial ones. Commercial loans to establish or extend a business were not common. Most were charitable loans needed by a poor person or by someone facing a temporary emergency.[16] It is quite clear that the well-being of the poor is a central concern of the texts on interest. "If you lend money to any of my people with you who is poor, you shall not be to him as a creditor, and you shall not exact interest from him" (Ex 22:25). The legislation on interest is one part of an extensive set of laws designed to protect the poor and prevent great extremes of wealth and poverty among the people of God.

Failing to understand this, the Christian church attempted to apply the texts on interest in a legalistic way. Several church councils wrestled with the question. Eventually, all interest on loans was prohibited in 1179 (Third Lateran Council). But the results were tragic. Medieval monarchs invited Jews, who were not bound by the church's teaching, into their realms to be money lenders. Anti-Semitism was one demonic result. Increasingly, theologians developed casuistic schemes for circumventing the prohibition.[17] Tragically, the misguided preoccupation with the letter of the law and the resulting adoption of an unworkable, legalistic application helped discredit or at least obscure the important biblical teaching that the God of the poor is Lord of economics—Lord even of interest rates. Legalistic utilization of the texts on interest thus helped create the modern mentality which views loans, banking, indeed the whole field of economics, as completely independent and autonomous. From the standpoint of revealed faith, of course, such a view is heretical. It stems from modern secularism, not from the Bible.[18]

This history warns us against a wooden application. But it dare not lead to timid silence. These texts unquestionably teach that the borrowers' need, rather than careful calculation of potential profit, must be decisive for the Christian lender. (Low-interest or no-interest loans for development provided by Christian organizations to Christians in the Third World are an example of meaningful, contemporary application of God's Word on interest.)

In applying the biblical teaching on the year of jubilee, the sabbatical year, gleaning and tithing, then, we must discover the underlying principles. Then we can search for contemporary strategies to give flesh to these basic principles. The texts we have examined clearly show that God wills justice, not mere charity. Therefore Christians should design and institute new structures that can effectively eliminate indigence among believers, and drastically reduce the scandalous extremes of wealth and poverty between rich and poor members of the one body of the risen Jesus.

Jesus' New Community

Let us see how the first-century Christians reaffirmed the Old Testament teaching. Jesus walked the roads of Galilee announcing the startling news that the kingdom of peace and righteousness was at hand. Economic relationships in the new community of his followers were a powerful sign confirming this awesome announcement.

The Hebrew prophets had predicted more than that Israel would be destroyed because of her idolatry and oppression of the poor. They had also proclaimed a message of hope—the hope of a future messianic kingdom. The days are coming, they promised, when God will raise up a righteous branch from the Davidic line. Peace, righteousness and justice will then abound in a new, redeemed society. When the shoot from the stump of Jesse comes, Isaiah predicted, the poor and meek will finally receive their due: "With righteousness he shall judge the poor, and decide with equity for the meek of the earth" (Is 11:4; see also Is 9:6-7; 61:1; Jer 23:5; Hos 2:18-20).

The essence of the good news which Jesus proclaimed was that the expected messianic kingdom had come.[19] Certainly the kingdom Jesus announced disappointed popular Jewish expectations. He did not recruit an army to drive out the Romans. He did not attempt to establish a free Jewish state. But neither did he remain alone as an isolated, individualistic prophet. He called and trained disciples. He established a visible community of disciples joined together by their submission to him as Lord. His new community began to live the values of the promised kingdom which was already breaking into the present. As a result, all relationships, even economic ones, were transformed in the community of Jesus' followers.

They shared a common purse (Jn 12:6).[20] Judas administered the common fund, buying provisions or giving to the poor at Jesus' direction (Jn 13:29). Nor did this new community of sharing end with Jesus and the Twelve. It included a number of women whom Jesus had healed. The women traveled with Jesus and the disciples, sharing their financial resources with them (Lk 8:1-3; see also Mk 15:40-41).[21]

From this perspective, some of Jesus' words gain new meaning and power. Consider his advice to the rich young man.

When Jesus asked the rich young man to sell his goods and give to the poor, he did not say "Become destitute and friendless." Rather, he said, "Come, follow me" (Mt. 19:21). In other words, he invited him to join a community of sharing and love, where his security would not be based on individual property holdings, but on openness to the Spirit and on the loving care of new-found brothers and sisters.[22]

Jesus invited the rich young man to share the joyful common life of his new kingdom.

Jesus' words in Mark 10:29-30 have long puzzled me: "Truly, I say to you, there is no one who has left house or brothers or sisters or mother or father or children or lands, for my sake and for the gospel, who will not receive a hundredfold *now in this time, houses and brothers and sisters and mothers and children and lands,* with persecutions, and in the age to come eternal life." Matthew 6 contains a similar saying. We are all very—indeed embarrassingly—familiar with the way Jesus urged his followers to enjoy a carefree life unburdened by anxiety over food, clothing and possessions (Mt 6:25-33). But he ended his advice with a promise too good to be true: "But seek first his kingdom and his righteousness, and all these things [that is, food, clothing and so on] shall be yours as well." These promises used to seem at least a trifle naive. But his words came alive with meaning when I read them in the context of the new community of Jesus' followers. Jesus began a new social order, a new kingdom of faithful followers who were to be almost completely available to each other.

The common purse of Jesus' disciples symbolized that almost unlimited liability for each other. In that new community there would be genuine economic security. Each would indeed have many more loving brothers and sisters than before. The economic resources available in difficult times would in fact be compounded a hundredfold and more. The resources of the entire community of obedient disciples would be available to anyone in need. To be sure, that kind of unselfish, sharing lifestyle would challenge surrounding society so pointedly that there would be persecutions. But even in the most desperate days, the promise would not be empty. Even if persecution led to death, children of martyred parents would receive new mothers and fathers in the community of believers.

In the community of the redeemed, all relationships are being transformed. Jesus and his first followers vividly demonstrate that the old covenant's pattern of economic relationships among the people of God is continued and deepened.

The Jerusalem Model

However embarrassing it may be to some, the massive economic sharing of the earliest Christian church is indisputable. "Now the company of those who believed were of one heart and soul, and no one said that any of the things which he possessed was his own, but they had everything in common" (Acts 4:32). Everywhere in the early chapters of Acts, the evidence is abundant and unambiguous (Acts 2:43-47; 4:32-37; 5:1-11; 6:1-7). The early church continued the pattern of economic sharing practiced by Jesus.

Economic sharing in the Jerusalem church started in the earliest period. Immediately after reporting the three thousand conversions at Pentecost, Acts notes that "all who believed were together and had all things in common" (2:44). Whenever anyone was in need, they shared. Giving surplus income to needy brothers and sisters was not enough. They regularly dipped into capital reserves, selling property to aid the needy. Barnabas sold a field he owned (4:36-37). Ananias and Sapphira sold property, although they lied about the price. God's promise to Israel that faithful obedience would eliminate poverty among his people came true (Deut 15:4)! *"There was not a needy person among them,* for as many as were possessors of lands or houses sold them; . . . and distribution was made to each as any had need" (Acts 4:34-35).

Two millenniums later the texts still throb with the first community's joy and excitement. They ate meals together "with glad and generous hearts" (Acts 2:46). They experienced an exciting unity as all sensed they "were of one heart and soul" (4:32). They were not isolated individuals, struggling alone to follow Jesus. A new community, in which all areas of life (including economics) were being transformed, became a joyful reality.

The evangelistic impact of their demonstration of oneness is striking. The texts repeatedly relate the transformed economic relationships in the Jerusalem church to the phenomenal evangelistic outreach. "And day by day, attending the temple together and breaking bread in their homes, they partook of food with glad and generous hearts, praising God *and having favor with all the people*. And the Lord added to their number day by day" (Acts 2:46-47). The joy and love exhibited in their common life was contagious. I mentioned that the author records in Acts 4 that they had all things in common instead of clinging to their private possessions. In the very next verse he adds, *"And with great power* the apostles gave their testimony to the resurrection of the Lord Jesus" (v. 33). Jesus' prayer that the loving unity of his followers would be so striking that it would convince the world that he had come from the Father has been answered—at least once! It happened in the Jerusalem church. The unusual quality of their life together gave power to the apostolic preaching.

The account in Acts 6 is particularly instructive. Apparently there was a significant minority of Hellenists in the Jerusalem church. (Hellenists were Greek-speaking Jews, perhaps even Greeks that had converted to Judaism.) Somehow, the Jewish-speaking majority had overlooked the needs of the Hellenist widows until they complained about the injustice. The church's response is startling. The seven men chosen to look after this matter were all from the minority group! Every one of their names is Greek.[23] The church turned over their entire program and funds for needy widows to the minority group that had been discriminated against. What was the result of this new act of financial fellowship? *"And the word of God increased;* and the number of disciples multiplied greatly in Jerusalem" (Acts 6:7).

Redeemed economic relationships in the early church resulted in an increase of the Word of God. What a sobering thought! Is it perhaps the same today? Would similar economic changes produce a dramatic increase of believers today? Probably so. Are those who talk about the importance of evangelism prepared to pay *that* price?

But what is the price to be paid? What was the precise nature of the Jerusalem church's costly *koinōnia*? The earliest church did not insist on absolute economic equality. Nor did they abolish private property. Peter reminded Ananias that he had been under no obligation either to sell his property or to donate the proceeds to the church (Acts 5:4). Sharing was voluntary, not compulsory.[24] But love for brothers and sisters was so overwhelming that many freely abandoned legitimate claims to private possessions. "No one said that any of the things which he possessed was his own" (4:32). That does not mean that everyone donated everything. Later in Acts we see that John Mark's mother, Mary, still owned her own house (12:12). Others also undoubtedly retained some private property.

The tense of the Greek words confirms this interpretation. In both Acts 2:45 and 4:34, the verbs are in the imperfect tense. In Greek the imperfect tense denotes continued, repeated action over an extended period of time. Thus the meaning is, "They often sold possessions," or, "They were in the habit of regularly bringing the proceeds of what was being sold."[25] The text does not suggest that the community decided to abolish all private property or that everyone instantly sold everything. Rather it suggests that over a period of time, whenever there was need, believers regularly sold lands and houses to aid the needy.

What then was the essence of the transformed economic relationships in the Jerusalem church? The best way to describe their practice is to speak of almost unlimited liability and near total availability. Their sharing was not superficial or occasional. Regularly and repeatedly, "they sold their possessions and goods and distributed them to all, *as any had need*" (2:45). If the need was greater than current cash reserves, they sold property. They simply gave until the needs were met. The needs of the sister and brother, not legal property rights or future financial security, were decisive. They made their financial resources unconditionally available to each other. Oneness in Christ for the earliest Christian community meant almost unlimited economic liability for, and sweeping economic availability to, the other members of Christ's body.

Unfortunately most Christians ignore the example of the Jerusalem church. Perhaps it is because of the economic self-interest of affluent Christians. At any rate, we have developed a convenient rationale for relegating the pattern of the Jerusalem church to the archivists' attic of irrelevant historical trivia. Why did Paul have to take a collection for the Jerusalem church a few decades later? A recent book offers the familiar response:

> The trouble in Jerusalem was that they turned their capital into income, and had no cushion for hard times, and the Gentile Christians had to come to their rescue. It is possible not to live for bread alone, not to be overcome by materialist values, and at the same time to act responsibly; and this is why the Church may be grateful for the protest of the commune movement, but still consider that is has no answer.[26]

But were the Jerusalem Christians really irresponsible, naive communal-types whom we should respect but certainly not imitate? It is absolutely essential to insist that the Jerusalem principle of almost unlimited economic liability and sweeping financial availability does not necessarily require communal living. It did not in Jerusalem. The Christian commune is only one of many faithful models. We dare not let the communal hobgoblin distort our discussion of the Jerusalem model.

But why did the Jerusalem church run into financial difficulty? It is quite unlikely that their economic sharing was to blame. Rather, it was due to a unique set of historical circumstances. Jerusalem attracted an unusually large number of poor. Since Jews considered alms given in Jerusalem particularly meritorious, the many pilgrims to the city were especially generous. As a result vast crowds of impoverished beggars flocked to the city. In addition, a disproportionately large number of older people gravitated to the Holy City to die or wait for the Messiah (see Lk 2:25, 36). There was also an unusually large number of rabbis living in Jerusalem because it was the center of Jewish faith. Rabbis depended on charity, however, since they were not paid for teaching. Their students likewise were often poor. Hence the large number of religious scholars in Jerusalem swelled the ranks of the destitute.[27]

Nor was that all. Natural disasters struck at midcentury. The Roman historians Suetonius and Tacitus report recurring food shortages and famines during the reign of the Emperor Claudius

(A.D. 41-54). Josephus dates such shortages in Palestine around A.D. 44 to 48.[28] Famine in Palestine was so severe at one point that the Antioch church quickly sent assistance (Acts 11:27-30).

Special reasons within the first church itself also caused unusual poverty. Jesus' particular concern for the poor and oppressed probably attracted a disproportionately large number of impoverished persons into the early church. Persecution too must have wreaked havoc with the normal income of Christians. Acts records considerable open persecution (8:1-3; 9:29; 12:1-5; 23:12-15). Undoubtedly Christians also experienced subtle forms of discrimination in many areas including employment.[29] Finally, the Twelve must have given up their livelihood when they moved from their native Galilee to Jerusalem. Hence their support increased the demand on the resources of the Jerusalem church.

These are some of the many reasons why the first community of Christians faced financial difficulty at midcentury. But misguided generosity was hardly a significant factor. In fact, it was probably precisely the unusually large number of poor in their midst that made dramatic sharing such an obvious necessity. That the rich among them gave with overflowing generosity to meet a desperate need in the body of Christ indicates not naive idealism but unconditional discipleship.

The costly sharing of the first church stands as a constant challenge to Christians of all ages. They dared to give concrete, visible expression to the oneness of believers. In the new messianic community of Jesus' first followers after Pentecost, God was redeeming all relationships. The result was far-reaching economic liability for and financial availability to the other brothers and sisters in Christ.

Whatever the beauty and appeal of such an example, however, was it not a vision which quickly faded? Most people believe it was. But the actual practice of the early church proves the contrary.

Economic Koinonia

Paul broadened the vision of economic sharing among the people of God in a dramatic way. He devoted a great deal of time to raising money for Jewish Christians among gentile congregations. In the process he developed *intra*church assistance (within one local church) into *inter*church sharing among all the scattered congregations of believers.

From the time of the exodus, God had taught his chosen people to exhibit transformed economic relations among themselves. With Peter and Paul, however, biblical religion moved beyond one ethnic group and became a universal, multiethnic faith. Paul's collection demonstrated that the oneness of that new body of believers entails economic sharing across ethnic and geographic lines.

Paul's concern for economic sharing in the body of Christ began early. Famine struck Palestine in A.D. 46. In response the believers at Antioch gave *"every one according to his ability,* to send relief to the brethren who lived in Judea"* (Acts 11:29). Paul helped Barnabas bring this economic assistance from Antioch to Jerusalem.[30]

That trip was just the beginning of Paul's extensive concern for economic sharing. For several years he devoted much time and energy to his great collection. He discusses his concern in several letters. Already in Galatians he expresses eagerness to assist the poor Jerusalem Christians (Gal 2:10). He mentions it in the letter to Rome (Rom 15:22-28). Briefly noted in 1 Corinthians 16:1-4, the collection became a major preoccupation in 2 Corinthians 7—9. He also arranged for the collection in the churches of Macedonia, Galatia, Corinth, Ephesus and probably elsewhere.[31]

Paul knew he faced certain danger and possible death. But he still insisted on personally accompanying the offering. It was while delivering this financial assistance that Paul was arrested for the last time. His letter to the Romans shows that he was not blind to the danger (Rom 15:31). Repeatedly friends and prophets warned Paul as he and the representatives of the contributing churches journeyed toward Jerusalem (Acts 21:4, 10-14). But Paul had a deep conviction that this financial symbol of Christian unity mattered far more even than his own life. "What are you doing, weeping and breaking my heart?" he chided friends imploring him not to accompany the others to Jerusalem. "For I am ready not only to be imprisoned but even to die at Jerusalem for the name of the Lord Jesus" (Acts 21:13). And he continued the journey. His passionate commitment to economic sharing with brothers and sisters led to his final arrest and martyrdom (see Acts 24:17).

Why was Paul so concerned with the financial problems of the Jerusalem church? Because of his understanding of fellowship. Koinonia is an extremely important concept in Paul's theology. And it is central in his discussion of the collection.

The word *koinōnia* means fellowship with someone or participation in something. Believers enjoy fellowship with the Lord Jesus (1 Cor 1:9).[32] Experiencing the koinonia of Jesus means having his righteousness imputed to us. It also entails sharing in the self-sacrificing, cross-bearing life he lived (Phil 3:8-10). Nowhere is the Christian's fellowship with Christ experienced more powerfully than in the Eucharist. Sharing in the Lord's Supper draws the believer into a participation (koinonia) in the mystery of the cross: "The cup of blessing which we bless, is it not a participation [koinonia] in the blood of Christ? The bread which we break, is it not a participation [koinonia] in the body of Christ?" (1 Cor 10:16).

Paul's immediate inference is that koinonia with Christ inevitably involves koinonia with all the members of the body of Christ. "Because there is one bread, we who are many are one body, for we all partake of the one bread" (1 Cor 10:17; see also 1 Jn 1:3-4). As seen in Ephesians 2, Christ's death for Jew and Gentile, male and female, has broken down all ethnic, sexual and cultural dividing walls. In Christ there is one new person, one new body of believers. When the brothers and sisters share the one bread and the common cup in the Lord's Supper, they symbolize and actualize their participation in the one body of Christ.

That is why the class divisions at Corinth so horrified Paul. Apparently wealthy Christians feasted at the Eucharistic celebration while poor believers went hungry. Paul angrily denied that they were eating the Lord's Supper at all (1 Cor 11:20-22). In fact, they were profaning the Lord's body and blood because they did not discern his body (1 Cor 11:27-29).

But what did Paul mean when he charged that they did not discern the Lord's body? To discern the Lord's body is to understand and live the truth that fellowship with Christ is inseparable from membership in his body where our oneness in Christ far transcends differences of race or class. Discernment of that one body of believers leads to sweeping availability to and responsibility for the other sisters and brothers. Discernment of that one body prompts us to weep with those who weep and rejoice with those who rejoice. Discernment of that one body is totally incompatible with feasting while other members of the body go hungry. Those who live a practical denial of their unity and fellowship in Christ, Paul insists, drink judgment on themselves when they go to the Lord's table. In fact, they do not really partake of the Lord's Supper at all.

Once we understand the implication of Paul's teaching on discerning the body in the Lord's Supper, we dare not rest content until the scandal of starving Christians is removed. As long as any Christian anywhere in the world is hungry, the Eucharistic celebration of all Christians everywhere in the world is imperfect.

For Paul, the intimate fellowship in the body of Christ has concrete economic implications, for he uses precisely this same word, *koinōnia,* to designate financial sharing among believers. Early in his ministry, the Jerusalem leaders endorsed his mission to the Gentiles after a dramatic debate. When they extended the "right hand of fellowship" (koinonia), they stipulated just one tangible expression of that fellowship. Paul promised financial assistance for his fellow Christians in Jerusalem (Gal 2:9-10).[33]

Paul frequently employs the word *koinōnia* as a virtual synonym for "collection." He speaks of the "liberality of the fellowship" (koinonia) that the Corinthians' generous offering would demonstrate (2 Cor 9:13, my translation; see also 8:4).[34] He employed the same language to report the Macedonian Christians' offering for Jerusalem. It seemed good to the Macedonians "to make fellowship [koinonia] with the poor among the saints at Jerusalem (Rom 15:25, my translation). Indeed, this financial sharing was just one part of a total fellowship. The gentile Christians had come to share in (he uses the verb form of *koinōnia*) the spiritual blessings of the Jews. Therefore it was fitting for the Gentiles to share their material resources. Economic sharing was an obvious and crucial part of Christian fellowship for St. Paul.[35]

Paul's first guideline for sharing in the body of believers was general: Give all you can. Each person should give "as he may prosper" (1 Cor 16:2). But that does not mean a small donation that costs nothing. Paul praised the Macedonians who "gave according to their means . . . and beyond their means" (2 Cor 8:3). The Macedonians were extremely poor. Apparently they faced particularly severe financial difficulties just when Paul asked for a generous offering (2 Cor 8:2). But still they gave beyond their means. No hint here of a mechanical ten per cent for pauper and millionaire. Giving as much as you can is the Pauline pattern.

Second, giving was voluntary (2 Cor 8:3). Paul specifically noted that he was not issuing a command to the Corinthians (2 Cor 8:8).

Legalism is not the answer.

Paul's third guideline is the most startling. The norm, he suggests, is something like economic equality among the people of God. "I do not mean that others should be eased and you burdened, but that as a matter of equality your abundance at the present time should supply their want, so that their abundance may supply your want, that there may be equality." To support his principle, Paul quotes from the biblical story of the manna. "As it is written, 'He who gathered much had nothing over, and he who gathered little had no lack' " (2 Cor 8:13-15).

According to the Exodus account, when God started sending daily manna to the Israelites in the wilderness, Moses commanded the people to gather only as much as they needed for one day (Ex 16:13-21). One omer (about four pints) per person would be enough, Moses said. Some greedy souls, however, apparently tried to gather more than they could use. But when they measured what they had gathered, they discovered that they all had just one omer per person. "He that gathered much had nothing over, and he that gathered little had no lack" (16:18).

Paul quotes from the biblical account of the manna to support his guideline for economic sharing. Just as God had insisted on equal portions of manna for all his people in the wilderness, so now the Corinthians should give "that there may be equality" in the body of Christ.

This may be startling and disturbing to rich Christians in the Northern Hemisphere. But the biblical text clearly shows that Paul enunciates the principle of economic equality among the people of God to guide the Corinthians in their giving. "*It is a question of equality. At the moment your surplus meets their need, but one day your need may be met from their surplus. The aim is equality*" (NEB).[36]

It is exciting to see how the biblical teaching on transformed economic relationships among God's people created in the early church a concern for the poor which was unique in late antiquity. Writing about A.D. 125, the Christian philosopher Aristides painted the following picture of economic sharing in the church.

They walk in all humility and kindness, and falsehood is not found among them, and they love one another. They despise not the widow, and grieve not the orphan. He that hath, distributeth liberally to him that hath not. If they see a stranger, they bring

him under their roof, and rejoice over him, as it were their own
brother: for they call themselves brethren, not after the flesh, but
after the spirit and in God; but when one of their poor passes
away from the world, and any of them see him, then he provides
for his burial according to his ability; and if they hear that any of
their number is imprisoned or oppressed for the name of their
Messiah, all of them provide for his needs, and if it is possible that
he may be delivered, they deliver him. And if there is among them
a man that is poor and needy, and they have not an abundance of
necessaries, they fast two or three days that they may supply the
needy with their necessary food.[37]

By A.D. 250 the church at Rome supported fifteen hundred needy
persons. According to the German scholar Martin Hengel, this kind
of economic sharing was unique in the late Roman Empire.[38]

That this transformed lifestyle made a powerful impression on
outsiders is clear from a grudging comment by a pagan emperor.
During his short reign (A.D. 361-63), Julian the Apostate tried to
stamp out Christianity. But he was forced to admit to a fellow pagan
"that the godless Galileans [Christians] feed not only their poor but
ours also." With chagrin he acknowledged that the pagan cult which
he had tried to revive had failed miserably in the task of aiding the
poor.[39]

The practice of second-century Christians, however interesting it
may be, is, of course, not normative today. In fact, many would
eagerly insist that neither is the practice of Paul at Corinth or the
first Christians in Jerusalem. What relevance then does their economic sharing have for the contemporary church?

Certainly the church today need not slavishly imitate every detail
of the life of the early church depicted in Acts. It is scriptural teaching, not the action of the Jerusalem church, that is normative. But
that does not mean that we can simply dismiss the economic sharing
described in Acts and the Pauline letters.

Over and over again God specifically commanded his people to
live together in community in such a way that they would avoid extremes of wealth and poverty. That is the point of the legislation concerning the jubilee and the sabbatical year. That is the point of the
legislation on tithing, gleaning and loans. Jesus, our only perfect
model, shared a common purse with the new community of his disciples. Again and again, Jesus instructed his followers to share with

those in need. The first-century Christians were simply implementing what both the Old Testament and Jesus commanded.

The powerful evangelistic impact of the economic sharing at
Jerusalem indicates that God approved and blessed the practice of
the Jerusalem church. When in some places Scripture commands
transformed economic relationships among God's people and in
other places describes God's blessing on his people as they implement these commands, then we can be sure that we have discovered
a normative pattern for the church today.

What is striking, in fact, is the fundamental continuity of biblical
teaching and practice at this point. The Bible repeatedly and pointedly reveals that God wills transformed economic relationships
among his people. Paul's collection was simply an application of the
basic principle of the jubilee. The particular method, of course, was
different because the people of God at his time were a multiethnic
body living in different lands. But the principle was the same. Since
the Greeks at Corinth were now part of the people of God, they
were to share with the poor Jewish Christians at Jerusalem—that
there might be equality.

Conclusion
We have looked carefully at the kind of economic relationships God
desires among his people. What does this biblical revelation mean
for affluent Christians in the Northern Hemisphere? Only one conclusion seems possible to me.

Present economic relationships in the worldwide body of Christ
are unbiblical and sinful, a hindrance to evangelism and a desecra-
tion of the body and blood of Jesus Christ. The dollar value of the
food North Americans throw in the garbage each year equals about
one-fifth of the total annual income of all the Christians in Africa.[40]
It is a sinful abomination for one part of the world's Christians living
in the Northern Hemisphere to grow richer year by year while our
brothers and sisters in the Third World ache and suffer for lack of
minimal health care, minimal education, and even—in some cases—
just enough food to escape starvation.

We are like the rich Corinthian Christians who feasted without
sharing their food with the poor members of the church (1 Cor
11:20-29). Like them we fail today to discern the reality of the one
worldwide body of Christ. The tragic consequence is that we pro-

fane the body and blood of the Lord Jesus we worship. Christians in
the United States spent $5.7 billion on new church construction
alone in the six years from 1967 to 1972.[41] Would we go on building
lavishly furnished expensive church plants if members of our own
congregations were starving? Do we not flatly contradict Paul if we
live as if African or Latin American members of the body of Christ
are less a part of us than the members of our home congregation?[42]

The present division between the haves and have nots in the body
of Christ is a major hindrance to world evangelism. Hungry people
in the Third World find it difficult to accept a Christ preached by
people who always symbolize (and often defend the affluence of)
the richest society on earth.

Lost opportunities and past and present sin, however, must not
blind us to present potential. We live in a world dangerously divided
between rich and poor. If a mere fraction of North American and
European Christians would begin to apply biblical principles on economic sharing among the worldwide people of God, the world
would be utterly astounded. There is probably no other step that
would have such a powerful evangelistic impact today. Is it not likely
that millions and millions of unbelievers would confess Christ?
Jesus' prayer might be answered. The mutual love and unity within
Christ's body might convince the world that Jesus indeed came from
the Father (Jn 17:20-23).

The church is the most universal body in the world today. It has
the opportunity to live a new model of sharing at a crucial moment
in world history. Because of its concern for the poor, the church in
the past pioneered in developing schools and hospitals. Later, secular governments institutionalized the new models. In the late twentieth century, a dangerously divided world awaits a new model of
economic sharing.

The Bible clearly teaches that God wills fundamentally transformed economic relationships among his people. Do we have the
faith and obedience to start living the biblical vision?

5

A Biblical Attitude toward Property & Wealth

In the house of the righteous there is much treasure. [Proverbs 15:6]
Blessed are you poor, for yours is the kingdom of God. [Luke 6:20]

The title of this chapter, "A Biblical Attitude toward Property and Wealth," promptly suggests an important question: Does the Bible sanction or condemn private property? Unfortunately, for many this is the only important question raised by the title. The biblical viewpoint is strikingly different. The Bible teaches many things about property and wealth.

Private Property
The Ten Commandments sanction private property implicitly and explicitly.[1] God forbids stealing, indeed even coveting, the house, land or animals of one's neighbors (Ex 20:15, 17; Deut 5:19, 21; see also Deut 27:17; Prov 22:28). Apparently Jesus likewise assumed the legitimacy of private property. His disciple Simon Peter owned a house that Jesus frequented (Mk 1:29). Jesus commanded his followers to give to the poor and loan money even when there was no reasonable hope of repayment (Mt 6:2-4; 5:42; Lk 6:34-35). Such advice would have made little sense if Jesus had not also assumed that the possession of property and money was legitimate so that one could make loans. As we saw in the previous chapter, not even the dramatic economic sharing in the first Jerusalem church led to a rejection of private ownership. Throughout bib-

lical revelation the legitimacy of private property is constantly affirmed.[2]

But the right of private property is not absolute. From the perspective of biblical revelation, property owners are not free to seek their own profit without regard for the needs of their neighbor. Such an outlook derives from the secular laissez-faire economics of the deist Adam Smith, not from Scripture.

Smith published a book in 1776 which has profoundly shaped Western society in the last two centuries.[3] (Since the Keynesian revolution, of course, Smith's ideas have shaped Western societies less than previously, but his fundamental outlook, albeit in somewhat revised form, still provides the basic ideological framework for many North Americans.) Smith argued that an invisible hand would guarantee the good of all if each person would pursue his or her own economic self-interest in the context of a competitive society. Supply and demand for goods and services must be the sole determinant of prices and wages. If the law of supply and demand reigns and if all seek their own advantage within a competitive, nonmonopolistic economy, the good of society will be served. Owners of land and capital therefore have not only the right but also the obligation to seek as much profit as possible.

Such an outlook may be extremely attractive to successful North Americans. Indeed laissez-faire economics has been espoused by some as *the* Christian economics.[4] In reality, however, it is a product of the Enlightenment.[5] It reflects a modern, secularized outlook rather than a biblical perspective.

It is interesting to note the striking parallel between the laissez-faire and the pagan Roman attitude toward private property. Carl F. H. Henry, former editor of *Christianity Today,* rightly contrasts the biblical and Roman understandings: "The Roman or Justinian view derives ownership from natural right; it defines ownership as the individual's unconditional and exclusive power over property. It implies an owner's right to use property as he pleases . . . irrespective of the will of others." And Henry admits that this pagan view "still remains the silent presupposition of much of the free world's common practice today."[6]

According to biblical faith, Yahweh is Lord of all things. He is the sovereign Lord of history. Economics is not a neutral, secular sphere independent of his lordship. Economic activity, like every other area of life, should be subject to his will and revelation.

How does the biblical view that Yahweh is Lord of all of life require a modification of the common belief that the right of private property is absolute and inviolable? The Bible insists that God alone has an absolute right to property. Furthermore, it teaches that this Absolute Owner places significant limitations on how his people acquire and use his property.

The psalmist summarized the biblical view of Yahweh's absolute ownership: "The earth is the LORD's and the fulness thereof, the world and those who dwell therein" (Ps 24:1). "Whatever is under the whole heaven is mine," God informed Job (Job 41:11; see also Ps 50:12; Deut 26:10; Ex 19:5). In chapter four we examined the year of jubilee. It is precisely because absolute ownership of the land rested with Yahweh rather than the Israelite farmers that he could command the redistribution of land every fiftieth year: "The land shall not be sold in perpetuity, *for the land is mine;* for you are strangers and sojourners with me" (Lev 25:23; see also Deut 10:14). Because he is the creator and sustainer of all things, God alone has absolute property rights.

As absolute owner, God places limitations on the acquisition and use of property. According to the Old Testament, "the right to property was in principle subordinated to the obligation to care for the weaker members of society."[7] That is the clear implication of the legislation on the jubilee, the sabbatical year, gleaning and interest. Property owners did not have the right to harvest everything in their fields. They were to leave some for the poor. When an Israelite farmer purchased land, he really only bought the use of the land until the year of jubilee (Lev 25:15-17). Indeed, even the right to use the land for the intervening years was not absolute. If a relative of the seller appeared, the purchaser had to sell the land back promptly. Or if the seller recovered financial solvency, he had the right to buy back his land immediately (Lev 25:25-28). The purchaser's right of ownership was subordinate to the original owner's right to earn a living.

God was concerned to avoid extremes of wealth and poverty among his people. He wanted each family to possess the means to earn its own way. These human rights, even of the less advantaged who regularly fell behind the more aggressive, more prosperous persons, were more significant than the property rights of the person able to pay the market price for land. Thus the rights of the poor and disadvantaged to possess the means to earn a just living have precedence over the rights of the more prosperous to make a profit.[8]

At the same time, biblical principles by no means support a communist economic system. Biblical principles point in the direction of *decentralized private* ownership which allows families to control their economic destiny. As stewards of the land and other economic resources that belong ultimately to God, they have the responsibility and privilege of earning their own way and sharing generously with others as they have need. This kind of decentralized economic system empowers all people to be co-creators with God. It also protects everyone against centralized economic power (as when the state owns the means of production or when small groups of elite control huge multinational corporations), which threatens freedom and promotes totalitarianism.

The Old Testament attitude toward property stems from the high view of persons held in Israel. Old Testament scholars have pointed out that Israel, unlike other ancient civilizations such as Babylon, Assyria and Egypt, considered all citizens equal before the law. In other societies the social status of the offender (royal official, poor man, priest) determined how his offense was judged and punished. In Israel all citizens were equal before the law. Because of this high view of persons, property seemed less significant by comparison.

> This equality before the law is accompanied by a new respect for human life. Whereas in neighboring states offenses connected with property such as theft, robbery, etc., were frequently punished with the death penalty, this was no longer the case in the law of the Old Testament. The life of even the most degraded person is worth more than the richest possession.[9]

The case of slaves illustrates this point. In all other ancient civilizations slaves were viewed as mere property. The owner was completely free to treat the slave according to his whim. But in Israel the slave was a person, not a piece of property. Specific laws guaranteed him certain rights (Ex 21:20, 26-28; Deut 23:15-16). "The fact that, in accordance with God's order, the life of every individual, even of the poorest, is of greater value than all material things—this fact represents an insurmountable stumbling-block to all economic developments which make profits for the few out of human misery."[10]

A Carefree Attitude toward Possessions

Jesus calls his followers to a joyful life of carefree unconcern for possessions:

> I bid you put away anxious thoughts about food to keep you alive and clothes to cover your body. Life is more than food, the body more than clothes. Think of the ravens: they neither sow nor reap; they have no storehouse or barn; yet God feeds them. You are worth far more than the birds! Is there a man among you who by anxious thought can add a foot to his height? If, then, you cannot do even a very little thing, why are you anxious about the rest?
>
> Think of the lilies: they neither spin nor weave; yet I tell you, even Solomon in all his splendour was not attired like one of these. But if that is how God clothes the grass, which is growing in the field today, and tomorrow is thrown on the stove, how much more will he clothe you! How little faith you have! And so you are not to set your mind on food and drink; you are not to worry. For all these are things for the heathen to run after; but you have a Father who knows that you need them. No, set your mind upon his kingdom, and all the rest will come to you as well. (Lk 12:22-31 NEB; see also 2 Cor 9:8-11)

Jesus' words are anathema to Marxists and capitalists alike: to Marxists because they worship Mammon by claiming that economic forces are the ultimate causal factors in history; to capitalists because they worship Mammon by idolizing economic efficiency and success as the highest goods.[11] Indeed, at another level, Jesus' words are anathema to the ordinary, comfortable "Christian." In fact, I must confess that I cannot read them without an underlying sense of uneasiness. The beauty and appeal of the passage always overwhelm me. But it also reminds me that I have not, in spite of continuing struggle and effort, attained the kind of carefree attitude Jesus depicts.

What is the secret of such carefree living? First, many people cling to their possessions instead of sharing them because they are worried about the future. But is not such an attitude finally unbelief? If we really believe that God is who Jesus said he is, then we can begin to live without anxiety for the future. Jesus taught us that God is our loving Father. His word *abba* is a tender, intimate word like *papa* (Mk 14:36). If we really believe that the almighty creator and sustainer of the cosmos is our loving papa, then we can begin to cast aside anxiety about earthly possessions.

Second, such carefree living presupposes an unconditional commitment to Jesus as Lord. We must genuinely want to seek first the kingdom of heaven. Jesus was blunt. We cannot serve God and possessions. "No one can serve two masters; for either he will hate the one and love the other, or he will be devoted to the one and despise the other. You cannot serve God and mammon" (Mt 6:24). Mammon is not some mysterious pagan God. The word *mammon* is simply the Aramaic word for wealth or property.[12] Like the rich young ruler and Zacchaeus, we must decide between Jesus and riches. Like the merchant in Jesus' parable, we must decide between the kingdom of heaven and our affluent life: "The kingdom of heaven is like a merchant in search of fine pearls, who, on finding one pearl of great value, went and sold all that he had and bought it" (Mt 13:45-46; see also v. 44). Either Jesus and his kingdom matter so much that we are ready to sacrifice everything else, including our possessions, or we are not serious about Jesus.

If Jesus is truly Lord and if we trust in a loving heavenly Father, then we can take courage to live without anxiety about possessions. That kind of carefree unconcern for possessions, however, is not merely an inner spiritual attitude. It involves concrete action. Immediately following the moving statement about the carefree life of the ravens and lilies, Jesus says, "Sell your possessions, and give alms; provide yourselves with purses that do not grow old, with a treasure in the heavens that does not fail. . . . For where your treasure is, there will your heart be also" (Lk 12:33-34).

If there are poor people who need assistance, Jesus' carefree disciple will help—even if that means selling possessions. People are vastly more important than property. "Laying up treasure in heaven" means exactly the same thing. "In Jewish literature, the good deeds of a religious person are often described as treasures stored up in heaven."[13] One stores up treasure in heaven by doing righteousness on earth. And aiding the poor is one of the most basic acts of righteousness. Jesus does not mean, of course, that we earn salvation by assisting the needy. But he does mean to urge his followers— out of gratitude for God's forgiving grace—to be so unconcerned with property that they eagerly sell it to aid the poor and oppressed. Such activity is an integral part of living a life of joyful unconcern for possessions.

But a difficult question remains. Did Jesus mean that we should sell all our possessions? How literally should we understand what he said in Luke 6:30: "Give to every one who begs from you; and of him who takes away your goods do not ask them again"? Jesus sometimes engaged in typical Jewish hyperbole to make a point. He hardly meant in Luke 14:26 that one must actively hate father and mother in order to be his disciple. But we have become so familiar with Jesus' words, so accustomed to compromising their call to radical discipleship and unconditional commitment, that we weaken his real intent. What 99 per cent of all North Americans need to hear 99 per cent of the time is this: "Give to everyone who begs from you," and "Sell your possessions." It is certainly true that Jesus' followers continued to own some private property. But Jesus clearly taught that the kind of substantial sharing he desired would involve selling possessions. His first followers at Jerusalem took him seriously. If Christians today in affluent countries want to experience Jesus' carefree outlook on property and possessions, they will need to do the same.

Other parts of the New Testament continue the same theme. Bishops must not be lovers of money (1 Tim 3:3; Tit 1:7). Deacons likewise dare not be "greedy for gain" (1 Tim 3:8). In many churches today, "success" in business is one of the chief criteria for selection to the church board. Is that not a blatant reversal of biblical teaching on the importance of possessions? Even those who are rich should be careful not to set their hope in "uncertain riches." Instead, they should trust in God and share generously (1 Tim 6:17-18). "Keep your life free from love of money, and be content with what you have; for he has said, 'I will never fail you nor forsake you' " (Heb 13:5). Our future is secure not because of our possessions but because it rests in the hands of a loving, omnipotent Father. If we truly trust in him and are unconditionally submitted to his lordship, we can confidently imitate Jesus' carefree unconcern for property and possessions.

The Rich Fool

Most Christians in the Northern Hemisphere simply do not believe Jesus' teaching about the deadly danger of possessions. We all know that Jesus warned that possessions are highly dangerous—so dangerous, in fact, that it is extremely difficult for a rich person to be a Christian at all. "It is easier for a camel to go through the eye of a needle than for a rich man to enter the kingdom of God" (Lk 18:25). But we do not believe Jesus. Christians in the United States live in the richest society in the history of the world, surrounded by a billion needy neighbors. Yet we demand that our government foster an ever-expanding economy in order that our incomes might increase each year. We insist on more and more. If Jesus was so un-American that he considered riches dangerous, then we must ignore or reinterpret his message.

But he said it all the same. Matthew, Mark and Luke all record the terrible warning: "How hard it is for those who have riches to enter the kingdom of God!" (Lk 18:24; Mt 19:23; Mk 10:23). The context of this saying shows why possessions are dangerous. Jesus spoke these words to his disciples immediately after the rich young man had decided to cling to his wealth rather than follow Jesus (Lk 18:18-23). Riches are dangerous because their seductive power frequently persuades us to reject Jesus and his kingdom.

The sixth chapter of 1 Timothy underlines and reinforces Jesus' teaching. Christians should be content with the necessities of food and clothing (1 Tim 6:8). Why? "Those who desire to be rich fall into temptation, into a snare, into many senseless and hurtful desires that plunge men into ruin and destruction. For the love of money is the root of all evils; it is through this craving that some have wandered away from the faith and pierced their hearts with many pangs" (1 Tim 6:9-10). A desire for riches prompts people to do anything for the sake of economic success. The result, Scripture warns, is anguish now and damnation later.

That economic success tempts people to forget God was already a biblical theme in the Old Testament. Before they entered the Promised Land, God warned the people of Israel about the danger of riches.

Take heed lest you forget the LORD your God . . . lest, when you have eaten and are full, and have built goodly houses and live in them, and when your herds and flocks multiply, and your silver and gold is multiplied, and all that you have is multiplied, then your heart be lifted up, and you forget the LORD your God. . . . Beware lest you say in your heart, "My power and the might of

my hand have gotten me this wealth." (Deut 8:11-14, 17)
An abundance of possessions can easily lead us to forget that God is
the source of all good. We trust in ourselves and our wealth rather
than in the Almighty.

Not only do possessions tempt us to forsake God. War and neglect
of the poor often result from the pursuit of wealth. "What causes
wars, and what causes fightings among you? . . . You desire and do
not have; so you kill. And you covet and cannot obtain; so you fight
and wage war" (Jas 4:1-2). A cursory reading of world history confirms this point.

Instead of fostering more compassion toward the poor, riches
often harden the hearts of the wealthy. Scripture is full of instances
in which rich persons are unconcerned about the poor at their door-
step (Is 5:8-10; Amos 6:4-7; Lk 16:19-31; Jas 5:1-5). Dom Helder
Camara, a Brazilian archbishop who has devoted his life to seeking
justice for the poor, makes the point forcefully:

> I used to think, when I was a child, that Christ might have been
> exaggerating when he warned about the dangers of wealth.
> Today I know better. I know how very hard it is to be rich and still
> keep the milk of human kindness. Money has a dangerous way of
> putting scales on one's eyes, a dangerous way of freezing people's
> hands, eyes, lips and hearts.[14]

Possessions are positively dangerous because they often encourage
unconcern for the poor, because they lead to strife and war, and
because they seduce people into forsaking God.

The usage of the word *covetousness* (it occurs nineteen times in the
New Testament) reflects the biblical understanding of the dangers
of riches. The Greek word *pleonexia* (translated "covetousness")
means "striving for material possessions."[15]

Jesus' parable of the rich fool vividly portrays the nature of covetousness. When a man came running to Jesus for help in obtaining
his share of a family inheritance, Jesus refused to consider the case.
Perceiving the real problem, Jesus instead warned of the danger of
covetousness. "Take heed, and beware of all covetousness [*pleonexia*]; for a man's life does not consist in the abundance of his possessions" (Lk 12:15). Knowing that the man was obsessed with material things, Jesus told him a story about a rich fool.

> The land of a rich man brought forth plentifully; and he thought
> to himself, "What shall I do, for I have nowhere to store my

crops?" And he said, "I will do this: I will pull down my barns, and build larger ones; and there I will store all my grain and my goods. And I will say to my soul, Soul, you have ample goods laid up for many years; take your ease, eat, drink, be merry." But God said to him, "Fool! This night your soul is required of you; and the things you have prepared, whose will they be?" So is he who lays up treasure for himself, and is not rich toward God. (Lk 12:16-21)

The rich fool is the epitome of the covetous person. He has a greedy compulsion to acquire more and more possessions, even though he does not need them. And his phenomenal success at piling up more and more property and wealth leads to the blasphemous conclusion that material possessions can satisfy all his needs. From the divine perspective, however, this attitude is sheer madness. He is a raving fool.

One cannot read the parable of the rich fool without thinking of our own society. We madly multiply more sophisticated gadgets, larger and taller buildings, and faster means of transportation—not because such things truly enrich our lives but because we are driven by an obsession for more and more. Covetousness, a striving for more and more material possessions, has become a cardinal vice of Western civilization.

The New Testament has a great deal to say about covetousness. It is divine punishment for sin. In its essence, it is idolatry. Scripture teaches that greedy persons must be expelled from the church. Certainly no covetous person will inherit the kingdom.

In Romans 1 Paul indicates that God sometimes punishes sin by letting sinners experience the ever more destructive consequences of their continuing rebellion against him. "And since they did not see fit to acknowledge God, God gave them up to a base mind and to improper conduct. They were filled with all manner of wickedness, evil, *covetousness,* . . . murder, strife, deceit" (Rom 1:28-29). Covetousness is one of the sins with which God punishes our rebellion. The parable of the rich fool suggests how the punishment works out. Since we are made for communion with the Creator, we cannot obtain genuine fulfillment when we seek it in material possessions. Hence we seek ever more frantically and desperately for more houses and bigger barns. Eventually we worship our possessions. As Paul indicates, covetousness is finally sheer idolatry (Eph 5:5; Col 3:5).

Paul actually commanded the Corinthians to exercise church discipline against covetous persons (1 Cor 5:11). Christians today are not at all surprised that he urged the Corinthians to excommunicate a church member living with his father's wife (1 Cor 5:1-5). But we quietly overlook the fact that Paul went right on to urge Christians not to associate or even eat meals with persons who claim to be Christians but who are guilty of greed! Are we not guilty of covetousness when we demand an ever higher standard of living while millions of children starve to death each year? Is it not time for the church to begin applying church discipline to those guilty of this sin?[16] Would it not be more biblical to apply church discipline to people whose greedy acquisitiveness has led to "financial success" than to elect them to the board of elders?

Such action may be the last means we have of communicating the biblical warning that greedy persons will not inherit the kingdom. "Do you not know that the unrighteous will not inherit the kingdom of God? Do not be deceived; neither the immoral, nor idolators, nor adulterers, nor homosexuals, nor thieves, *nor the greedy* [the covetous], nor drunkards, nor revilers, nor robbers will inherit the kingdom of God" (1 Cor 6:9-10). Covetousness is just as sinful as idolatry and adultery.

The same vigorous, unambiguous word appears in Ephesians: "Be sure of this, that no fornicator or impure man, or one who is covetous (that is, an idolater), has any inheritance in the kingdom of Christ" (Eph 5:5). These biblical passages should drive us all to our knees. I am afraid that I have been repeatedly and sinfully covetous. The same is true of the vast majority of Western Christians.

Possessions are dangerous. They lead to a multitude of sins, including idolatry. Western Christians today desperately need to turn away from their covetous civilization's grasping materialism.

The Ring and the Beloved
Possessions are dangerous. But they are not innately evil.[17] Biblical revelation begins with creation. And created things, God said, are good (Gen 1).

Biblical faith knows nothing of the ascetic notion that forsaking food, possessions or sex is inherently virtuous. To be sure, these created goods are, as St. Augustine said, only rings from our Beloved. They are not the Beloved himself. Sometimes particular cir-

cumstances—such as an urgent mission or the needs of the poor—
may require their renunciation. But these things are part of God's
good creation. Like the ring given by the Beloved, they are signs of
his love. If we treasure them as good tokens of his affection instead
of mistaking them for the Beloved, they are marvelous gifts which
enrich our lives.

God's provision for Israel's use of the tithe symbolizes the scriptural perspective (Deut 14:22-27). Every third year, as we saw earlier, the tithe was given to the poor. In the other years, however, the
people were to go to the place of worship and have a fantastic feast.
They were to have a great big, joyful celebration! "Before the LORD
your God, in the place which he will choose, to make his name dwell
there, you shall eat the tithe of your grain, of your wine, and of your
oil, and the firstlings of your herd and flock" (Deut 14:23). Those
who lived far from the place of worship could sell the tithe of their
produce and take the money with them. Listen to God's directions
for the party: "Spend the money for whatever you desire, oxen, or
sheep, or wine or strong drink, whatever your appetite craves; and
you shall eat there before the LORD your God and rejoice" (Deut
14:26). God wants his people to celebrate the glorious goodness of
his creation.

Jesus' example fits in perfectly with the Old Testament view. Certainly he said a great deal about the danger of possessions. But he
was not an ascetic. He was happy to join in marriage celebrations
and even contribute the beverage (Jn 2:1-11). He dined with the
prosperous. Apparently he was sufficiently fond of feasts and celebrations that his enemies could spread the false rumor that he was a
glutton and a drunkard (Mt 11:19). Christian asceticism has a long
history, but Jesus' life undermines its basic assumptions.

A short passage in 1 Timothy succinctly summarizes the biblical
view. In the latter days people will forbid marriage and advocate
abstinence from foods. But this is misguided, "for everything created by God is good, and nothing is to be rejected if it is received
with thanksgiving" (1 Tim 4:4).

The biblical teaching on the goodness of creation does not contradict the other biblical themes we have explored. It is also true that
possessions are dangerous and that God's people must practice self-
denial to aid the poor and feed the hungry. But it is important to
focus the biblical mandate to liberate the poor without distorting

other aspects of Scripture. It is not because food, clothes and property are inherently evil that Christians today must lower their standard of living. It is because others are starving. Creation is good. But the one who gave us this gorgeous token of his affection has asked us to share it with our sisters and brothers.

Righteousness and Riches

Does obedience guarantee prosperity? Is it true that "in the house of the righteous there is much treasure" (Prov 15:6)? Is the reverse also true? Are riches a sure sign of righteousness?

The Bible certainly does not romanticize poverty. It is a curse (2 Sam 3:29; Ps 109:8-11). Sometimes it is the result of sin, but not always. A fundamental point of the book of Job is that poverty and suffering are not always due to disobedience. In fact, they can be redemptive (Is 53). Even so, poverty and suffering are not inherently good. They are tragic distortions of God's good creation.

Prosperity, on the other hand, is good and desirable. God repeatedly promised his people Israel that obedience would bring abundant prosperity in a land flowing with milk and honey (Deut 6:1-3). "All these blessings shall come upon you . . . if you obey the voice of the LORD your God. . . . And the LORD will make you abound in prosperity, in the fruit of your body, and in the fruit of your cattle, and in the fruit of your ground" (Deut 28:2, 11; see also Deut 7:12-15). That God frequently rewards obedience with material abundance is a clear teaching of Scripture.

But the threat of a curse always accompanied the promise of blessing (Deut 6:14-15; 8:11-20; 28:15-68). As we discovered in the last two chapters, one of God's most frequent commands to his people was to feed the hungry and to bring justice to the poor and oppressed. For repeatedly ignoring this command, Israel experienced God's curse. Israel's prosperity in the days of Amos and Isaiah was not the result of divine blessing. It was the result of sinful oppression of the poor. God consequently destroyed the nation.

More biblical texts warn of God's punishment of the rich and powerful because of their neglect or oppression of the poor than tell us that material abundance results from obedience.[18] The two statements, however, are not mutually contradictory. Both are true. It is the biblical balance that we need.

The Bible does teach that God rewards obedience with prosperity. But it denies the converse. It is a heresy, particularly common in the West, to think that wealth and prosperity are always a sure sign of righteousness. They may be the result of sin and oppression, as in the case of Israel (see chapter three). The crucial test is whether the prosperous are obeying God's command to bring justice to the oppressed.[19] If they are not, they are living in damnable disobedience to God. On biblical grounds, therefore, one can be sure that prosperity in the context of injustice results from oppression rather than obedience and that it is not a sign of righteousness.

The connection between righteousness, prosperity and concern for the poor is explicitly taught in Scripture. The picture of the good wife in Proverbs 31 provides one beautiful illustration. This woman is a diligent businessperson who buys fields and engages in trade (vv. 14, 16, 18). She is a righteous woman who fears the Lord (v. 30). Her obedience and diligence clearly bring prosperity. But material possessions do not harden her heart against the poor: "She opens her hand to the poor, and reaches out her hands to the needy" (v. 20). Psalm 112 is equally explicit:

Blessed is the man who fears the LORD,
   who greatly delights in his commandments! . . .
Wealth and riches are in his house; . . .
   The LORD is gracious, merciful, and righteous.
It is well with the man who deals generously and lends,
   who conducts his affairs with justice. . . .
He has distributed freely, he has given to the poor.
   (Ps 112:1, 3-5, 9)

The righteous person distributes his riches freely to the poor. He works to establish justice for the oppressed. That kind of life is a sign that one's prosperity results from obedience rather than oppression.

God wills prosperity with justice. As John V. Taylor has pointed out so beautifully, the biblical norm for material possessions is "sufficiency."[20] Proverbs 30:8-9 is a perfect summary:

Give me neither poverty nor riches;
   feed me with the food that is needful for me,
lest I be full, and deny thee,
   and say, "Who is the LORD?"
or lest I be poor, and steal,
   and profane the name of my God.

Western Christians, however, must be careful not to distort the biblical teaching that God sometimes rewards obedience with material abundance. Wealthy persons who make Christmas baskets and give to relief have not satisfied God's demand. God wills justice for the poor. And justice, as we have seen, means things like the jubilee and the sabbatical remission of debts. It means economic structures that check the emergence of extremes of wealth and poverty. It means massive economic sharing among the people of God. Prosperity without that kind of biblical concern for justice unambiguously signifies disobedience.

We have seen that the Old Testament teaches that material possessions sometimes result from divine blessing. But is this view compatible with Jesus' saying: "Blessed are you poor, for yours is the kingdom of God" (Lk 6:20)? Does Jesus consider poverty itself a virtue? Furthermore, how can one reconcile the Lucan version of this beatitude with Matthew's version: "Blessed are the poor *in spirit*" (Mt 5:3)?

The development of the idea of the "pious poor" in the centuries just prior to Christ helps answer these questions. Already in the Psalms the poor were often identified as the special objects of God's favor and protection precisely because they were oppressed by the wicked rich (see, for example, Psalm 8).[21] When Greece and then Rome conquered Palestine, Hellenistic culture and values were foisted on the Jews. Those who remained faithful to Yahweh often suffered financially. Thus the term *poor* came to be used to describe faithful Jews. "It was virtually equivalent to pious, God-fearing, and godly and reflects a situation where the rich were mainly those who had sold out to the incoming culture and had allowed their religious devotion to become corrupted by the new ways. If the poor were the pious, the faithful and largely oppressed, the rich were the powerful, ungodly, worldly, even apostate."[22]

In such a setting the righteous are often poor, hungry and sad, not just "in spirit" but in physical life. Matthew has not "spiritualized" Jesus' words. He has simply captured another aspect of Jesus' original meaning. Jesus was talking about those faithful persons who so hungered for righteousness that they sacrificed even their material prosperity when that became necessary. Jesus did not mean that poverty and hunger are desirable in themselves. But in a sinful world where, frequently, success and prosperity are possible only if one transgresses God's law, poverty and hunger are indeed a blessing. The kingdom is for precisely such people.

Jesus' comment in Mark 10:29-30 adds further clarification. He promised that those who forsake all for the kingdom will receive a hundredfold even in this life. He even included houses and lands, part of the good creation intended for our enjoyment. In the same sentence, however, he also promised persecution. Sometimes—perhaps most of the time—the wicked, powerful and rich will persecute those who dare to follow Jesus' teaching without compromise. Hunger and poverty often result. In such a time the poor and hungry disciples are indeed blessed.

I fear that we may be at the threshold of such an age. The time may soon come when those who dare to preach and live what the Bible teaches about the poor and possessions will experience terrible persecution. Indeed that day has already arrived in some lands. Many Christians in Latin America have experienced torture, some even death, because they identified with the poor. If the wars of redistribution envisaged by Heilbroner become a reality, if affluent lands go to war to protect their unfair share of the world's food and resources, then persecution in affluent countries will inevitably occur.[23]

In such an age faithful Christians will continue to assert that property rights are not absolute. They will courageously insist that the right of individuals and nations to use land and resources as they please is subordinate to the right of all people to have the resources to earn a just living. They will understand more profoundly than today Jesus' carefree unconcern for possessions. As they see fellow church members choose security and affluence rather than faithfulness and persecution, they will realize how dangerous indeed are possessions and wealth. Certainly they will not despise the good gifts of creation. But, when forced to choose between possessions and the kingdom, they will gladly forsake the ring for the Beloved.

6

Structural Evil & World Hunger

Come now, you rich, weep and howl for the miseries that are coming upon you. Your riches have rotted and your garments are moth-eaten. Your gold and silver have rusted, and their rust will be evidence against you and will eat your flesh like fire. You have laid up treasure for the last days. Behold, the wages of the laborers who mowed your fields, which you kept back by fraud, cry out; and the cries of the harvesters have reached the ears of the Lord of hosts. You have lived on the earth in luxury and in pleasure; you have fattened your hearts in a day of slaughter. [James 5:1-5]

I read some time ago that Upton Sinclair, the author, read this passage (James 5:1-5) . . . to a group of ministers. Then he attributed the passage to Emma Goldman, who at the time was an anarchist agitator. The ministers were indignant, and their response was, "This woman ought to be deported at once!" [unpublished sermon (1 June 1975) by Dr. Paul E. Toms, former president of the National Association of Evangelicals]

In the early 1950s Northeast High School in Philadelphia was famous for its superb academic standards and its brilliant, long-standing athletic triumphs. The second oldest school in the city, Northeast had excellent teachers and a great tradition. And it was almost entirely White. Then in the mid fifties, the neighborhood began to change. Black people moved in. Whites began to flee in droves to the Greater Northeast, a new, all-White section of Philadelphia.

Quite naturally, a new high school became necessary in this developing, overwhelmingly White area.

When the excellent new school was completed in 1957, it took along the name Northeast High School, with its fond memories and traditions and many connotations of academic excellence and athletic triumph. The inner-city school was renamed Edison High. The new school took all the academic and athletic trophies and awards, school colors and songs, powerful alumni and all the money in the treasury. Worst of all, the teachers were given the option of transferring to new Northeast High. Two-thirds of them did.[1]

The Black students who now attended Edison High had an old, rapidly deteriorating building, frequent substitute teachers and no traditions. Nor did the intervening years bring many better teachers or adequate teaching materials. The academic record since 1957 has been terrible. In fact, Edison High has only one claim to uniqueness. It has one national record. More students from Edison High died in Vietnam than from any other high school in the United States.

Who was guilty of this terrible sin? Local, state and federal politicians who had promoted de facto housing segregation for decades? The school board? Parents who had, at best, only a partial picture of what was going on? Christian community leaders? White students at the new Northeast High whose excellent education and job prospects have been possible, in part, precisely because of the poor facilities and bad teachers left behind for the Black students at Edison? Who was guilty?

Many would deny any personal responsibility. "That's just the way things are!" And they would be quite right. Long-standing patterns in jobs and housing had created a system which automatically produced Edison High. But that hardly silences the query about responsibility. Do we sin when we participate in evil social systems and societal structures that unfairly benefit some and harm others?

The Bible and Structural Evil

Neglect of the biblical teaching on structural injustice or institutionalized evil is one of the most deadly omissions in many parts of the church today. What does the Bible say about structural evil, and how does that deepen our understanding of the scriptural perspective on poverty and hunger?

Christians frequently restrict the scope of ethics to a narrow class of "personal" sins. In a study of over fifteen hundred ministers, researchers discovered that the theologically conservative pastors speak out on sins such as drug abuse and sexual misconduct.[2] But they fail to preach about the sins of institutionalized racism, unjust economic structures and militaristic institutions which destroy people just as much as do alcohol and drugs.

There is an important difference between consciously willed, individual acts (like lying to a friend or committing an act of adultery) and participation in evil social structures. Slavery is an example of the latter. So is the Victorian factory system where ten-year-old children worked twelve to sixteen hours a day. Both slavery and child labor were legal. But they destroyed people by the millions. They were institutionalized, or structural, evils. In the twentieth century, as opposed to the nineteenth, evangelicals have been more concerned with individual sinful acts than with our participation in evil social structures.

But the Bible condemns both. Speaking through his prophet Amos, the Lord declared, "For three transgressions of Israel, and for four, I will not revoke the punishment; because they sell the righteous for silver, and the needy for a pair of shoes—they that trample the head of the poor into the dust of the earth, and turn aside the way of the afflicted; a man and his father go in to the same maiden, so that my holy name is profaned" (Amos 2:6-7). Biblical scholars have shown that some kind of legal fiction underlies the phrase "selling the needy for a pair of shoes."[3] This mistreatment of the poor was *legal!* In one breath God condemns both sexual misconduct and legalized oppression of the poor. Sexual sins and economic injustice are equally displeasing to God. God revealed the same thing through his prophet Isaiah:
Woe to those who join house to house,
 who add field to field,
until there is no more room,
 and you are made to dwell alone in the midst of the land.
The LORD of hosts has sworn in my hearing:
"Surely many houses shall be desolate,
 large and beautiful houses, without inhabitant. . . .
Woe to those who rise early in the morning,
 that they may run after strong drink,

who tarry late into the evening
  till wine inflames them!" (Is 5:8-9, 11)
Equally powerful is the succinct, satirical summary in verses 22 and
23 of the same chapter: "Woe to those who are heroes at drinking
wine, and valiant men in mixing strong drink, who acquit the guilty
for a bribe, and deprive the innocent of his right!" Here God condemns in one breath both those who amass large landholdings at the
expense of the poor and those who have fallen into drunkenness.
Great economic inequality is just as abominable to our God as drunkenness.

   Some young activists have supposed that as long as they were
fighting for the rights of minorities and opposing militarism, they
were morally righteous, regardless of how often they shacked up for
the night with a guy or a girl in the movement. Some of their elders,
on the other hand, have supposed that, because they did not smoke,
drink and lie, they were morally upright even though they lived in
segregated communities and owned stock in companies that exploit
the poor of the earth. God, however, has declared that robbing your
workers of a fair wage is just as sinful as robbing a bank. Voting for a
racist because he is a racist is just as sinful as sleeping with your
neighbor's wife. Silent participation in a company that carelessly
pollutes the environment and thus imposes heavy costs on others is
just as wrong as destroying your own lungs with tobacco.

   God clearly reveals his displeasure at evil *institutions* in Amos 5:10-
15. (To understand this passage, we need to remember that Israel's
court sessions were held at the city gate.) "They hate him who re-
proves in the gate.... I know how many are your transgressions,
and how great are your sins—you who...take a bribe, and turn
aside the needy in the gate.... Hate evil, and love good, and establish justice in the gate." "Let justice roll down like waters" (Amos
5:24) is not abstract verbalization. The prophet means justice in the
legal system. He means, Get rid of the corrupt legal system that
allows the wealthy to buy their way out of trouble but gives the poor
long prison terms.

   Nor is it only the dishonest and corrupt individuals in the legal
system who stand condemned. God clearly revealed that laws themselves are sometimes an abomination to him.

   Can wicked rulers be allied with thee,
     who frame mischief by statute?

They band together against the life of the righteous,
and condemn the innocent to death.
But the LORD has become my stronghold,
and my God the rock of my refuge.
He will bring back on them their iniquity
and wipe them out for their wickedness;
the LORD our God will wipe them out. (Ps 94:20-23)
The Jerusalem Bible has an excellent rendition of verse 20: "You
never consent to that corrupt tribunal that imposes disorder as law."
God wants his people to know that wicked governments "frame mischief by statute." Or, as the New English Bible puts it, they contrive
evil "under cover of law."

God proclaims the same word through the prophet Isaiah:
Woe to those who decree iniquitous decrees,
and the writers who keep writing oppression,
to turn aside the needy from justice
and to rob the poor of my people of their right. . . .
What will you do on the day of punishment,
in the storm which will come from afar?
To whom will you flee for help,
and where will you leave your wealth?
Nothing remains but to crouch among the prisoners
or fall among the slain.
For all this [God's] anger is not turned away
and his hand is stretched out still. (Is 10:1-4)
It is quite possible to make oppression legal. Then, as now, legislators devised unjust laws, and the bureaucracy (the scribes or writers) implemented the injustice. But God shouts a divine woe against
those rulers who use their official position to write unjust laws and
unfair legal decisions. Legalized oppression is an abomination to our
God. Therefore, God calls his people to oppose political structures
that frame mischief by statute.

The just Lord of the universe will also destroy wicked rulers and
unjust social institutions (see 1 Kings 21). God cares about evil economic structures and unjust legal systems—precisely because they
destroy people by the hundreds and thousands and millions.

Another side to institutionalized evil makes it especially pernicious. Structural evil is so subtle that one can be ensnared and hardly
realize it. God inspired his prophet Amos to utter some of the harsh-

est words in Scripture against the cultured upper-class women of his day: "Hear this word, you cows of Bashan . . . who oppress the poor, who crush the needy, who say to [your] husbands, 'Bring, that we may drink!' The Lord GOD has sworn by his holiness that, behold, the days are coming upon you, when they shall take you away with hooks, even the last of you with fishhooks" (Amos 4:1-2).

The women involved may have had little direct contact with the impoverished peasants. They may never have realized clearly that their gorgeous clothes and spirited parties were possible only because of the sweat and tears of toiling peasants. In fact, they may even have been kind on occasion to individual peasants. (Perhaps they gave them "Christmas baskets" once a year.) But God called these privileged women "cows" because they profited from social evil. Before God they were personally and individually guilty.[4]

If one is a member of a privileged class that profits from structural evil, and if one does nothing to try to change things, he or she stands guilty before God.[5] Social evil is just as displeasing to God as personal evil. And it is more subtle.

In the first edition of this book, I said that social evil hurts more people than personal evil. That may be true in the Third World, but I no longer believe that it is true in North America and Western Europe. Within the industrialized nations, the agony caused by broken homes, sexual promiscuity, marital breakdown and divorce probably equals the pain caused by structural injustice. That is not to deny or de-emphasize the latter. It is merely to underline that both kinds of sin devastate our Western society today.

The prophets told how the God of justice responds to oppressive social structures. God cares so much about the poor that he will destroy social structures that tolerate and foster great poverty. Repeatedly God declared that he would destroy the nation of Israel because of *both* its idolatry *and* its mistreatment of the poor (for example, Jer 7:1-15).

The *both/and* is crucial. We dare not become so preoccupied with horizontal issues of social justice that we neglect vertical evils such as idolatry. Modern Christians seem to have an irrepressible urge to fall into one extreme or the other. But the Bible corrects our one-sidedness. God destroyed Israel and Judah because of both their idolatry and their social injustice.

Here, however, our focus is on the fact that God destroys oppressive social structures. Amos's words, which could be duplicated from many other places in Scripture, make this divine response clear:

Because you trample upon the poor and take from him exactions of wheat, you have built houses of hewn stone, but you shall not dwell in them. (5:11)

Woe to those who lie upon beds of ivory, and stretch themselves upon their couches, and eat lambs from the flock, . . . but [who] are not grieved over the ruin of Joseph! Therefore they shall now be the first of those to go into exile. (6:4, 6-7)

Hear this, you who trample upon the needy, and bring the poor of the land to an end, saying, "When will the new moon be over, that we may sell grain? And the sabbath, that we may offer wheat for sale . . . and deal deceitfully with false balances, that we may buy the poor for silver and the needy for a pair of sandals? (8:4-6)

Behold, the eyes of the Lord GOD are upon the sinful kingdom, and I will destroy it from the surface of the ground. (9:8)

Within a generation after the time of the prophet Amos, the northern kingdom of Israel was completely wiped out.

Probably the most powerful statement of God's work to destroy evil social structures is in the New Testament—in Mary's Magnificat. Mary glorified the Lord who "has put down the mighty from their thrones, and exalted those of low degree; [who] has filled the hungry with good things, and the rich he has sent empty away" (Lk 1:52-53). The Lord of history is at work pulling down sinful societies where wealthy classes live by the sweat, toil and grief of the poor.

Institutionalized Evil Today

What does this biblical teaching mean for affluent Westerners? If Amos were alive today, would he deliver the same judgments on us as he did against the unrighteous Israelites of his own day?

The answer, I think, is yes. Stan Mooneyham has written of "the stranglehold which the developed West has kept on the economic throats of the Third World." He believes that "the heart of the problems of poverty and hunger are human systems which ignore, mistreat and exploit man. . . . If the hungry are to be fed, . . . some of the systems will require drastic adjustments while others will have to be scrapped altogether."[6] Together we must examine the evidence for this evaluation.

I cite the disturbing data which follows neither with sadistic enjoyment of an opportunity to flagellate the affluent, nor with a desire to create feelings of irresolvable guilt. God has no interest in "guilt trips." But I do believe the God of the poor wants us all to feel deep pain over the agony and anguish that torment the poor. And I also believe we must call sin by its biblical name.

All developed countries are directly involved. So too are the wealthy elite in poor countries. Ancient social patterns, inherited values and cherished philosophical perspectives in developing countries also contribute in an important way to create and preserve poverty.[7] It would be naive to simplify complex realities and isolate one scapegoat. But surely *our* first responsibility is to pluck the beam from our own eye. Our most desperate need is to understand and change what we are doing wrong.

How then are we a part of unjust structures that contribute to world hunger? We will briefly probe the historical origins of the present problem and then examine four current issues: international trade; consumption of natural resources; food consumption and food imports; and multinational corporations in the Third World.

Origins and Growth
One quarter of the world's people wallow in the mire of deep poverty. Forty thousand children die each day of malnutrition and related diseases. One billion people have annual incomes of less than $50 a year.[8] While one person in four slowly starves, we who have enough resources to end such misery seem strangely indifferent to their plight. In fact, we persist in demanding that our governments preserve and even increase our incredibly high standard of living. The result is an ever-widening gap between the rich and the poor.

How did we get into this situation? One part of the answer—and only one part—can be found if we look briefly at the history of colonialism. Respected development economist Mahbub ul Haq, for years a senior economist at the World Bank, writes that "the basic reasons for inequality between the presently developed and developing nations lie fairly deep in their history. In most parts of the Third World, centuries of colonial rule have left their legacy of dependency."[9]

It is now generally recognized by historians that the civilizations

Europe discovered were not less developed or underdeveloped in any sense. True, the civilizations of Asia, Africa and the Americas were different from those of Europe, and they lack both Christian faith and military technology. But in almost no sense were they underdeveloped.

In his classic of development literature *Asian Drama,* Gunnar Myrdal places much of the blame for the economic stagnation of Southeast Asia at the feet of European colonizers: "In general, the colonial regimes in South Asia were inimical to the development of manufacturing industry in the colonies. This was even more true when they gradually gave up, after the 1850's and 1870's, the crudely exploitative policies of early colonialism and began to encourage investment and production. It was predominately or exclusively the production of raw materials for export that was encouraged."[10]

Most colonizing countries used their colonies to enhance their own national status in the world community. Such was the mood of the mercantilist era. Strong nation-states became the ultimate objective, and control over land and wealth around the world was the key to power.[11] The creation of colonies was extremely useful. But, preoccupied with the status of the mother country, colonizers seldom exhibited much regard for the economic, social and cultural conditions of the indigenous peoples.

In his book *Bread and Justice* James B. McGinnis cites the example of the town of Potosi, Bolivia. Potosi was a thriving urban area in the seventeenth century when the Spaniards came to mine the area's gold and silver. At first the Spanish miners produced booming economic growth. But

> when the silver ran out, Potosi's boom ended and the area was left to "underdevelop." . . .
>
> The underdevelopment of Potosi, then, began with the abuse of its people and resources through the European colonial system. The Latin American economy was geared by the Europeans to meet their own needs, not those of the local people. The underdevelopment which is characteristic of this "ghost" town today, has its roots in the history of military conquests. Underdeveloped countries today are full of "ghost" towns like Potosi, and nearly all were European colonies at one time.
>
> The arrival of the Europeans in Asia, Africa, and Latin America—what is known today as the Third World—fundamentally

altered the processes of development which were taking place at the time. In some cases, these societies were more advanced than others; and all, of course, had problems to surmount. But the people in these areas were constructing societies which, although not industrialized, were often highly sophisticated and complex. They were able to meet their physical and psychological needs through their own institutions. The military conquest of Third World people led to the plunder and destruction of some of the world's greatest civilizations.[12]

As McGinnis emphasizes, such examples are widespread. Consider an article in a recent issue of the *Wall Street Journal*. Examining the current attempt of Gabon to build a transnational railroad, it asks why one was not built in colonial days. The author answers:

The French built only what they needed to find and export Gabon's raw materials. In fact, colonials' habit of building only those roads and ports and power plants that served their purposes, while ignoring the rest of the country, still stifles Third World economies. "They inherited a legacy that condemned them to underdevelopment," complains the UN's Mr. Doo Kingue, whose own country, Camaroon, was colonized by Germans, English and French.[13]

It would be simplistic, of course, to suggest that the impact of colonialism and subsequent economic and political relations with Western nations was entirely negative. It was not. One thinks for instance of the spread of literacy and improved health care. Furthermore, one can only thank God for the opportunities to spread the gospel around the world during the colonial period. Christian values often undercut ancient social evils such as the caste system in India. What a tragedy, however, that so much of the impact of the Christian West on the developing political and economic structures of the colonies was shaped by economic self-interest rather than the biblical principles of justice. It is quite likely that, if the whole biblical message had been shared and lived in social and economic life, the Third World would know less misery today. If Christian attitudes toward property and wealth had ruled the colonizers' actions, if the principles of jubilee, the sabbatical year and continual uplifting of the poor had been an integral part of the colonial venture and international economic activity since then, there would probably be no need for this book today.

Unfortunately, however, they were not. Nor has there been any major sustained effort on the part of the developed nations since then to restore or institute just economic relations between first and third worlds. The wealthy nations continue to pursue their own self-interest with only marginal interest in the economic progress (or regress) of the poor nations.[14]

As a result the legacy lives on. What began as unfair colonial relationships between the rich and the poor countries has grown and developed into the structural network that rules the international economic order today. Not surprisingly, many of the injustices perpetuated in the early days of colonialism have become cemented in the institutions that govern contemporary economic activity. In her book *Aspects of Development and Underdevelopment,* published by Cambridge University Press, Joan Robinson shows how trade structures and land and labor institutions in the Third World, as well as international financial structures, all developed largely from the foundation which was laid in the colonial era.[15]

It is true, of course, that many economists today, armed with an economic theory born and bred in the developed Western world, argue that present economic relations between rich and poor countries are perfectly appropriate. Current patterns of trade, international finance and foreign investment cause them little concern. But such relations look different when viewed from the perspective of the rampant injustice of the colonial era.

Herein lies the insidiousness of structural injustice. Initial injustices, unless corrected, mushroom. The longer injustice continues without redress, the more serious and the more intractable the problems become. It is like a small lie that must grow and multiply many times to protect the first, "small" lie.

It is comfortably easy to believe that the poverty of the Third World is entirely or largely a product of its people's laziness, lack of intelligence, corruption or proclivity to proliferate. But that is to ignore the historical data of the centuries of colonialism.

Not all contemporary problems, however, can be blamed on the past. Present international economic structures are also unfair.

International Trade

The industrialized nations have carefully crafted the patterns of international trade for their own economic benefit. In colonial days, as we have seen, the mother countries regularly made sure that economic affairs were organized to their own advantage.[16]

Such advantage was largely achieved through manipulation of commodity trade. Institutions and policies were implemented to increase the quantity of useful goods going to the colonizing countries and at the same time to subdue any local efforts to improve manufacturing capacities. As a result, many Third World countries became heavily dependent on trade with the developed countries of the West.

Even today most less developed countries depend highly on international trade for a major share of their livelihood. In Ecuador, for example, merchandise trade comprises some 33 per cent of the nation's Gross Domestic Product. In Honduras the figure is 41 per cent, in Kenya 29 per cent, in the Philippines 21 per cent, and in Guyana it is as high as 66 per cent. By contrast, the figure for the United States is a relatively small 8 per cent.[17] As a consequence, favorable patterns of international trade are vital to Third World nations.

The industrialized countries have continued to impose restrictive tariffs and import quotas to keep out many of the goods produced in the less developed countries.[18] Tariff structures and import quotas affecting the LDCs are in fact one fundamental aspect of present injustice in today's international economic structures. Since most LDCs are dependent on trade, such restrictions are harmful to them; their removal would be most helpful. But the developed world has largely refused to do that. In the early 1960s, for instance, the Kennedy round of tariff negotiations lowered the tariffs on goods traded among the rich industrial nations by 50 per cent. But it did little to lower tariffs on goods from poorer countries. The relative situation of the poor countries actually grew worse.[19]

Traditionally, developed countries have allowed many agricultural and other primary products (minerals, cocoa, rubber, sisal and so on) to enter relatively duty-free. But they have been less lenient with manufactured goods. The more manufacturing and processing done by the poor country, the higher the tariff. The tariff on candy bars, for example, is five times higher than on raw cocoa beans.[20]

The reasons for the imposition of such trade restrictions are rather clear. In colonial times they were imposed in order to limit the competition to the mother country's own fledgling industrial enterprises and to facilitate the transfer of needed primary products. Today, restrictions are maintained mainly because their removal would threaten the interests of certain well-organized and politically entrenched groups. Both labor and management in the developed countries want to be able to buy cheap raw materials in order to profit from processing and manufacturing them here.

More recently, "voluntary" quotas on manufactured goods from poor countries have become common. The United States threatens new tariff barriers on certain manufactures exported by poor countries unless they "voluntarily" limit the volume exported to us. The result is fewer jobs in hungry lands and lower export earnings.

Brazil's attempt to develop a coffee-processing industry provides one illustration. Coffee used to provide Brazil with approximately one-half of its total export earnings. Brazil's coffee exports increased 90 per cent between 1953 and 1961. But the total revenue earned from coffee dropped by 35 per cent. In 1966 Brazil decided to process its own coffee in order to supply more jobs and earn more income for its people. But when it seized 14 per cent of the U.S. market, the U.S. coffee manufacturers (Tenco, General Foods, Standard Brands and others) charged the Brazilians with unfair competition. What did the U.S. government do? It threatened to cut off aid to Brazil, warning that it might not renew the International Coffee Agreement (which keeps coffee prices somewhat stable). Brazil eventually was forced to tax its instant coffee exports, and its nascent industry was seriously damaged.[21]

On textiles, which many developing countries such as India could supply cheaply to developed countries, the developed world has placed quota restrictions, and the ailing domestic industries in the developed countries are exerting strong pressure for these quotas to be even more restrictive.

In his text *Economic Development,* Theodore Morgan summarizes the situations as follows:

> The overall pattern is plain. Primary and simple products have low duties, though some have quotas. Simple manufactures have higher duties; and complex manufactures still higher. There are sharp obstacles to major cuts in tariff and nontariff barriers because of the resistance of domestic businessmen, labor groups,

and regions, which fear injury from increased imports.[22]
The result is to deprive poor countries of millions of jobs and billions
of dollars from increased exports. Mahbub ul Haq has estimated
that "Third World countries today lose $20 billion to $25 billion a
year in export income because they get frustrated by First World
tariff and non-tariff barriers."[23]

By and large the countries of the Third World have been his-
torically bound to produce primary commodities for export. In
many cases colonial governments coercively discouraged manufacturing industries and actively encouraged the production and export of certain agricultural products and other raw materials. In
other cases powerful landowners were able to squelch local industrialization efforts so that agricultural export enterprises remained
highly profitable.[24] As soon as the developed countries began indus-
trializing, they set up tariffs and quotas to discourage industrialization in the Third World. For all these reasons LDCs have specialized
in primary products and have tended to import manufactured
products from the industrialized nations.

Some would argue that such a pattern conforms nicely to the economic theory of comparative advantage. This theory suggests that
each country ought to specialize in and trade that group of commodities for which it has a cost advantage in production. The United
States thus has a comparative advantage in computers and some
appliances, Japan in automobiles and televisions, and Colombia in
coffee and bananas. The theory of comparative advantage would
thus tell Colombia not to worry too much about industrialization.
If they invest heavily in coffee and bananas they will be as well off as
possible. While this theory may be instructive, it can also be myopic.
In particular, it pays no special attention to the long-term effects of
such specialization. In fact, the trade patterns that have emerged
create special and serious problems for the exporters of primary
products.

In the first place, many Third World economists have charged
that LDC reliance on primary products has destined them to suffer
continually declining relative terms of trade. They cite such evidence as Brazil's being able in 1954 to buy one U.S. jeep for fourteen
bags of coffee, while in 1968 the same U.S. jeep cost Brazil forty-five
bags of coffee.[25] Tanzania could buy a tractor in 1963 for five tons
of sisal; in 1970, by contrast, the same tractor cost ten tons of sisal.[26]

The *World Development Report 1982* shows how Sri Lanka, which has been dependent on its exports of tea, rubber and coconut products, has suffered severe terms-of-trade losses over the last thirty years.[27]

Although some cases are extreme and are surrounded by special intervening circumstances, economists generally recognize that over the last thirty years the low income LDCs have experienced a serious decline in the relative prices of agricultural commodities.[28] At the same time, middle income LDCs, which tend to export more minerals (including oil) than agricultural products, have been more fortunate. Prices on these commodities do not show the same unequivocal downward trend.[29] Sometimes certain agricultural commodities enjoy short surges in prices, such as coffee did in 1977 and sugar does periodically. But in general the declining trend is clear. Hans Singer, a respected economist at the United Nations, argues, "It is a matter of historical fact that ever since the seventies [the 1870s] the trend of prices has been heavily against sellers of food and raw materials and in favor of the sellers of manufactured articles. The statistics are open to doubt and to objection in detail, but the general story which they tell is unmistakable."[30]

A second pernicious problem to which primary-product exporters are vulnerable is that prices fluctuate widely. Violent fluctuation in prices of primary products is harmful to the developing countries' economies. It makes planning almost impossible, since they depend on export earnings for the vital foreign exchange needed to buy essential imported goods. Some countries are dependent on just one commodity for virtually all their exports. Bangladesh depends on jute, Zambia on copper. Hence their economies fluctuate violently with the world price of the commodity they export. It is like living perpetually on a roller coaster, one moment enjoying the benefits of high prices, the next enduring a harrowing tumble into the trenches of low prices.

We have looked briefly at several aspects of present international trade patterns which work to the disadvantage of the developing nations: high tariffs and low quotas (especially on manufactured goods) imposed by the industrialized nations; a thirty-year pattern of declining relative terms of trade; and wild fluctuations in prices of primary commodity exports.

What has been the response of the LDCs?

Proposals from the Third World

Less developed countries have protested against the unjust patterns of international trade for decades. At the Bandung Afro-Asian Conference in 1955 and at the 1964 UN Conference on Trade and Development, LDCs urged the wealthy nations to support trade patterns that were not so detrimental to them. But the affluent turned a deaf ear. In 1972 the American *Journal of Commerce* reported that Washington was ignoring all the reform proposals of the LDCs. The *Journal* concluded: "In other words, just about every major proposal put forth in the interests of protecting the LDCs from further deterioration in the terms of trade is drawing a negative reaction in Washington."[31]

In 1973, however, the United States and other developed countries began to realize they could not ignore Third World desires quite so casually. In that year OPEC was able to create a strong international cartel in oil. Since then OPEC has raised the price of a barrel of oil some 600 per cent (after adjusting for inflation).

Presently, there is a general feeling that OPEC has already fallen apart or may soon do so. The combination of world recession and conservation measures in oil-importing countries has led to a decrease in the demand for OPEC oil, which in turn has fanned the dissension in the ranks of OPEC leaders. The consequences, for the moment, are slightly lower prices for oil; although relatively stable, the prices will probably not rise sharply in the near future unless the recession ends dramatically and world demand for oil rises rapidly. But this is not to say that OPEC is dead. Quite the contrary. Oil still sells at a price significantly higher than it would have sold without OPEC. Because of the recession OPEC's power has waned somewhat, but not permanently and not significantly. OPEC remains a primary force in world economic affairs.

When it became obvious that the OPEC venture was no fluke (as the industrialized countries hoped it would be), a new respect for Third World power slowly emerged. Both sides began to realize that industrialized nations were just as dependent on the poor countries as the poor were on the rich. In fact, many vital raw materials necessary for industrial production were and are largely imported from the LDCs (see table 13).

Because of different economic factors, OPEC-like cartels are not likely to succeed for most of these products. But this did not dampen

U.S. Imports of Selected Minerals from Principal LDC Suppliers

Mineral	Major LDC suppliers with per cent supplied by each		Total per cent of U.S. imports supplied by LDCs	Total per cent of U.S. use supplied by LDCs
Aluminum	Jamaica	36	82	77
Bauxite	Guinea	22		
Cobalt	Zaire	27	45	41
Colombium	Brazil	84	91.7	91.7
	Nigeria	7		
Copper	Chile	23	50.9	7
	Zambia	12		
	Peru	10		
Graphite	Mexico	57	88.6	88.6
	Brazil	10		
	China	10		
Iron ore	Venezuela	14	30.8	8
	Brazil	8		
Tin	Malaysia	44	97.3	78
	Thailand	20		
	Bolivia	17		
Tungsten	China	18	70.7	37
	Thailand	9		

Source: John P. Lewis and Valeriana Kallab, eds., U.S. Foreign Policy and the Third World: Agenda 1983 *(New York: Praeger, 1983), table A.6.*

Table 13

the optimistic spirits of the LDCs. In 1974 they introduced into the United Nations proposals for the formation of a New International Economic Order (NIEO). That same year the general assembly adopted a "Declaration and Action Program" and a "Charter of Economic Rights and Duties of States" for the New International Economic Order. There were eight key proposals:[32]

1. *Prices of primary products and raw materials.* The prices, the developing nations insisted, should increase immediately. Furthermore, they should be tied directly to the prices of the manufactured products which the poor nations must import from rich nations. A

common fund should be set up which would be used to finance buffer stocks of twenty or thirty key commodities so that wild fluctuations in commodity prices could be ironed out.

2. *Tariffs and other barriers to trade.* Developed countries should remove tariffs and other trade barriers to products from the developing nations.

3. *National sovereignty over national resources.* LDCs should have the "right" to nationalize foreign holdings with fair compensation.

4. *Foreign aid.* Rich nations should increase both emergency food aid and grants for long-term development. The UN should achieve its target of 0.7 per cent of GNP on official development assistance by the developed countries (see table 10, p. 42).

5. *Industry.* The developing world should increase its share of world manufactured-goods output from about 10 per cent in 1975 to 25 per cent by the year 2000.

6. *International debt.* Debt should be rescheduled for many developing countries, and for the poorest it should be cancelled. (Many developing countries spend a large proportion of their current aid meeting interest and capital repayment on previous "aid.")

7. *Technology.* Arrangements should be made for the transfer of technology from developed to developing countries—other than through multinational companies, of which developing countries are understandably, in the light of some of their recent experiences, suspicious.

8. *International monetary arrangements.* The poor nations should have a larger role in the International Monetary Fund and other international monetary arrangements which affect trade and development. In order to promote trade and help countries with balance-of-payment problems, the International Monetary Fund originally created Special Drawing Rights (SDRs) worth about $3 billion per year. James P. Grant, president of the Overseas Development Council, showed how unequally assets were distributed, however: "Under the distribution formula that was established, . . . three-quarters of these assets were made available virtually without cost to the rich countries, since these countries . . . set up the system and determined how SDRs would be allocated."[33]

One should not accept these proposals simply because Third World leaders made them. Indeed, some valid criticisms of them have been made.[34] But, as Oxford economist Donald Hay has argued, the proposals merit careful, sympathetic attention.[35]

Unfortunately, little has happened. None of the proposals has been implemented. Initially, the developed countries made it appear that they would grant some concessions. In practice, however, they have been exceptionally stingy with anything but palliative measures. Some of the proposals have been attempted half-heartedly (the commodity fund, for example). But most of them have either been ignored into oblivion or negotiated to death.[36]

Consider item seven. One of the ways for transferring technology and sharing resources was to be through agreements concerning the Law of the Sea. Under the sea lies a wealth of unclaimed resources. Because no nation can justly claim property rights to the oceans, the untapped wealth of the ocean floor seems to offer a chance for the Third World to gain without sacrifice from the wealthy nations. The seabed is a "common heritage of mankind" whose riches should benefit all. However, the LDCs do not possess the sophisticated technology needed to mine the resources. Hence the possibility for the transfer of technology from rich to poor.

Negotiations began in 1973 and continued steadily until 1981. Then, at the last minute in 1981, when the final details were to be worked out and the treaty signed by all participating nations, the United States, under the direction of President Ronald Reagan, backed out. The reason given was that the administration feared the transfer of technology would jeopardize the economic advantage of U.S.-based mining companies. The Law of the Sea, a mechanism that might have greatly assisted the poorer countries, has thus been effectively scuttled.[37]

A similar fate probably awaits the 1980 report of the Brandt commission. An international commission of leaders from both developed and less developed countries issued the report *North-South: A Program for Survival* in 1980.[38] The purpose of the report was to reopen the lines of communication between the rich nations of the North and the poor nations of the South. The report stressed the mutual interdependence of all countries of the globe. It emphasized that the wealthy countries could not expect peaceful international relations while over half of the globe struggles with poverty. It also emphasized that poor countries could not expect to develop without the support of their wealthy counterparts. The report encouraged cooperation instead of confrontation. It made significant recommendations which dealt with the control of multinationals, the encouragement of local development in LDCs, the resolution of the global energy crisis, the institution of a new world monetary order, and the establishment of new trade relationships. The proposals reflect the thinking of the New International Economic Order, but they are widely recognized as realistic and workable. Tragically, however, the report has not generated much response from any major developed country except England.

The Brandt report did lead to a potentially significant international summit of twenty-two world leaders in Cancun, Mexico, in October 1981. Many hoped that progress on the Brandt proposals would occur. One week before leaving for Cancun, however, President Reagan infuriated Third World participants with a militant speech that implicitly rejected all the major recommendations of the Brandt commission.

At Cancun, British Prime Minister Margaret Thatcher seemed impressed by an Indian proverb used by Indian Prime Minister Indira Gandhi to compare the economic problems of the West and India: "I complained of having no shoes until I met a man with no feet." But the industrialized nations made virtually no concessions.

President Reagan refused to make any specific commitments, only agreeing "in principle" to some sort of global negotiations. Six months later an editorial in the *Third World Quarterly,* a development journal reflecting Third World opinion, complained, "Six months after Cancun there was little to suggest that the Global Round of negotiations might be launched in the foreseeable future. The U.S. administration had not changed its position."[39] Tragically, the Brandt report will probably be ignored until it too disappears in the annals of neglected opportunities.

Abstract analysis of unjust trading patterns may seem dull for comfortable North Americans. But experiencing the effects can be sheer agony. In *What Do You Say to a Hungry World?* Stan Mooneyham tells the story of Juan Díaz, a coffee worker in El Salvador, a country which depends on coffee exports for a major share of its earnings.

He and three of his five daughters spend long, hard days in the coffee fields of Montenango. On a good day, Juan picks enough coffee to earn $1.44; his daughters make a total of $3.35. With $1.24 of these wages, Juan and his wife Paula are able to feed their

family for one day. In bad times, Juan and his daughters make as
little as $.56 a day—less than half the money they need just to eat.

At the end of the six-week coffee season, Juan does odd jobs
around the hacienda—provided there is work to be done. He can
earn about $.90 there for an eight-hour day. Paula Díaz supple-
ments her husband's earnings by working in the market. When
people have enough money to purchase the tomatoes, cabbages
and other home-grown vegetables she sells, Paula can make about
$.40 a day.

The hacienda provides a simple dwelling for the Díaz family,
but no modern facilities. Candles are used for light, water has to
be hauled from a well and furnishings consist of little more than a
table and some chairs. Aside from a dress and shoes for each of
the girls during the coffee season, the family has not been able to
buy much else in the last five years. Whatever money doesn't go
for food is spent for visits to the health clinic ($.40 each time), the
high interest on bills at the company store, expenses for the children in school, and for the burial of Juan's father, who died last
year.

"You know, I look forward to a better life for my children,"
Juan says, "I dream that if it is possible—if I can possibly afford it
—my children will not follow in my footsteps, that they will break
out of this terrible way of life. But the money problems we face
every day blot out those dreams. I feel bad, nervous, I don't sleep
nights worrying about how I'll get something for them to eat. I
think and think but don't find any answers. I work hard; my wife
and daughters do, too. We all do. But still we suffer. Why?"[40]
One big reason is that present patterns of international trade are
fundamentally unjust. While their genesis was in the colonial period,
the trade relations built up since then continue to afflict LDCs. In
chapters seven to nine we shall examine proposals for constructive
change—in our personal lifestyles, the church and society at large.
For the present, it is enough to see that current trade patterns make
it impossible to live in the affluent West without being involved in
social structures that contain serious injustice and help keep millions
of people hungry.

Consumption of Nonrenewable Resources
Unfortunately, international trade is not the only way that we are

implicated in structural evil. Wealthy nations contribute heavily to the depletion of the world's nonrenewable resources. In so doing they seriously threaten the possibilities for development of the Third World.

Table 14, column 7, shows the enormous proportion of these eight nonrenewable natural resources consumed by the developed nations of the world to sustain our affluent consumer society. As 27.6 per cent of the world's population, we account for 83 to 94 per cent of total world consumption—and this despite the fact that during the period from 1974 to 1976 the Western world was in the worst

Rich Countries' Consumption of Nonrenewable Natural Resources 1974-76

	1	2	3	4	5	6	7
						E.E.C.	Europe N. America
					Australia	Scandinavia	U.S.S.R.
			West		New	N. America	Japan
	U.S.	U.K.	Germany	Canada	Zealand	Australasia	Australasia
% of World Population	5.4	1.4	1.5	0.6	0.4	13.4	27.6
% of Annual World Consumption of Resource							
Petroleum	28.5	3.5	4.8	3.1	1.3	53.7	83.0
Natural Gas	47.4	3.0	3.1	3.9	0.5	65.0	92.1
Aluminum	32.8	3.4	6.5	2.5	1.4	57.0	90.2
Copper	21.2	5.7	8.6	2.8	1.4	52.8	89.1
Lead	22.3	6.0	5.8	1.4	1.9	51.7	86.0
Nickel	24.1	4.7	8.2	1.8	0.6	50.6	94.2
Tin	23.8	6.4	6.1	2.0	1.7	51.6	84.1
Zinc	18.5	4.3	6.1	2.6	2.0	45.7	85.6

Sources: World Metal Statistics published by World Bureau of Metal Statistics. BP statistical review of the World Oil Industry, 1976.

Table 14

recession it had known in over forty years! Column 6 shows that even among the developed nations, the nominally "Christian" nations of the European Economic Community, Scandinavia, North America and Australasia with only 13.4 per cent of the world's population account for over half the world's total annual consumption of all but one of these resources—and this without the help of Japan, the U.S.S.R. and 200 million people in the "poorer" countries of Eastern and Southern Europe.

Our per capita energy consumption offers one vivid example of the staggering imbalance in resource consumption. Table 15 shows

Per Capita Energy Consumption—1970 and 1980

	Kilograms per person (coal equivalent)	
	1970	1980
United States	10,870	10,410
Canada	8,779	10,241
West Germany	5,124	5,727
U.S.S.R.	4,048	5,595
Great Britain	5,029	4,835
France	3,814	4,351
Japan	3,098	3,690
Italy	2,647	3,318
Mexico	1,055	1,770
Brazil	449	761
Philippines	263	328
India	142	191
Zaire	68	67
Ethiopia	27	29

Source: U.S. Bureau of the Census, Statistical Abstract of the U.S., 1982-83, pp. 876-77.

Table 15

that the average person in the United States consumes 358 times as much energy per year as the average person in Ethiopia. Canadians and Americans even consume about twice as much energy as people in West Germany, France or England. In 1979, the Harvard Business School published *Energy Future,* which pointed out that Americans could use 30 to 40 per cent less energy with no damage to our lifestyle.[41] What an incredible commentary on our wastefulness!

The statistical disparities of this table on energy consumption become much more meaningful when put into real-life situations. In 1973-74 and again in 1978-79 Westerners complained about the lack of gasoline for their family cars and grumbled about the long lines at the gas pumps. It was an inconvenience, to be sure; but few, if any, went hungry because of it. In India, however, the situation was different. There farmers waited in line for days for a small can of fuel to run their irrigation pumps. Many of them received no gasoline at all and were consequently forced to return to earlier, less productive farming methods. The result was less food and more hunger. In the United States reduced energy consumption is a matter of inconvenience, or a luxury foregone. In India and other LDCs it can be a matter of life or death.

We have seen that the rich nations consume a high per cent of the nonrenewable resources used each year. But may that not be merely the result of our industrialization and the material abundance it has created? The statistics on resource use are really no surprise since consumption of natural resources goes along, hand and glove, with the process of industrialization. Indeed, if LDCs advance materially, as they must, they too will begin to use greater amounts of nonrenewable resources. Consequently it is not the simple statistics on resource use that are of the greatest interest. They merely point out the well-known disparity between relative states of development (as well as North American wastefulness). Rather we must ask two deeper questions. First, does the extravagant use of natural resources by the developed world improve or hinder the development prospects of the Third World? Second, are there really limits to growth, and if so where do they arise?

On the first question experts disagree. Many professional world watchers insist that the Third World cannot expect to develop unless the industrialized world continues to purchase a high volume of natural resources from the Third World. The Brandt commission report concurs. On the other hand, some argue that it was largely the contact between the first and third worlds that led to the underdevelopment of the world's poor nations in the first place. These people are skeptical of development schemes which rely heavily on the First World. They argue that developed nations rape the Third World. Just as the Spaniards took precious metals out of Latin America, so too the developed countries continue to wrest raw materials from their weaker neighbors. They achieve this primarily via unfairly bargained agreements between multinational mining and extraction companies and LDC governments. According to this second viewpoint, LDCs are selling their birthright of natural resources to the rich countries for a relatively few luxury goods for their nations' wealthy elite.

Both sides are partially correct. Given the present state of things, the Third World must look to the developed world for markets for its goods (hopefully with more favorable trading patterns), and it must look to the developed world for needed technology. But increased trading with the industrialized nations will benefit the Third World only if the First World changes significantly. Instead of quietly condoning arrangements that are counterproductive to LDCs, the governments of wealthy nations could begin to insist on more equitable resource trading agreements. Western nations could encourage development of Third World economies so that poor nations could begin to make better use of their natural resources. At the same time the First World could show less preoccupation with its own ever-increasing consumption.

The question of limits to growth is even more difficult to answer with certainty because of its speculative nature. We frequently hear admonitions against worrying excessively about declining resources. Technology will prevail, optimists confidently assure us. Technological progress will create alternatives to presently essential, but increasingly scarce, natural resources. At the same time, others less optimistic confront us with warnings that we are being too profligate in a resource-scarce world. International development expert Lester Brown, for instance, has argued, "It has long been part of the conventional wisdom within the international development community that the two billion people living in the poor countries could not aspire to the lifestyle enjoyed by the average North American because there was not enough iron ore, petroleum and protein in the world to provide it."[42]

If Brown is right, then it becomes incumbent on Western society to begin seeking ways to reduce our consumption of these scarce resources. We must make them available to the poorer nations. Such a call stands in stark contrast to U.S. infatuation in the early '80s with getting its economy growing again. (To be sure, as we will see in chapter nine, economic growth does not always require greater resource consumption. The type of growth being promoted in the United States, however, is the kind that would.)

Some new light has been shed on this issue by *The Global 2000 Report to the President* released in 1980.[43] The study tried to project what world conditions would be in the year 2000 if present trends continue. The report is not optimistic. In an opening section the report states:

> Environmental, resource, and population stresses are intensifying and will increasingly determine the quality of human life on our planet. These stresses are already severe enough to deny many millions of people basic needs for food, shelter, health, and jobs, or any hope for betterment. At the same time, the earth's carrying capacity—the ability of biological systems to provide resources for human needs—is eroding. The trends reflected in the Global 2000 study suggest strongly a progressive degradation and impoverishment of the earth's natural resource base.[44]

The report does not, in contrast to the statement by Brown, find any serious threat of severe shortages of commonly used metals. Nor does it forecast any serious deficiencies in the energy supply (as long as much of the new demand is satisfied by nuclear power!).[45]

Severe problems do, however, loom large. The dangers arise not so much because vital metal and energy resources are disappearing, but because the increasing use of these materials threatens the carrying capacity of the world environment. For example, as the economy of the United States grows, the demand for energy increases. One of the currently proposed plans to meet this new demand is through increasing the number of coal-fired power plants. But when coal is burned, great amounts of sulfur and nitrogen oxides are released into the air.[46] This in turn creates the acid rain that has already done major damage to lakes, forests and farms in northeastern United States and Canada. Another potentially dangerous effect of increased energy consumption is the rising level of carbon dioxide in the atmosphere. While its ultimate effects are unknown, many scientists expect the increased level of carbon dioxide to cause a general global warming, which would have a significant negative impact on world agriculture and general environmental stability.

Industrial activity and high levels of natural resource consumption thus adversely affect our most precious resources: air, water and cultivable land. According to the report, atmospheric pollution, a deteriorating agricultural base and increasing water pollution combined with ever more common fresh-water shortages all lie in wait for us in the future if current trends do not change.

All such ecological strains result from industrialization, affluence and population growth. The more goods we produce, the more energy we burn, the more agricultural products we grow, the greater the danger of imminent cataclysm. Presently the greatest contributors to these problems are the nations of affluence. As E. F. Schumacher bluntly puts it:

> It is obvious that the world cannot afford the U.S.A. Nor can it afford Western Europe or Japan. . . . Think of it—one American drawing on resources that would sustain fifty Indians! . . . The poor don't do much damage; the modest people don't do much damage. Virtually all the damage is done by, say, 15 per cent. . . . The problem passengers on Space-Ship Earth are the first-class passengers and no one else.[47]

Yet the developed nations call for ever more production and consumption. Is such profligacy the outcome of pure greed? Perhaps, in part. But there is a deeper structural problem. When developed economies stop growing, they stagnate. People are thrown out of work. Welfare rolls grow. Discontent among social groups is sown. Social confrontations increase.[48]

In bygone days no one really suspected that growing economies represented a threat to the quality of life of future generations. Now, however, there is good reason to believe that continued material economic growth in the developed world cannot be justified; highly industrialized countries are already contributing more than their share to the erosion of the earth's carrying capacity.

Our resource use therefore represents the most devious type of structural evil. If we stop growing, our society is threatened; yet to foster material growth increasingly endangers a fragile biosphere and, by extension, undermines the poor countries' opportunity to

develop. It will take all of our insight and then some to see our way
out of this dilemma. Technology, though useful, will not provide
the sole answer. A return to biblical principles must be our starting
point.

Food Consumption Patterns

Our eating patterns—a third area where we are caught in institutionalized sin—may seem to us personal and private. But they are
tightly interlocked with complex economic structures, including
national and international agricultural policies and the decisions of
multinational corporations engaged in agribusiness.

Dr. Georg Borgstrom, an internationally known food specialist
and professor of food science and human nutrition at Michigan
State University, has pointedly underscored the way North Americans consume a disproportionate share of the world's supply of
food. He has insisted that we ought to measure world population
not merely in terms of people but also in terms of the total "feeding
burden" of the globe. In a fascinating paper presented in 1974 he
pointed out that, if we count livestock as well as people, the earth
already had in 1974 not 4 billion but 19 billion "population equivalents," that is, inhabitants. (He computed the amount of protein
required by the livestock and calculated how many people that
protein would feed.)[49] So the feeding burden of the United States
was not 210 million people in 1974. Rather, the "U.S. total feeding
burden in biological terms was consequently 1.6 billion."[50] Though
India had three times as many people as the United States, it had
far less livestock. Counting livestock, India had only 1.2 billion
"population equivalents." So who has the sacred cows?

Another indication that something is wrong comes from a review
of trade statistics. Rich countries have regularly imported more
food from poor nations than they have exported to them. Poor
LDCs have been feeding the affluent minority. Table 16 shows that
in 1979 the developed nations exported $22,259 million worth of
food to poor nations; but they imported $32,810 million worth of
food. In 1980 and 1981 the picture began to change, with net loss to
the poor in 1980 falling to $2,720 million and with an actual surplus
of $2,100 million for the poor in 1981.

There may be cause for optimism here, but also reason for cau-
tion. The world was in recession. Whereas the food imported by

wealthy countries tends to be luxury foods (such as exotic fruits or nuts and beef), the food imported by poor countries is more often nutritionally vital (for example, basic grains). In times of recession, as now, wealthy countries forgo a bit of their luxury food; but basic grains remain just as necessary all the time, so poor countries continue to import them. Hence the trade balance we see for 1980-81. But, as the developed world moves out of its recession, we will likely see the food situation revert again to a net loss to poor countries. Witness the trends which followed the 1975 world recession.

Food Exports and Imports (in millions of U.S. dollars)

	Food exports from developed world to LDCs		Food imports by developed world from LDCs		Net loss of food by poor countries
1 Year	2 All developed countries	3 The U.S.A.	4 All developed countries	5 The U.S.A.	6 Column 4 minus column 2
1955	2,090	735	6,870	2,470	4,780
1960	3,150	1,470	7,160	2,450	4,010
1965	3,130	1,594	7,045	2,373	3,915
1970	4,542	1,767	9,864	3,400	5,322
1975	14,496	6,141	18,226	5,380	3,730
1976	13,315	5,317	22,909	7,008	9,594
1977	14,884	5,183	29,880	8,577	14,996
1978	18,597	7,099	30,289	8,988	11,692
1979	22,259	8,012	32,810	9,045	10,551
1980	31,339	11,346	34,059	9,997	2,720
1981	33,861	13,076	31,761	9,310	−2,100

Sources: U.N.'s Handbook of International Trade and Development Statistics, 1972; *and* U.N.'s Monthly Bulletin of Statistics, *February and May 1983.*

Note: Centrally planned economies are not included.

Table 16

But what about North America? Canada and the United States both still export more food than they import. But this picture changes dramatically when one compares U.S. food exports from and imports to only the less developed countries. The facts in table 16 are as clear as they are astonishing. Every year except when the U.S. economy is in serious recession (1975, 1980, 1981) the United States imports more food from poor nations than it exports to them.

Data about the world fish catch tell the same story. In 1973 the world fish catch was 65.7 million tons. Had the catch been divided evenly, each person in the world would have received thirty-four pounds.[51] Not surprisingly, it was not so divided. The developed nations, with one-quarter of the world's people, took about three-quarters of the year's fish catch. Peru has the largest anchovy fisheries in the world, but little of the anchovy protein goes to feed the millions of poor Peruvians; most of it fattens livestock in the United States and Europe. The story with tuna is similar. Professor Borgstrom has pointed out that two-thirds of the total world tuna catch ends up in the United States. One-third of this tuna goes for catfood![52] Obviously Americans do not import so much food because we need it, but because we want it and have enough money to pay for it.

Why is it that countries with a less-than-adequate food supply for their own people willingly send us more food than they get in return? The obvious answer is that food exports by poor nations pay for their imports of high technology, oil and luxury goods. But poor people are less interested in those things than in food to feed their families. So we still face the question. Why does food needed to end starvation and malnutrition in poor nations get exported to rich nations?

The answer is double-pronged. The first prong is purely economic: Much food grown or gathered in LDCs is not available to its own poor people simply because the poor cannot afford it. They have no land on which to grow their own crops to sell. Nor can they find productive work in the squalid, overpopulated cities.

The second prong of the answer is historical, once again stretching back to the colonial era.[53] In those days export crops were actively promoted—to the detriment of food production for local consumption. Plantations were planned to produce export crops. Local people, frequently dispossessed of their land, were turned into either slaves or poorly paid agricultural workers. Those who managed to keep some land were "encouraged" to produce foodstuffs desired in the mother countries. Growing food for the mother country was seen as the colony's highest priority. John Stuart Mill, the respected nineteenth-century British economist, "reasoned that colonies should not be thought of as civilizations or countries at all but as 'agricultural establishments' whose sole purpose was to supply the 'larger community to which they belong.' "[54]

Colonial days have ended for the most part, but the vestiges remain. The plantations created have not willingly been returned to the descendants of their original owners. New owners (whether the local elite or multinational corporation) of the same large holdings still look to the industrialized countries as their trading partners since the peasant community has little to offer in the way of goods desired by the landowner. Owners of large landholdings could grow beans, corn or rice for the local population, but the local people do not have the assets to produce anything marketable. So instead the owners look to a country like the United States for their market. They send us cotton, beef, coffee, bananas or other agricultural products, and we send them the goods they desire in return. As time goes on, the landowners and other persons of wealth look increasingly to the developed world for economic partnership. Besides withholding land from the peasant community, this relationship leads to the introduction of labor-saving farm technology. Fewer workers are needed to work the large estates, and people are left unemployed with nowhere else to go. In such a way the structures favor the wealthy and oppress the poor.

It is perhaps in this context that the divine wisdom of the jubilee principle is best understood. The jubilee calls for redistribution of society's pool of productive assets. When members of a society lose their assets, by whatever means, it is difficult for them to participate in economic activity. People with no assets can produce no goods. With no goods to trade, they cannot purchase necessities.

In almost all of today's LDCs the process of displacing people from the land began many years ago and has continued to the present. Seldom has anything like the jubilee occurred, and so the problems have grown. And the longer they grow, the more impossible they become.

Why are we so perplexed by the existence of hunger and poverty today? Is it really any wonder? People were impoverished a long time ago, and steps have never been taken to right the initial injustices or to restore productive capabilities to the poor. This is why in good times we import more food from poor countries than we send back to them. Injustice has become deeply embedded in national and international economic and social life.

Two illustrations may help. Borgstrom has said that "the Mexican border is the scene of the world's biggest meat transfers." In the mid 1970s Americans imported approximately one million cattle every year from Mexico. That amount was half as much as Mexicans had left for themselves.[55]

Nor is it merely that Americans consume beef that hungry Mexicans need. American demand for beef also encourages unjust structures in Mexico. Until oil prices dropped in 1982, Mexico's economy had for twenty years been growing at the exceptionally high annual rate of 6-7 per cent. But unemployment and the income differential between rich and poor had also spurted forward. Why? Because the government had encouraged large farms and urban factories rather than a pattern of development that would benefit everyone. Almost all increasing farm production came from fewer than 5 per cent of the farms.[56] The U.S. government's General Accounting Office recently reported that Mexico's shift to producing more food for export (most of it for the U.S. market) has resulted in higher food prices in Mexico, a greater scarcity of food there, and a more unequal distribution of income.[57] As a result of Mexico's approach to development, and other factors as well, the 1980 *World Development Report* indicated that 20 per cent of all Mexicans received 58 per cent of the total income, while 40 per cent of the people got less than 10 per cent.[58] The result is unemployment and hunger, especially in the countryside.

Because oil prices have dropped and because Mexico's corrupt government has misused billions of dollars in foreign loans, it finds itself in an awful predicament. The new president, Miguel Hurtado de la Madrid, is preaching austerity, but his programs of slowing wage growth and decreasing food subsidies will hurt the poor much more than the rich. Not only did the poor share little in the economic growth of the last two decades, but they are now being asked to shoulder the burdens brought about by the government's financial indiscretions.

Mexico might have decided to adopt a development strategy—using people rather than machines, and fostering small farms—that would have provided food for the masses rather than beef for export. But there were too many powerful influences telling it not to. Americans could not have corrected this injustice merely by not purchasing the beef, but certainly the U.S. demand for Mexican beef helped promote the present unjust structures in Mexico.

The picture is similar throughout Central America.[59] Roughly 50 per cent of its cultivated land is used to grow export crops. Beef exports (largely to the United States for hamburgers, sausages and frozen pizza) have soared in the past twenty-five years—partly because Central American beef costs 40 per cent less than American beef. During the past twenty years over one-half of all the loans made by the World Bank and the Inter-American Development Bank for agriculture and rural development in Central America went to promote the production of beef for export.

Unfortunately, beef exports produced tragedy in Central America. Malnutrition has increased along with land concentration. Since the early 1960s per capita beef consumption in Central America declined by 20 per cent. The poor there simply could not compete with wealthy Americans. A study by the Pan American Health Organization showed that between 1965 and 1975 malnutrition rose by 67 per cent among children five years and under. In fact, 50 per cent of the children in Central America died before the age of six—largely because of malnutrition and related diseases.

One reason hunger and malnutrition have grown is that the profitable beef exports encouraged large landholders to increase their holdings at the expense of the poor. (Large landholdings, of course, have been common since the earliest days of Spanish colonialism.) By 1973 in Costa Rica the 5 per cent of the ranchers with the largest holdings owned 55 per cent of the pastureland; the 40 per cent with the smallest holdings owned 2 per cent of the pastureland. Land that had formerly grown corn or beans for local consumption was devoted to beef for export. And since a thousand-acre ranch needed only five workers, while a thousand acres in rice or beans required one hundred persons, many rural laborers lost their jobs and joined the lines of the unemployed in the cities. Why do fully 50 per cent of all the people in El Salvador, Guatemala and Honduras have annual incomes of less than $100 per person? Beef—and other export crops that end up on American tables—is part of the answer.

Not all the examples come from Latin America.[60] In the Philippines 77 per cent of all children between the ages of one and five suffer from malnutrition. Seventy-six per cent of all rural families fall below the UN poverty threshold. Land ownership and income distribution are, of course, unequal; 1.6 per cent of the families own 38 per cent of the land producing rice and corn. The richest 5 per cent of the population receive 25 per cent of the total family income, while the poorest 50 per cent get only 18 per cent.

Again the tragic story goes back to colonial days. Before the Spanish conquerers arrived in the early 1600s, local villages owned the land cooperatively. But the Spanish demand for surplus crops for taxes allowed the better-off Filipinos who collected the taxes for the Spanish colonialists to amass larger and larger holdings. After the United States replaced Spain in 1898, export cropping (and land concentration) increased still further. After 1960 export cropping grew even faster, as American pineapple producers moved from Hawaii to the Philippines to take advantage of cheaper wages. (They saved 47 per cent in production costs.) From 1960 to 1980 the amount of land devoted to export crops increased from 15 per cent to 30 per cent.

The government of President Ferdinand Marcos has promoted a national development policy based on export crops by ruthlessly suppressing movements of workers who press for higher wages or land reform. (The average wage for a sugar-cane laborer working thirteen to fourteen hours a day is $7.00 a week.) Both Amnesty International and the International Commission of Jurists have documented the existence of thousands of political prisoners. Electric-shock torture, water torture, extended solitary confinement and beatings are widespread. Meanwhile American military aid to Marcos continues to increase.

Who is responsible for the children dying in Central America or the Philippines? The wealthy national elite who want to increase their affluence? The American companies that work closely with the local elite? The Americans who go to MacDonalds to eat the beef needed by hungry children in Central America?

Once again we dare not make the simplistic assumption that if we stop eating food imported from the Third World, hungry children there will promptly enjoy it. More extensive economic and political changes are required. Chapter nine examines some of the ways we can promote such changes. My purpose here is simply to show that our eating patterns are interlocked with destructive social and economic structures that leave millions hungry and starving.

Multinationals in the Less Developed World

We have seen how international structures and institutions are woven with threads spun from injustice, threads so tightly knit in the fabric of international economic activity that the injustice is easily overlooked. With multinational corporations the injustices are perhaps easier to see, but they are harder to remove.

Multinational corporations (MNCs) are children of the affluent West. Most of them began years ago as small, localized firms, but over time, for a variety of reasons and by a variety of means, they expanded into sprawling corporations. For the most part their growth has been gradual and they have evolved alongside the economy as a whole. Consequently the developed world, although at times exasperated at the apparent indifference of large corporations to wider social goals, has learned to work constructively with them and, to a certain extent, to control their power.

After World War 2, again for a variety of reasons, these big corporations moved in droves to set up overseas operations. Most of their activity went to other developed countries, but increasingly they moved into less developed countries as well. Development economist Michael Todaro notes that in 1962 private investment in foreign countries was $2.4 billion. By the mid seventies annual investment in LDCs was running around $9 billion.[61] By a different calculation the book value of foreign investment in non-OPEC LDCs in 1967 was about $21 billion; by 1975 the figure had increased to around $44 billion.[62] Unfortunately, serious problems can arise when a large, technologically advanced, managerially sophisticated firm, whose goal is to create profit for shareholders back home, goes to do business in a materially poor, governmentally unsophisticated, dependent LDC.

Nonetheless, before the negative side of multinationals became known, people promoted them as a major engine of economic development and growth in LDCs. It was thought that MNCs could help in a number of ways: (1) by providing access to scarce capital resources; (2) by increasing the flow of foreign exchange to LDCs;

(3) by providing LDC governments with healthy businesses from which to generate the tax revenues needed for development projects; and (4) by introducing technology and training workers in technical and managerial skills.[63] On paper the possibilities looked promising. Had the LDCs been equally powerful bargaining and trading partners, this might have gone well. But it soon became apparent that MNCs were not going to be the savior of the less developed world. Instead, increasing evidence emerged that they would to some degree be counterproductive to the true progress and development of the LDCs. In retrospect this should really have been no surprise to people with a biblical view of sin. Powerful agents regularly dominate and take advantage of weaker ones. Interested primarily if not exclusively in profits for themselves, MNCs took advantage of the LDCs they courted.

What is so bad with multinationals? Richard Barnet answers the question this way: "If we take as the development priority the requirement that minimum basic needs in food, shelter, health, water, and education must be met early in the development process, then the contribution of the multinationals based on the record is almost certain to be negative."[64] In considering Barnet's claim, three dimensions must be brought out: simple economic effects, political effects and ideological effects.

First, *the economic effects*. Donald Hay outlined three problems in his paper at the International Consultation on Simple Lifestyle sponsored by the World Evangelical Fellowship and the Lausanne Committee for World Evangelization. First, multinationals do not really contribute the amount of capital they usually profess to.[65] Instead they borrow heavily from the banks in host countries, thereby reducing the funds available to local entrepreneurs and diminishing the level of indigenous business involvement. Second, multinationals are naturally more concerned about their own profit than the welfare of the host countries. This sometimes results, for example, in the shutting down of an entire subsidiary operation, an action that is devastating in impact on the relatively small LDC while only marginally significant for the MNC. MNCs may also artificially vary their profit picture to avoid local taxes by selling their finished product to the parent company at below-market price. A third problem Hay finds is that MNCs frequently promote "the wrong sort of development" to the LDCs. He argues that MNCs usually produce highly differentiated products for the wealthy instead of necessities for the poor. By so doing MNCs reinforce the dualistic structures that keep the majority in poverty and a minority in the mainstream of developed world economics.[66]

On *the political side*, Barnet argues that MNCs may work to ensure political stability even though political change may be essential for widespread social and economic development. MNCs, he contends, are not interested in the basic needs of the poor, but in ensuring stable markets so that profits are not jeopardized.[67] As a result MNCs all too often end up staunchly supporting oppressive military regimes that are not interested in the basic needs of the poor. In addition, MNCs have built up a strong bargaining position because over the years LDCs have become increasingly more dependent on their presence. (Many of them have annual sales which are greater than the GNPs of many LDCs.) By threatening to leave and thereby throwing a dependent economy into chaos, MNCs can often extort one-sided agreements on such issues as tax concessions, profit repatriation limits, indigenous training requirements and so on. Once the MNC is established, it becomes a pressure group "lobbying" for preferred treatment for foreign firms. Barnet says that they can thus divert government spending away from development projects for the poor and toward expenditures on "roads, harbors, [and] subsidies for high technology, to develop the infrastructure to support profitable private investment."[68]

While economic and political problems could conceivably be resolved by an understanding international community, the resolution of *ideological issues* is more in doubt. By default, MNCs happen to be on the cutting edge of First World contact with the people of Third World nations. MNCs thus communicate to a poverty-stricken world what life is like in affluent nations. But not only do they impress on the poor how Westerners live; they also encourage them, through lavish advertising campaigns, to try and live the same way.

The result is that many poor people are enticed into spending a disproportionate share of their income on goods that do them no good. Soft drinks are an example of unnecessary but frequently purchased goods.[69] Perhaps the most well-known and pernicious case involves the Nestlé Corporation and its persistence in marketing infant formula to Third World mothers who were better off nursing their children. The practice of dressing company representatives to look like nurses and having them recommend to mothers that they feed their infants formula was one of the most devious types of product promotion.

Aggressive advertising by large Western MNCs who have promoted bottle-feeding has drastically reduced the number of breast-fed babies in the Third World. In its 1982-83 report UNICEF noted that the percentage of breast-fed infants in Brazil declined from 96 per cent in 1940 to 40 per cent in 1974. In Chile it fell from 95 per cent in 1955 to 20 per cent today. (Fortunately, the worst abuses have recently been curtailed—in part because of an international boycott of Nestlé products.) UNICEF estimates that one million children a year would be saved within a decade if breast-feeding could again replace infant formula.[70]

In a moment of candor H. W. Walter, chairman of the board of International Flavors and Fragrances, put it bluntly:

> How often we see in developing countries that the poorer the economic outlook, the more important the small luxury of a flavored soft drink or smoke. . . . To the dismay of many would-be benefactors, the poorer the malnourished are, the more likely they are to spend a disproportionate amount of whatever they have on some luxury rather than on what they need. . . . Observe, study, learn. . . . We try to do it at IFF. It seems to pay off for us. Perhaps it will for you.[71]

Todaro sums up the ideological argument: "MNCs typically produce *inappropriate products* (those demanded by a small minority of the population), stimulate *inappropriate consumption patterns* through advertising and their monopolistic market power, and do this all with *inappropriate* (capital-intensive) *technologies of production.*"[72] The judgment of Oxford economist Donald Hay is that "multinational companies, themselves the creations of the developed countries, are on balance detrimental to less developed countries."[73]

Once again we must ask, Who is at fault? Is it the host governments, for letting in multinationals with their interests so contrary to what the country as a whole needs? Or is it the MNCs, for not taking a more charitable stance toward the poor? Or is it the people in the developed world, for unknowingly supporting MNCs by purchasing their products or owning their stock? The answer is, All three. All three share some responsibility for the negative impact of multinational corporations on Third World countries.

We are all implicated in structural evil. International trade patterns are unjust. The prodigious consumption of natural resources severely threatens the world environment and the development opportunities of the Third World. Food consumption patterns are interlocked with past and present injustices that have never been rectified. And multinational corporations often hinder rather than promote meaningful development in less developed nations. Every person in developed countries is involved in these structural injustices. Unless you have retreated to some isolated valley and grow or make everything you use, you participate in unjust structures which contribute directly to the hunger of a billion malnourished neighbors.

We cannot, of course, conclude that international trade or investment by multinational corporations in poor countries is necessarily immoral. Nor would the economies of the developed world be destroyed if present injustices in the system were corrected. The proper conclusion is that injustice has become deeply embedded in some of our fundamental economic institutions. Biblical Christians—precisely to the extent that they are faithful to Scripture—will dare to call such structures sinful.

The reader without a degree in economics probably wishes international economics were less complex or that faithful discipleship in our time had less to do with such a complicated subject. But former UN Secretary General Dag Hammarskjöld was right: "In our era, the road to holiness necessarily passes through the world of action."[74] To give the cup of cold water effectively in the Age of Hunger frequently requires some understanding of international economic and political structures. The story of bananas helps clarify these complex issues.

The Story of Bananas
On April 10, 1975, North Americans learned that United Brands, one of three huge U.S. companies that grow and import bananas, had arranged to pay $2.5 million (only $1.25 million was actually paid) in bribes to top government officials in Honduras. Why? To persuade them to impose an export tax on bananas that was less than half of what Honduras had requested.[75] In order to increase profits for a U.S. company and to lower banana prices, the Honduran gov-

ernment agreed, for a bribe, to cut drastically the export tax, even though the money was desperately needed in Honduras.

The story actually began in March 1974. Several banana-producing countries in Central America agreed to join together to demand a one-dollar tax on every case of bananas exported. Why? Banana prices for producers had not increased in the previous twenty inflation-ridden years. But the costs for manufactured goods had constantly escalated. As a result the real purchasing power of exported bananas had declined by 60 per cent. At least half of the export income for Honduras and Panama came from bananas. No wonder they were poor. (As we have already seen, half of the inhabitants of Honduras earn less than one hundred dollars a year.)

What did the banana companies do when the exporting countries demanded a one-dollar tax on bananas? They adamantly refused to pay. Since three large companies (United Brands, Castle and Cooke, and Del Monte) controlled ninety per cent of the marketing and distribution of bananas, they had powerful leverage. In Panama the fruit company abruptly stopped cutting bananas. In Honduras the banana company allowed 145,000 crates to rot at the docks. One after another the poor countries gave in. Costa Rica finally settled for twenty-five cents a crate; Panama, for thirty-five cents; Honduras, thanks to the large bribe, eventually agreed to a thirty-cent tax.[76]

One can easily understand why a UN fact-finding commission in 1975 concluded, "The banana-producing countries with very much less income are subsidizing the consumption of the fruit, and consequently the development of the more industrialized countries."[77]

Why don't the masses of poor people demand change? They do. But they have little power. Dictators representing tiny, wealthy elites that work closely with American business interests rule many Latin American countries.

The history of Guatemala, also a producer of bananas for United Brands, shows why change is difficult. In 1954 the CIA helped overthrow a democratically elected government in Guatemala. Why? Because it had initiated a modest program of agricultural reform that seemed to threaten unused land owned by the United Fruit Company (the former name of United Brands). The U.S. secretary of state in 1954 was John Foster Dulles. His law firm had written the company's agreements with Guatemala in 1930 and 1936. The CIA

director was Allen Dulles, brother of John Foster Dulles and previous president of United Fruit Company. The assistant secretary
of state was a major shareholder in United Fruit Company.[78] In
Guatemala and elsewhere change is difficult because U.S. companies work closely with wealthy, local elites to protect their mutual
economic interests.

In the past, most Americans knew little about the injustice in
Central America. That began to change in the early 1980s. With
major radical guerrilla movements' gaining ground in El Salvador
and Guatemala, President Reagan made a vigorous military response with greatly increased U.S. military aid. Front-page head-
lines on Central America became a regular feature of American
newspapers. In 1981 Reagan authorized $19 million for secret CIA
military support for right-wing guerrillas attacking the new socialist
government of Nicaragua. The stated goal was to stop alleged arms
shipments from the Soviet Union and Cuba through Nicaragua to
the guerrillas in El Salvador. The real aims, however, were the in-
timidation and destabilization of the left-wing Nicaraguan government and its actual overthrow.[79] In August 1983, when Reagan dis-
patched a large Navy flotilla to sail menacingly off the Nicaraguan
coast, it seemed possible that major fighting could erupt in Central
America.

The civil wars raging in Central America today undoubtedly have
many roots.[80] Certainly the fact that some of the guerrilla movements have turned in despair to Marxist countries for support and
supplies complicates the problems. Soviet shipment of arms must be
condemned. But President Reagan's attempt to solve the problems
primarily via a military response is both immoral and foolish. The
root causes of the violence and war are the long-standing economic
injustice and desperate poverty of the masses of poor people in the
region. If half of your children are dying of malnutrition before
they reach the age of six, you do not need Marxist-Leninists to tell
you something needs to change.

Tragically there will always be those eager to provide plausible
rationalizations. Andrew M. Greeley, a prominent sociologist at the
University of Chicago, has mocked those who try to make Americans
feel guilty about their economic relationships with the Third World:
"Well, let us suppose that our guilt finally becomes too much to bear
and we decide to reform. . . . We inform the fruit orchards in Cen-

tral America that we can dispense with bananas in our diets. . . . Their joy will hardly be noticed as massive unemployment and depression sweep those countries."[81]

One wonders if Greeley is naive or perverse. The point is not—and Greeley surely knows this—that we should stop importing bananas. It is rather that multinational firms and huge agribusinesses, in complicity with all the buyers of bananas in the developed world, are engaged in a sordid business which keeps the poor from escaping their poverty trap. The point is further that we should encourage the reorganization of economic structures and promote programs here and in Central America that will help poor people in producing countries share in the benefits of agricultural production and trade.

The example of bananas shows how all of us are involved in unjust international economic structures. The words of the apostle James seem to speak directly to our situation.

Come now, you rich, weep and howl for the miseries that are coming upon you. . . . Your gold and silver have rusted, and their rust will be evidence against you. . . . Behold, the wages of the laborers who mowed your fields, which you kept back by fraud, cry out; and the cries of the harvesters have reached the ears of the Lord of hosts. You have lived on the earth in luxury and in pleasure; you have fattened your hearts in a day of slaughter. (Jas 5:1-5)

The Repentance of Zacchaeus

What should be our response, brothers and sisters? For biblical Christians the only possible response to sin is repentance. Unconsciously, to at least some degree, we have become entangled in a complex web of institutionalized sin. Thank God we can repent. God is merciful. He forgives. But only if we repent. And biblical repentance involves more than a hasty tear and a weekly prayer of confession. Biblical repentance involves conversion. It involves a whole new lifestyle. The One who stands ready to forgive us for our sinful involvement in terrible economic injustice offers us his grace to begin living a radically new lifestyle of identification with the poor and oppressed.

Sin is not just an inconvenience or a tragedy for our neighbors. It is a damnable outrage against the Almighty Lord of the universe. If God's Word is true, then all of us who dwell in affluent nations are trapped in sin. We have profited from systemic injustice—sometimes only half knowing, sometimes only half caring and always half hoping not to know. We are guilty of an outrageous offense against God and neighbor.

But that is not God's last word to us. If it were, honest acknowledgment of our involvement would be almost impossible. If there were no hope of forgiveness, admission of our sinful complicity in evil of this magnitude would be an act of despair.[82] But there is hope. The One who writes our indictment is the One who died for us sinners.

John Newton was captain of a slave ship in the eighteenth century. A brutal, callous man, he played a central role in a system which fed thousands to the sharks and delivered millions to a living death. But eventually, after he gave up his career as captain, he saw his sin and repented. His familiar hymn overflows with joy and gratitude for God's acceptance and forgiveness.

Amazing grace! How sweet the sound,
    that saved a wretch like me;
I once was lost, but now am found,
    was blind but now I see.
'Twas grace that taught my heart to fear,
    and grace my fears relieved;
How precious did that grace appear
    the hour I first believed.

John Newton became a founding member of the society for the abolition of slavery. The church which he pastored, St. Mary Woolnoth in the City of London, was a meeting place for abolitionists. William Wilberforce frequently came to him for spiritual counsel. Newton delivered impassioned sermons against the slave trade, convincing many people of its evil. He campaigned against the slave trade until he died in the year of its abolition, 1807.

We are participants in a system that dooms even more people to agony and death. If we have eyes to see, God's grace will also teach our hearts to fear and tremble, and then also to rest and trust.

But only if we repent. Repentance is not coming forward at the close of a service. It is not repeating a spiritual law. It is not mumbling a liturgical confession. All of these things may help. But they are no substitute for the kind of deep inner anguish that leads to a new way of living.

Biblical repentance entails conversion; literally the word means "turning around." The Greek word *metanoia,* as Luther insisted so vigorously, means a total change of mind. The New Testament links repentance to a transformed style of living. Sensing the hypocrisy of the Pharisees who came seeking baptism, John the Baptist denounced them as a brood of vipers. "Bear fruit that befits repentance," he demanded (Mt 3:8). Paul told King Agrippa that, wherever he preached, he called on people to "repent and turn to God and perform deeds worthy of... repentance" (Acts 26:20).

Zacchaeus should be our model. As a greedy Roman tax collector, Zacchaeus was enmeshed in sinful economic structures. But he never supposed that he could come to Jesus and still continue enjoying all the economic benefits of that systemic evil. Coming to Jesus meant repenting of his complicity in social injustice. It meant publicly giving reparations. And it meant a whole new lifestyle.

What might genuine, biblical repentance mean for affluent Christians entangled in their society's sinful structures? Part 3 examines this question.

Part
3

Implementation

Where should we change?

A prominent Washington think tank once assembled a large cross section of distinguished religious leaders to discuss the problems of world hunger. The conferees expressed deep concern. They called for significant structural change. But their words rang hollow. They were meeting at an expensive, exclusive resort in Colorado!

Simpler personal lifestyles are essential. But personal change is insufficient. A friend of mine has forsaken the city for a rural community. He grows almost all his own food, lives simply and places few demands on the poor of the earth. This person has considerable speaking and writing talents which could promote change in church and society, but unfortunately he uses them less than he might because of the time absorbed by his "simple" lifestyle.

We need to change at three levels. Simple personal lifestyles are crucial to symbolize, validate and facilitate our concern for the hungry. The church must change so that its common life presents a new model for a divided world. Finally, the structures of secular society, both here and abroad, require revision.

7

The Graduated Tithe & Other Less Modest Proposals: Toward a Simpler Lifestyle

Before God and a billion hungry neighbors, we must rethink our values regarding our present standard of living and promote more just acquisition and distribution of the world's resources.[1] *[The Chicago Declaration of Evangelical Social Concern (1973)]*

Those of us who live in affluent circumstances accept our duty to develop a simple life-style in order to contribute more generously to both relief and evangelism.[2] *[Lausanne Covenant (1974)]*

The rich must live more simply that the poor may simply live.[3] *[Dr. Charles Birch (1975)]*

I once heard a state senator from Pennsylvania argue that his constituents were so nearly poor that they simply could not afford to pay another cent in taxes. He cited a letter from an irate voter as proof. This good person had written him announcing that her family could not possibly pay any more taxes. Why, she said, they already paid the government income taxes and sales taxes—and besides that they bought licenses for their two cars, summer camper, houseboat and motorboat!

We affluent Westerners have a problem. We actually believe that we can just barely get along on the twenty, twenty-five or thirty-five thousand that we make. We are in an incredible rat race. When our income goes up by another $1,000, we convince ourselves that we *need* about that much more to live—comfortably. The state senator was not joking. He agreed that more taxes would have threatened his constituent with poverty and destitution.

How can we escape this delusion? How will we respond to the desperate plight of the world's poor? Forty thousand children died today because of inadequate food. One billion people live in desperate poverty. The problem, we know, is that the world's resources are not fairly shared. North Americans live on an affluent island amid a sea of poverty-stricken people.

How will we respond to this gross inequality? Former President Richard Nixon enunciated one response in a June 13, 1973, speech to the nation: "I have made this basic decision: In allocating the products of America's farms between markets abroad and those in the United States, we must put the American consumer first."[4] Such a statement may be good politics, but it certainly is not good theology.

But how much should we give? Should we congratulate the Christian millionaire who tithes faithfully?

John Wesley gave a startling answer. One of his frequently repeated sermons was on Matthew 6:19-23 ("Lay not up for yourselves treasures upon earth . . ." KJV).[5] Christians, Wesley said, should give away all but "the plain necessaries of life"—that is, plain, wholesome food, clean clothes and enough to carry on one's business. One should earn what one can, justly and honestly. Capital need not be given away. But Wesley wanted all income given to the poor after bare necessities were met. Unfortunately, Wesley discovered, not one person in five hundred in any "Christian city" obeys Jesus' command. But that simply demonstrates that most professed believers are "living men but dead Christians." Any "Christian" who takes for himself anything more than the "plain necessaries of life," Wesley insisted, "lives in an open, habitual denial of the Lord." He has "gained riches and hell-fire!"[6]

Wesley lived what he preached. Sales of his books often earned him 1,400 pounds annually, but he spent only 30 pounds on himself. The rest he gave away. He always wore inexpensive clothes and dined on simple food. "If I leave behind me 10 pounds," he once wrote, "you and all mankind bear witness against me that I lived and died a thief and a robber."[7]

One need not agree with Wesley's every word to see that he was struggling to follow the biblical summons to share with the needy. How much should we give? Knowing that God disapproves of ex-

tremes of wealth and poverty, we should give until our lives truly
reflect the principles of Leviticus 25 and 2 Corinthians 8. Surely
Paul's advice to the Corinthians applies even more forcefully to
Christians today in the Northern Hemisphere: "I do not mean that
others should be eased and you burdened, but that *as a matter of
equality* your abundance at the present time should supply their
want . . . *that there may be equality*" (2 Cor 8:13-14).

The God of North America and Its Prophet

Why are we so unconcerned, so slow to care? We learn one reason
from the story of the rich young ruler. When he asked Jesus how to
obtain eternal life, Jesus told him to sell all his goods and give to the
poor. But the man went away sad because he had great possessions.
Now, as we are usually told, the point of the story is that if we want to
follow Christ, he alone must be at the center of our affections and
plans. Whether the idol be riches, fame, status, academic distinction
or membership in some in-group, we must be willing to abandon it
for Christ's sake. Riches just happened to be this young man's idol.
Jesus then is not commanding us to sell all our possessions. He is
only demanding total submission to himself.

This interpretation is both unquestionably true and unquestionably inadequate. To say no more is to miss the fact that wealth and
possessions are the most common idols for us rich Westerners. Jesus,
I suspect, meant it when he added, "Truly, I say to you, it will be
hard for a rich man [especially for the twentieth-century Westerner]
to enter the kingdom of heaven. Again I tell you, it is easier for a
camel to go through the eye of a needle than for a rich man to enter
the kingdom of God" (Mt 19:23-24).

We have become ensnared by unprecedented material luxury.
Advertising constantly convinces us that we really need one unnecessary luxury after another. The standard of living is the god of
twentieth-century America, and the adman is its prophet.

We all know how subtle the materialistic temptations are and how
convincing the rationalizations. Only by God's grace and with great
effort can we escape the shower of luxuries which has almost suffo-
cated our Christian compassion. All of us face this problem. Some
years ago I spent about fifty dollars on an extra suit. That's not much
of course. Besides, I persuaded myself, it was a wise investment
(thanks to the 75 per cent reduction). But that money would have

fed a starving child in India for about a year. In all honesty we have to ask ourselves: Dare we care at all about current fashions if that means reducing our ability to help hungry neighbors? Dare we care more about obtaining a secure economic future for our family than for living an uncompromisingly Christian lifestyle?

I do not pretend that giving an honest answer to such questions will be easy. Our responsibility is not always clear. One Saturday morning as I was beginning to prepare a lecture (on poverty!), a poor man came into my office and asked for five dollars. He was drinking. He had no food, no job, no home. The Christ of the poor confronted me in this man. But I didn't have the time, I said. I had to prepare a lecture on the Christian view of poverty. I did give him a couple of dollars, but that was not what he needed. He needed somebody to talk to, somebody to love him. He needed my time. He needed me. But I was too busy. "Inasmuch as you did it not to the least of these, you did it not . . ."

We need to make some dramatic, concrete moves to escape the materialism that seeps into our minds via the diabolically clever and incessant radio and TV commercials. We have been brainwashed to believe that bigger houses, more prosperous businesses, more luxurious gadgets, are worthy goals in life. As a result, we are caught in an absurd, materialistic spiral. The more we make, the more we think we need in order to live decently and respectably. Somehow we have to break this cycle because it makes us sin against our needy brothers and sisters and, therefore, against our Lord.

The Graduated Tithe

The graduated tithe is one of many models which can help break this materialistic stranglehold. I share it because it has proved helpful in our family. Obviously it is not the only useful model. Certainly it is not a biblical norm to be prescribed legalistically for others. I am aware that it is only a modest beginning.

When Arbutus and I decided to adopt a graduated scale for our giving in 1969, we started by sitting down and trying to calculate honestly what we would need to live for a year. We wanted a figure that would permit reasonable comfort but not all the luxuries. I suspect that we arrived at this base amount rather arbitrarily. The authors of *Limits to Growth* (1974) suggest a standard of living which everyone in the world could share without rapidly depleting our natural resources and provoking prompt ecological disaster.[8] Perhaps their figure of $1,800 (= $3,652 in 1983) per person per year might offer a rational way to arrive at one's base amount. Another more radical approach would be to use the U.S. government's definition of the poverty level for one's basic amount. In early 1976 that

Total income	Tithe: Per cent of additional thousand	Tithe: Per cent of the whole	Total given away	Personal expenditures and savings
10,000	–	10.0%	$ 1,000	$ 9,000
11,000	15%	10.5%	1,150	9,850
12,000	20%	11.3%	1,350	10,650
13,000	25%	12.3%	1,600	11,400
14,000	30%	13.6%	1,900	12,100
15,000	35%	15.0%	2,250	12,750
16,000	40%	16.6%	2,650	13,350
17,000	45%	18.2%	3,100	13,900
18,000	50%	20.0%	3,600	14,400
19,000	55%	21.8%	4,150	14,850
20,000	60%	23.8%	4,750	15,250
21,000	65%	25.7%	5,400	15,600
22,000	70%	27.7%	6,100	15,900
23,000	75%	29.8%	6,850	16,150
24,000	80%	31.9%	7,650	16,350
25,000	85%	34.0%	8,500	16,500
26,000	90%	36.2%	9,400	16,600
27,000	95%	38.3%	10,350	16,650
28,000	100%	40.5%	11,350	16,650

Table 17

would have meant a figure of $5,050 for a family of four.[9]

Somehow we arrived in 1969 at a base of $7,000. By 1973 we had increased it to $8,000. And in 1982 we increased it again to $10,000. (This time we had decided to use an approximation of the 1982 federal poverty level: $9,862 for a family of four.)

We decided to continue giving a tithe of 10 per cent on this basic amount. Then, for each additional thousand dollars of income above that basic amount, we would increase our giving by 5 per cent on that thousand. Table 17 shows how it works out.

Lots of questions arise. Do you use gross income or take-home pay? Farmers and business persons obviously must work with some figure of net income. Do you increase the base figure for inflation each year? At first we did. But then we decided that holding the base amount steady in spite of inflation would be a good way to keep pressing for a simpler lifestyle. Do you simply add $3,652 for each additional person? Obviously not. A single person cannot manage on $3,652! And a family unit of six children under ten does not need a base figure of $29,216.

What about taxes? At first we did not deduct taxes. Obviously one would have to do that eventually or the graduated tithe and taxes would take all his or her income. So in 1979 we began to deduct federal, state and city (but not property or sales) taxes from our income before we calculated the graduated tithe we would pay.

Other questions remain. For instance, one may have to take into account special expenditures for things like college education. There are many good reasons for doing things differently. Our pattern is in no way an ideal model. Each person and family will need to develop its own plan. The following suggestions may help those who want to develop their own version of the graduated tithe.

First, discuss the idea with the whole family. Everyone needs to understand the reasons so that the family can come to a common decision. Second, spell out your plan in writing at the beginning of the year. It is relatively painless, in fact exciting, to work it out theoretically. After you commit yourself to the abstract figures, it hurts less to dole out the cash each month! Third, discuss your proposal with a committed Christian friend or couple who share your concern for justice. Fourth, discuss major expenditures with the same people. It is easier for a slightly more objective observer to spot rationalizations than it is for you. They may also have helpful hints on simple living. Fifth, each year try to reduce your basic figure *and total expenditures.* (That does not mean you have no understanding of the need for capital investment to increase productivity. It simply means that you give more via Christian organizations for capital investment among the poor.)

As the perceptive reader has already noticed, this proposal for a graduated tithe is really a modest one. In fact, the proposal is probably so modest that it verges on unfaithfulness to Saint Paul. But it is also sufficiently radical that its implementation would revolutionize the ministry and life of the church.

Some Christians are experimenting with far more radical attempts to win the war on affluence.

Communal Living and Other Lifestyle Models
The model which permits the simplest standard of living is probably the commune. Housing, furniture, appliances, tools and car that would normally serve one nuclear family can accommodate ten or twenty people. Communal living releases vast amounts of money and people-time for alternative activities.

Many Christian communes have been initiated as conscious attempts to develop a more ecologically responsible and less unjust standard of living. But not all are so deliberate. At Church of the Redeemer in Houston, Texas, a simple communal lifestyle "just happened." This inner-city, Episcopal church was virtually dead fifteen years ago. Then a charismatic renewal occurred. Scores of needy persons requiring special love and nurture flocked to Redeemer. Communal living seemed the only answer.

By 1976 about three hundred and fifty people lived communally in approximately thirty-five different households. Each household had eight to fifteen members. In a typical household of eleven persons, two were wage-earners working at outside jobs. The rest were available to staff the numerous programs of the church.

Of the income of each household, 20 per cent went to the church. The remainder permitted a modest lifestyle for the members. In 1974 the households needed approximately $1,800 per person per year for all expenses. In one household I visited in 1976, adults received an allowance of $1 per week for incidental expenses. Jerry Barker explains how their simple lifestyle emerged.

It soon became obvious that the needs we were faced with would take lots of resources and so we began to cut expenses for things we had been accustomed to. We stopped buying new cars and new televisions and things of that sort. We didn't even think of them. We started driving our cars until they literally fell apart and then we'd buy a used car or something like that to replace it. We began to turn in some of our insurance policies so that they would not be such a financial drain on us. We found such a security in our relationship with the Lord that it was no longer important to have security for the future. . . . We never have had any rule about it, or felt this was a necessary part of the Christian life. It was just a matter of using the money we had available most effectively, particularly in supporting so many extra people. We learned to live very economically. We quit eating steaks and expensive roasts and things like that and we began to eat simple fare. . . . We'd often eat things that people would bring us—a box of groceries or a sack of rice.[10]

The standard of living of Christian communities varies. But almost all live far more simply than the average North American family. At Chicago's Reba Place, for example, eating patterns are based on the welfare level of the city (see chapter eight). Christian communes have a symbolic importance today out of all proportion to their numbers. They quietly question this society's affluence. And they offer a viable alternative.

Communal living, of course, is not for everyone. In fact, I personally believe that it is the right setting for only a small percentage of Christians. We need many more diverse models.

In her delightful book *Living More with Less*, Doris Longacre gives us quick glimpses of several hundred Christians who are learning the joy of sharing more.[11] Some still live in what I would consider substantial affluence. Others live far more simply than I do. But everyone is trying to spend less on themselves in order to share more.

That is what Robert Bainum did. Bainum was a successful Christian businessman—in fact, a millionaire. But in a personal conversation he recently told me that as he read the first edition of *Rich Christians in an Age of Hunger* God called him to share more with the poor of the earth. He gave away half of his wealth and then devoted his creative energy and organizational abilities to relief and development programs among the poor, both at home and abroad.[12]

In the mid 1970s Graham Kerr was the Galloping Gourmet for two hundred million TV viewers each week. He was rich and successful, but his personal life was falling apart. Since he came to Christ in 1975, his family life has been miraculously restored; he has abandoned his gourmet TV series and given away most of his money. His life now centers around using his knowledge of nutrition to develop a new kind of agricultural missionary who both shares the gospel and helps poor Third World people develop a better diet with locally available products. Graham and his wife, Treena, live a simple lifestyle—but not because they are ascetics. They live simply because they want to share as much as possible to evangelize the world and reduce poverty.[13]

Biblical Christians are experimenting with a variety of simpler lifestyles. An Age of Hunger demands drastic change. But we must be careful to avoid legalism and self-righteousness. "We have to beware of the reverse snobbery of spiritual one-up-manship."[14]

No one model is God's will for everyone. Our God loves variety and diversity. Does that mean, however, that we ought to fall back into typical Western individualism, with each person or family doing what is good in its own eyes? By no means.

Two things can help. First, we need the help of other brothers and sisters—in our local congregation, in our town or city, and around the world. We need to develop a process for discussing our economic lifestyles with close Christian friends in our congregation. We also need new ways to dialog about the shape of a faithful lifestyle with poor Christians.[15]

Second, certain criteria can help us determine what is right for us. I offer six—as suggestions, *not* as norms or laws.[16]

1. We ought to move toward a personal lifestyle that could be sustained over a long period of time if it were shared by everyone in the world.

2. We need to distinguish between necessities and luxuries, and normally we need to reject both our desire for the latter and our inclination to blur the distinction.

3. Expenditures for the purpose of status, pride, staying in fashion and "keeping up with the Joneses" are wrong.

4. We need to distinguish between expenditures to develop our particular creative gifts and legitimate hobbies and a general demand for all the cultural items, recreational equipment and current

hobbies that the "successful" of our class or nation enjoy. Each person has unique interests and gifts. We should, within limits, be able to express our creativity in those areas. But if we discover that we are justifying lots of things in many different areas, we should become suspicious.

5. We need to distinguish between occasional celebration and normal day-to-day routine. A turkey feast with all the trimmings at Thanksgiving to celebrate the good gift of creation is biblical (Deut 14:22-27). Unfortunately, most of us overeat every day, and that is sin.

6. There is no necessary connection between what we earn and what we spend on ourselves. We should not buy things just because we can afford them.

Some Practical Suggestions

The following are hints, not rules. Freedom, joy and laughter are essential elements of simple living. (See the Appendix for addresses and information about groups and organizations named.)

1. Question your own lifestyle, not your neighbor's.

2. Reduce your food budget by:

☐ gardening: try hoeing instead of mowing;

☐ substituting vegetable protein for animal protein. Cookbooks like *Recipes for a Small Planet* and *More with Less Cookbook* tell how to prepare delicious, meatless meals. One-third of our daily protein needs costs thirteen cents via peanut butter, seventy-three cents via veal cutlets;[17]

☐ joining a food co-op (if there's none in your area, write to The Co-operative League of the U.S.A. for materials on how to start one);

☐ fasting regularly;

☐ opposing (by speech and example) the flagrant misuse of grain for making beer and other alcoholic beverages (the United States annually uses enough grain—5.2 million tons—in the production of alcoholic beverages to feed 26 million people in a country like India);[18] and

☐ setting a monthly budget and sticking to it.

3. Lower energy consumption by:

☐ keeping your thermostat (at the home and office) at 68° F. or lower during winter months;

☐ supporting public transportation with your feet and your vote;

☐ using bicycles, carpools and, for short trips, your feet;

☐ making dishwashing a family time instead of buying a dishwasher; and

☐ buying a fan instead of an air conditioner.

4. Resist consumerism by:

☐ laughing regularly at TV commercials;

☐ developing family slogans like: "Who Are You Kidding?" and "You Can't Take It with You!";

☐ making a list of dishonest ads and boycotting those products; and

☐ using the postage-paid envelopes of direct-mail advertisers to object to their unscrupulous advertising.

5. Buy and renovate an old house in the inner city. (Persuade a few friends to do the same so you can enjoy Christian community.)

6. Reduce your consumption of nonrenewable natural resources by:

☐ resisting obsolescence (buying quality products when you must buy);

☐ sharing appliances, tools, lawnmowers, sports equipment, books, even a car (this is easier if you live close to other Christians committed to simple living); and

☐ organizing a "things closet" in your church for items used only occasionally—edger, clippers, cots for unexpected guests, lawnmowers, camping equipment, ladder.

7. Have one or two "homemade" babies and then adopt.

8. See how much of what you spend is for status and eliminate it.

9. Refuse to keep up with clothing fashions. (Virtually no reader of this book needs to buy clothes—except maybe shoes—for two or three years.)

10. Enjoy what is free.

11. Live on a welfare budget for a month. (Ron Jones's *Finding Community* will tell you how to calculate it.)[19]

12. Give your children more of your love and time rather than more things.

That's enough for a beginning.

The following will help further. The Shakertown Pledge Group publishes a "Bibliography on Simple Living," and Alternatives publishes an *Alternatives Celebrations Catalog* which provides exciting, inexpensive, ecologically sound alternative ideas for celebrating Christmas, Valentine's Day, Thanksgiving and other holidays.

Ernest Callenbach's *Living Poor with Style* and Art Gish's *Beyond the Rat Race* (especially chapter one) also have valuable suggestions.

Criteria for Giving
If ten per cent of all North American Christians adopted the graduated tithe, huge sums of money would become available for kingdom work. Where would that money do the most good?

Obviously Christians should not give all their money to relieve world hunger. Christian education and evangelism are extremely important and deserve continuing support. My family tries to give approximately as much to support evangelism as we do to activities promoting social justice. (What we like best are wholistic programs that combine both.) We regularly give some funds through non-church channels. Part of a graduated tithe might appropriately be given to political campaigns devoted to social justice.

The authors of *Christian Responsibility in a Hungry World* list the following suggestions for allocating that portion of giving devoted to hunger and development:
☐ 20 per cent for emergency relief
☐ 40 per cent for agricultural and rural community development programs
☐ 20 per cent to heighten awareness and change lifestyles in affluent countries
☐ 20 per cent for Christian witness in the area of public policy and structural change.[20]

But which relief and development agencies are doing the best job? This issue is important, but you must decide for yourself. Here are some general criteria for deciding where to channel your giving for development in hungry lands:

1. Do the funds support wholistic projects in the Third World, working simultaneously at an integrated program of evangelism, social change, education, agricultural development and so on?

2. Do the funds support truly indigenous projects? That involves several issues: (a) Are the leaders and most of the staff of the projects in the developing nations indigenous persons? They should be. (b) Do the projects unthinkingly adopt Western ideas, materials and technology or do they use materials suited to their own culture? (c) Did the project arise from the felt needs of the people rather than from some outside "expert"?

3. Are the projects primarily engaged in long-range development (that includes people development), or in emergency projects only?

4. Are the programs designed to help the poor masses understand that God wants sinful social structures changed and that they can help effect that change?

5. Do the programs work through and foster the growth of the church?

6. Are the programs potentially self-supporting after an initial injection of seed capital? And do the programs from the beginning require commitment and a significant contribution of capital or time (or both) from the people themselves?

7. Do the programs aid the poorest people in the poorest developing countries?

8. Is agricultural development involved? (It need not always be, but in a majority of cases it should be.)

9. Is justice rather than continual charity the result?[21]

10. Several crucial questions pertain to the North American agency through which one channels funds: (a) Does the organization spend more than 10 or 15 per cent of total funds on fund raising and administration? (b) Are Third World persons, North American minority persons and women represented among the board and top staff? (c) Is the organization audited annually by an independent CPA firm? (d) Are the board members and staff persons of known integrity? Is the board paid? (It should not be.) (e) Are staff salaries consistent with the biblical call for jubilee among all God's people? (f) Does the organization object to answering these questions?[22]

An example will help clarify the kind of wholistic program which meets most of the above criteria. This description comes from a Christian organization supporting wholistic development programs in the Third World.

Elizabeth Native Interior Mission [is] in southern Liberia. ENI is headed by Augustus Marwieh who became a Christian under Mother George, one of the first black American missionaries to Africa. Ten years ago Gus went to work at the struggling mission where he had been saved. The young people were leaving the villages to go to the capital city of Monrovia; there, most found only unemployment, alcohol, and prostitution. Local skills like log sawing, blacksmithing, and making pottery were dying out as the people became dependent on outside traders (usually foreigners) and became poorer and poorer. At least 90% of the people were illiterate, and many suffered from protein deficiency.

Today 160 churches have been started, and 10,000 people have become Christians. Eleven primary schools are operating, and they stress locally usable skills instead of the usual Liberian fare of Spot and Jane in English. A vocational school is forming that will help revive local trades and encourage new skills; and steps are being taken to form co-operatives which will avoid middlemen, replace foreign merchants, provide capital, etc.

One crucial element, especially in view of their protein shortage, is agriculture, and in the last ten years the people have made great strides. But they are so poor that *often the only farming tool they have is a machete* (a heavy knife). So Gus is burdened to start a revolving loan fund from which people can borrow to buy a hoe, a shovel, a water can, spraying equipment, a pick, or an ax. You and I buy tools like that on a whim for the garden in our backyards, but for these people such purchases are completely out of reach even though they need them to fight malnutrition. So next time you start feeling poor, remember Gus' people.[23]

There are scores of similar wholistic programs operated by biblical Christians in developing countries. And they desperately need additional funds. Organizations that enable us to share with them represent a contemporary way for God's people to live the jubilee.

The gulf between what affluent Northern Christians give and what they *could* give is a terrifying tragedy. *Christianity Today* reported that, in 1971 a *mere tithe* from the fifty-two largest U.S. denominations would be $17.5 billion annually. Instead they gave only $4.4 billion in *total church giving* that year.[24] (Only a tiny fraction of that $4.4 billion, of course, went to help poor people.) Even if another $4.4 billion in charitable contributions were given through nonchurch channels, the combined total of $8.8 billion still would be less than 5 per cent. We ought to quadruple that.

And it does make a difference. The U.S. government's foreign aid has become so meager that by 1974 thirty-two cents of every U.S. dollar given as economic aid to developing nations came from private contributions.[25] That does not mean that working for increased governmental foreign aid is unimportant. But it does mean that church contributions to developing nations are extremely significant.

I have focused on monetary giving in most of this chapter. But that is not the only way. Giving oneself is equally important. Some Christians choose low-paying jobs because the opportunity for service is great. Others decline overtime to permit more volunteer activity. Thousands of Christians have given two or more years to serve in developing countries.

There is a great need for sensitive persons who will live with people in rural villages, showing the poor that God wants them to help change the unjust structures which oppress them. Agricultural workers who can share intermediate technological skills are in high demand. "One person with practical skills who's prepared to work and live in a remote village is generally worth a dozen visiting university professors and business tycoons."[26] Time is money. Sharing time is just as important as sharing financial resources.

I am convinced that simpler living is a biblical imperative for contemporary Christians in affluent lands. But we must remain clear about our reasons. We are *not* committed to a simple lifestyle. We have only one absolute loyalty and that is to Jesus and his kingdom. But the head of this kingdom is the God of the poor! And hundreds of millions of his poor are starving.

An Age of Hunger summons affluent people to a lower standard of living. But a general assent to this statement will not be enough to escape the daily seductions of Madison Avenue. Each of us needs some *specific, concrete* plan. The graduated tithe and communal living offer two models. The examples of Robert Bainum and Graham and Treena Kerr suggest others. There are many more. By all means avoid legalism and self-righteousness. But have the courage to commit yourself to some *specific method* for moving toward a just personal lifestyle.

Will we dare to measure our living standards by the needs of the poor rather than by the lifestyle of our neighbors?

8

Watching Over One Another in Love

Extra ecclesiam, nulla salus.

Somehow the pressures of modern society were making it increasingly difficult for us to live by the values we had been taught. We thought our church should constitute a community of believers capable of withstanding these pressures, yet it seemed to go along with things as they were instead of encouraging an alternative. The "pillars" of the church seemed as severely trapped by material concerns and alienation as most non-Christians we knew.[1] [Dave and Neta Jackson]

The church should consist of communities of loving defiance. Instead it consists largely of comfortable clubs of conformity. A far-reaching reformation of the church is a prerequisite if it is to commit itself to Jesus' mission of liberating the oppressed.

If the analysis in the preceding chapters is even approximately correct, then the God of the Bible is calling Christians today to live in fundamental nonconformity to contemporary society. Affluent North American and European societies are obsessed with materialism, sex, economic success and military might. Things are more important than persons. Job security and an annual salary increase matter more than starving children and oppressed peasants. Paul's warning to the Romans is especially pertinent today: "Don't let the world around you squeeze you into its own mould" (Rom 12:2 Phillips). Biblical revelation summons us to defy many of the basic values of our materialistic, adulterous society.

But that is impossible! As individuals, that is. It is hardly possible for isolated believers to resist the anti-Christian values which pour from our radios, TVs and billboards. The values of our affluent society seep slowly and subtly into our hearts and minds. The only way to defy them is to immerse ourselves in Christian fellowship so that God can remold our thinking as we find our primary identity with brothers and sisters who are also unconditionally committed to biblical values.

That faithful obedience is possible only in the context of powerful Christian fellowship should not surprise us. The early church was able to defy the decadent values of Roman civilization precisely because it experienced the reality of Christian fellowship in a mighty way. For the early Christians koinonia was not the frilly "fellowship" of church-sponsored, biweekly bowling parties. It was not tea, cookies and sophisticated small talk in Fellowship Hall after the sermon. It was an almost unconditional sharing of their lives with the other members of Christ's body.

Christian fellowship meant costly, sweeping availability to and liability for the other sisters and brothers—emotionally, financially · and spiritually. When one member suffered, they all suffered. When one rejoiced, they all rejoiced (1 Cor 12:26). When a person or church experienced economic trouble, the others shared without reservation.[2] And when a brother or sister fell into sin, the others gently restored the straying person (Mt 18:15-17; 1 Cor 5; 2 Cor 2:5-11; Gal 6:1-3).[3] The sisters and brothers were available to each other, liable for each other, accountable to each other.

The early church, of course, did not always live out the New Testament vision of the body of Christ. There were tragic lapses. But the network of tiny house churches scattered throughout the Roman Empire did experience their oneness in Christ so vividly that they were able to defy and eventually conquer a powerful, pagan civilization.

John Wesley's early Methodist class meetings captured something of the spirit alive in the early church. These assembled in houses weekly, bringing together persons "united in order to pray together, to receive the word of exhortation, and to watch over one another in love, that they may help each other to work out their salvation."[4] The overwhelming majority of churches today, however, do not provide the context in which brothers and sisters can encourage, admonish and disciple each other. We desperately need new structures for watching over one another in love, new settings that will help us become truly one.

A Sociological Perspective

The sociology of knowledge underlines the importance of Christian community for biblical nonconformists. Sociologists of knowledge have studied the relationship between ideas and the social conditions in which ideas arise. They have discovered that the plausibility of ideas depends on the social support they have. "We obtain our notions about the world originally from other human beings, and these notions continue to be plausible to us in a very large measure because others continue to affirm them."[5] An Amish youth who migrates to New York City will soon begin to question earlier values. The sociological reason for this change is that the "significant others" who previously supported his ideas and values are no longer present.

The complicated network of social interactions in which one develops and maintains one's view of reality is called a plausibility structure. This plausibility structure consists of ongoing conversation with "significant others" as well as specific practices, rituals and legitimations designed to support the validity of certain ideas. As long as these social processes continue, we tend to accept the corresponding beliefs as true or plausible. But if the supportive structures disappear, doubt and uncertainty arise.

Hence the difficulty of a cognitive minority. A cognitive minority is a small group of people who hold a set of beliefs that differ sharply from the majority view in their society. Because they constantly meet people who challenge their fundamental ideas, members of a cognitive minority find it difficult to maintain their distinctive beliefs. According to well-known sociologist Peter Berger, a cognitive minority can maintain its unpopular ideas only if it has a strong community structure:

Unless our theologian has the inner fortitude of a desert saint, he has only one effective remedy against the threat of cognitive collapse in the face of these pressures. He must huddle together with like-minded fellow deviants—and huddle very closely indeed. Only in a countercommunity of considerable strength does cognitive deviance have a chance to maintain itself. The countercommunity provides continuing therapy against the creeping doubt as to whether, after all, one may not be wrong and the majority right. To fulfill its function of providing social support for the deviant body of "knowledge," the countercommunity must provide a strong sense of solidarity among its members.[6]

Berger's analysis relates directly to contemporary Christians determined to follow biblical teaching on the poor and possessions. Berger analyzed the problem of orthodox Christians who defy the dominant "scientific" ideas of contemporary secularism and maintain a biblical belief in the supernatural. But his analysis pertains just as clearly to the problem of living the ethics of Jesus' kingdom in a world that follows different standards. Most of our contemporaries—both inside and outside the churches—accept the dominant values of our consumption-oriented, materialistic culture. Genuine Christians, on the other hand, are committed to the very different norms revealed in Scripture. It should not surprise us that only a faithful remnant continues to cling to these values. But the fact that genuine Christians are a cognitive minority alerts us to the need for strong Christian community.

That does not mean that Christians should imitate the Amish and retreat to isolated rural solitude. We must remain at the center of contemporary society in order to challenge, witness against and, it is to be hoped, even change it. But precisely as we are in the world but not of it, the pressure to abandon biblical norms in favor of contemporary values will be intense. Hence the need for new forms of Christian community today.

The ancient Catholic dictum *extra ecclesiam, nulla salus* ("outside the church there is no salvation") contains a significant sociological truth. Certainly it is not impossible for individual Christians to maintain biblical beliefs even if a hostile majority disagrees. But if the church is to consist of communities of loving defiance in a sinful world, then it must pay more attention to the quality of its fellowship.

What are some promising models of Christian community for our time?

New Patterns of Christian Community
When one speaks of Christian community, some people instantly think of Christian communes. That is unfortunate. Communes

are only one of many forms for genuine Christian fellowship today. House churches or mission groups within larger congregations, individual house churches and small traditional churches,
all offer excellent contexts for living out the biblical vision of the
church.

I am thoroughly convinced, however, that the overwhelming
majority of Western churches no longer understand or experience
biblical koinonia to any significant degree. As mentioned earlier,
the essence of Christian community is open accountability to and
far-reaching liability for our sisters and brothers in the body of
Christ. That means that our time, our money and our very selves
are available to the brothers and sisters.

That kind of fellowship hardly ever happens in larger churches
of one hundred or more persons. It requires small communities of
believers like the early Christian house churches. The movement
which conquered the Roman Empire was a network of small house
churches. Frequently Paul speaks of "the church that meets in the
house of..." (Rom 16:5, 23; 1 Cor 16:19; Col 4:15; Philem 2; see
also Acts 2:46; 12:12; 20:7-12). It was only in the latter part of the
third century that the church started to build sanctuaries. The structure of the early church fostered close interaction and fellowship.[7]

What happens when God grants the gift of genuine Christian
fellowship? Deep, joyful sharing replaces the polite prattle typically
exchanged by Christians on Sunday morning. Sisters and brothers
begin to discuss the things that really matter to them. They disclose
their inner fears, their areas of peculiar temptation, their deepest
joys. And they begin to challenge and disciple each other according
to Matthew 18:15-17 and Galatians 6:1-3.

It is in that kind of setting—and perhaps only in that kind of
setting—that the church today will be able to forge a faithful lifestyle
for Christians in an Age of Hunger. In small house-church settings
brothers and sisters can challenge each other's affluent lifestyles.
They can discuss family finances and evaluate each other's annual
budgets. Larger expenditures (like those for houses, cars and long
vacations) can be evaluated honestly in terms of the needs of both
the individuals involved and God's poor around the world. Tips for
simple living can be shared. Voting patterns that liberate the poor,
jobs that are ecologically responsible, and charitable donations that
build self-reliance among the oppressed—these and many other is-

sues can be discussed openly and honestly by persons who have
pledged themselves to each other as brothers and sisters in Christ.

What models of the church foster that kind of Christian community?

A Congregation of House Churches

Congregations composed of clusters of house churches make up, in
my opinion, the most exciting, viable alternative to the typical congregation today. Living Word Community in Philadelphia and the
Church of the Savior in Washington, D.C., are two variations on
this theme.

Fifteen years ago Living Word (then called Gospel Temple) was a
typical, successful Pentecostal church. There was a large, growing
congregation of several hundred people from the greater Philadelphia area. The church had a young dynamic pastor, a packed sched-
ule of meetings, a full repertoire of church organizations and, according to the pastor, little real Christian fellowship.

In 1970 it decided to change drastically. The church jettisoned
all existing activities except the Sunday morning worship service.
Everyone was urged to attend "home meetings," where twelve to
twenty people met weekly for study, prayer, worship and shepherd-
ing. For a couple of years they wondered if they had made a gigantic
mistake. "To move from a pew to a living room chair and look at
people face to face was terrifying."[8] But a breakthrough occurred
when the leaders of the home meetings realized that most people
did not know how to meet each other's needs. The leaders started
making suggestions: "You two ladies go to Jane Brown's house and
make dinner for her because she is sick." "You three people paint
Jerry's apartment on Saturday."

Oneness and caring began to develop. These weekly gatherings
became the center of spiritual activity in the church. Counseling,
discipling, even evangelistic outreach all began to happen primarily
in the home meetings. One result was rapid growth. As soon as a
home meeting reached twenty-five persons, it was divided into two
home meetings.

In 1974 growth had already led to division into two weekend
services. By 1976 thirteen to fourteen hundred people were attending weekend services. There were fifty different home meetings and
four separate "Sunday" services.

One of these four weekend gatherings still occurs on Sunday morning in the original downtown sanctuary. For the others the congregation rents space from various churches and holds the weekend service on Saturday or Sunday evening. As a result the congregation has avoided costly building programs and has financial resources available for more important matters.

Genuine Christian community has emerged from this drastic restructuring. Because of the small home meetings, the pastors confidently assert that all eight hundred members of Living Word receive personal, pastoral care. Each individual's burdens and problems are known in his or her small home meeting.

Financial sharing was not part of the original vision. But it has begun to happen in a significant way. Members of home meetings have dug into savings and stocks to provide interest-free loans for two families who purchased house trailers for homes. When members went to sign the papers for an interest-free mortgage for another family's house, secular folk present for the transfer were totally perplexed! If a member of a home meeting needs a small amount of financial assistance ($50 or $100), the other members of his home meeting help out. A congregational fund meets larger needs. A food co-op and a store for used clothing and furniture supply basic needs inexpensively. A sizable portion of total congregational giving is used for economic sharing in the church.

Living Word has begun to develop an extensive concern for justice and the poor. The pastors preach about social justice. The church has worked in a major way with refugees from Southeast Asia. The church's relief fund contributes several thousand dollars each year to relieve world poverty.

Living Word has been successful in working with Black and Hispanic Americans. The Hispanic subcongregation of 150 persons is growing rapidly. In the summer of 1982, Living Word began an evangelistic outreach in the poorest Hispanic section of the city. Drug rehabilitation, job counseling, emergency food distribution and ministry to battered women are all part of this wholistic outreach. Some church members are relocating in this needy area and evangelistic efforts continue.

The people in Living Word have a deep commitment to living more simply. More understanding of injustice in economic structures are needed. But these concerns are developing at Living

Word. The creative upheaval of the last fifteen years has produced a flexible openness to new directions in discipleship. And the small house-church structure is an ideal context in which to forge new economic lifestyles.

Living Word has demonstrated that a traditional congregation can be transformed into a cluster of house churches. And the result has been not disruption but growth—in discipleship, Christian community and numbers.

The Church of the Savior in Washington, D.C., pioneered the small-group model at the end of World War 2.[9] All members must be in one of its many mission groups. Prospective members must take five classes over a period of about two years. The membership covenant, renewed annually, commits every member to four disciplines: daily prayer, daily Bible study, weekly worship and proportionate giving, beginning with a tithe of total gross income.

Consisting of five to twelve persons, the mission groups are the heart of the Church of the Savior. They are not merely prayer cells, Bible study gatherings, encounter groups or social action committees (although they are all of these). Gordon Cosby, pastor of Church of the Savior, emphasizes that it is in the mission groups that the members experience the reality of the body of Christ: "The mission group embodies the varied dimensions of church. It is total in scope. It is both inward and outward. It requires that we be accountable to Christ and to one another for the totality of our lives. It assumes that we share unlimited liability for one another."[10] Via verbal or written reports, each member of a mission group reports weekly on failure or success in following the covenanted disciplines, on new scriptural insight, and on the problems and joys of the week.

Economics figures prominently in the membership commitment. Part of the membership covenant reads, "I believe that God is the total owner of my life and resources. I give God the throne in relation to the material aspect of my life. God is the owner. I am the ower. Because God is a lavish giver, I too shall be lavish and cheerful in my regular gifts."[11]

The church has held out the goal of accountability of brothers and sisters to each other in the use of personal finances. Some mission groups regularly share income tax returns as a basis for discussing each other's family budgets and finances. Concern for more simple lifestyles is growing at Church of the Savior.

The goal of many of the mission groups is liberation for the poor. Members of the mission group called Jubilee Housing have renovated deteriorating housing in inner-city Washington. Along with other mission groups (Jubilee Jobs, Columbia Road Health Service, Family Place), they are bringing hope of genuine change to hundreds of people in the inner city. For Love of Children has fought for the rights of neglected children through court action, legislation, and monitoring of local and federal governmental activity.

In recent years several of the church's mission groups have dedicated themselves to peace and justice in the international arena. World Peacemakers has worked to develop peace-and-justice groups in churches throughout the United States, modeling them after their own group structure. COSIGN (The Church of the Savior International Good Neighbors) has made it possible for several hundred Americans to serve in the Thailand refugee camps. Now this mission group, along with the Central American Peace Institute and the Dayspring Refugee Mission, is providing direct relief to Central American refugees driven by violence from their homes into neighboring countries and the United States. At the same time these missions are working to change U.S. foreign policy which exacerbates the Central American refugee problem.

The Dunamis concept emerged in one of the mission groups. Different task forces select specific public policy issues and build relationships of love, prayer, pastoral concern and prophetic witness with senators and congresspersons. In 1983, Henri Nouwen traveled across the United States promoting local Dunamis groups' working on U.S. policy in Central America. The Dunamis approach of forming a pastoral/prophetic relationship with persons in political office could be applied at the local or state level.[12]

By 1976 increasing size seemed to threaten genuine community at Church of the Savior. (There were one hundred members plus fifty intern members.) As a result the church divided into seven fully autonomous sister communities. Gordon Cosby's hope was that these new communities would have a wide economic mix so that economic sharing and simple living could increase. Like Living Word in Philadelphia, Church of the Savior prefers to subdivide into small congregations rather than run the risk of diluting Christian community.

Thousands of churches today have small groups—encounter

groups, biweekly fellowship groups, serendipity groups, prayer cells and an infinite variety of action groups that aim at fellowship. Do these small groups fulfill the same function as Living Word's home meetings and Church of the Savior's mission groups? Hardly ever.

Though the numerous small groups flourishing in the churches today are useful and valuable, they seldom go far enough. Participants may agree to share deeply in one or two areas of life, but they do not assume responsibility for the other brothers' and sisters' growth toward Christian maturity in every area of life. Hardly ever do they dream that truly being sisters and brothers in Christ means costly, sweeping economic liability for each other or responsibility for the economic lifestyles of the other members. The crucial question is, Have the participants committed themselves to be brothers and sisters to each other so unreservedly that they enjoy nearly total liability for and accountability to each other?

Almost everyone expects most small groups to dissolve in six months or two years. Life will then continue as before. They are "limited liability" small groups, and they have genuine importance. But what people desperately need today is the church. From the biblical perspective, being the church means accepting liability for and availability and accountability to the other members of the local expression of Christ's body.

The Individual House Church
Another structure where true Christian community can happen is the individual house church. Virtually no expenses are involved. When it is impossible to find genuine Christian community in any other way, small groups of Christians should begin meeting in their own homes. (But they should promptly seek a relationship with other bodies of Christians. Lone rangers are not God's will for his church!) In his book on church structures, Howard A. Snyder proposed that denominations adopt the house church model for church planting, especially in the city. This structure is flexible, mobile, inclusive and personal. It can grow by division, is an effective means of evangelism and needs little professional leadership.[13]

An ideal house church arrangement is to have several families or single persons purchase houses within a block or two of each other. In many inner-city locations, especially in changing neighborhoods, inexpensive houses change hands rapidly. Living across the street or down the block from each other greatly facilitates sharing cars, washers, dryers, freezers and lawnmowers (or gardening equipment). Living close together also encourages Christian community. It quickly creates open relationships which foster honest mutual searching for a less unjust standard of living.

The Christian Commune

Thousands of communal experiments have occurred in the last decade. Many have been explicitly Christian. The Christian commune represents an alternative model for persons dissatisfied with our consumer-oriented society.

Reba Place Fellowship in Evanston, Illinois, began in 1957 with three people.[14] By 1983, there were 130 persons living with a common treasury. A small percentage of these live in large households, but most have their own apartments. They all live close to each other in the same neighborhood.

In addition to the 130 who share a common treasury, another 200 persons are part of Reba Place Church. These have their own private budgets but share the community's deep commitment to a simple lifestyle and generous sharing with each other and the poor.

The 130 who share a common treasury place their earnings in a central fund. The central fund pays directly for large expenditures like housing, utilities and transportation. Each month, every family and single person receives an allowance for food, clothing and incidentals. The food allowance is the same as that for people on welfare in Chicago. Because of the size and permanence of the community, no insurance is necessary (except that required by law). Not channeling cash into the rich insurance industry frees considerable money for other things. Community living also requires fewer automobiles, washing machines and lawnmowers.[15] The simple lifestyle at Reba Place enables this community to share generously with the poor in the immediate community and around the world.

One incident suggests the character of their availability to one another. One day a man with a serious drinking problem dropped in to talk with Virgil Vogt, one of the elders. When Virgil invited him to accept Christ and join the community of believers, the man grew uncomfortable and hastily insisted that he simply wanted money for a bus ticket to Cleveland.

"O.K." Virgil agreed, "we can give you that kind of help too, if

that's all you really want." He was quiet a moment, then he shook
his head. "You know something?" he said, looking straight at the
man. "You've just really let me off the hook. Because if you had
chosen a new way of life in the kingdom of God, then as your
brother I would have had to lay down my whole life for you. This
house, my time, all my money, whatever you needed to meet your
needs would have been totally at your disposal for the rest of your
life. But all you want is some money for a bus ticket. . . ." The man
was so startled he stood up and shortly left, without remembering
to take the money. The next Sunday he was sitting next to Virgil
in the worship service.[16]

Although not for everyone, Reba Place and other Christian communes offer one setting in which widespread liability for and accountability to other brothers and sisters can become a reality.[17]

The Bible and the daily newspaper issue the same summons.
Faithful people in an Age of Hunger must adopt simple lifestyles
and change unjust economic structures. But that is not a popular
path to tread in an affluent society. Unless Christians anchor themselves in genuine Christian community, they will be unable to live
the radical nonconformity commanded by Scripture and essential in
our time. Our only hope is a return to the New Testament vision of
the body of Christ. If that happens, the Lord of the church may
again create communities of loving defiance able to withstand and
conquer the powerful, pagan civilizations of East and West worship-
ing at the shrine of Mammon.

9

Structural Change

The present social order is the most abject failure the world has ever seen.... Governments have never learned yet how to so legislate as to distribute the fruits of the industry of their people. The countries of the earth produce enough to support all, and if the earnings of each was fairly distributed it would make all men toil some, but no man toil too much. This great civilization of ours has not learned so to distribute the product of human toil so that it shall be equitably held. Therefore, the government breaks down.[1] *[C. I. Scofield, author of the Scofield Bible notes, 1903]*

A group of devout Christians once lived in a small village at the foot of a mountain. A winding, slippery road with hairpin curves and steep precipices without guard rails wound its way up one side of the mountain and down the other. There were frequent fatal accidents. Deeply saddened by the injured people who were pulled from the wrecked cars, the Christians in the village's three churches decided to act. They pooled their resources and purchased an ambulance so that they could rush the injured to the hospital in the next town. Week after week church volunteers gave faithfully, even sacrificially, of their time to operate the ambulance twenty-four hours a day. They saved many lives, although some victims remained crippled for life.

One day a visitor came to town. Puzzled, he asked why they did not close the road over the mountain and build a tunnel instead. Startled at first, the ambulance volunteers quickly pointed out that this approach, although technically quite possible, was not realistic or advisable. After all, the narrow mountain road had been there for a long time. Besides, the mayor would bitterly oppose the idea. (He owned a large restaurant and service station halfway up the mountain.)

The visitor was shocked that the mayor's economic interests mattered more to these Christians than the many human casualties. Somewhat hesitantly, he suggested that perhaps the churches ought to speak to the mayor. After all, he was an elder in the oldest church in town. Perhaps they should even elect a different mayor if he proved stubborn and unconcerned. Now the Christians were shocked. With rising indignation and righteous conviction they informed the young radical that the church dare not become involved in politics. The church is called to preach the gospel and give its cup of cold water. Its mission is not to dabble in worldly things like changing social and political structures.

Perplexed and bitter, the visitor left. As he wandered out of the village, one question churned round and round in his muddled mind. Is it really more spiritual, he wondered, to operate the ambulances which pick up the bloody victims of destructive social structures than to try to change the structures themselves?

Ambulance Drivers or Tunnel Builders?

An Age of Hunger demands compassionate action and simplicity in personal lifestyles. But compassion and simple living apart from structural change may be little more than a gloriously irrelevant ego trip or proud pursuit of personal purity.

Eating less beef or even becoming a vegetarian will not necessarily feed one starving child. If millions of Americans and Europeans reduce their beef consumption but do not act politically to change public policy, the result will not necessarily be less starvation in the Third World. To be sure, if people give the money saved to private agencies promoting rural development in poor nations, then the result will be less hunger. But unless one also changes public policy, the primary effect of merely reducing one's meat consumption may simply be to enable the Russians to buy more grain at a cheaper price next year or to persuade farmers to plant less wheat. What is needed is a change in public policy. Our Age of Hunger demands structural change.

Many questions promptly arise. Granted, some structural change is necessary. But is our present economic system basically just, or do Christians need to work for fundamental restructuring? What specific structural changes would be consistent with biblical principles? Are these principles pertinent to *secular* society? Israel, after all, was a theocracy. Can we really expect unbelievers to live according to biblical ethics?

The Bible does not directly answer these questions. Although biblical revelation tells us that God and his faithful people are always at work liberating the oppressed, we do not find a comprehensive blueprint for a new economic order in Scripture. We do find, however, some principles apropos of justice in society.

Certainly the first application of biblical truth concerning just relationships among God's people should be to the church. As the new people of God, the church should be a new society incarnating the biblical principles on justice in society through its common life (Gal 3:6-9; 6:16; 1 Pet 2:9-10). Indeed, only as the church itself is a visible model of transformed socioeconomic relationships will any appeal to government possess integrity. Much recent Christian social action has been ineffective because Christian leaders were calling on the government to legislate what they could not persuade their church members to live.

Biblical principles, however, apply to secular societies as well as the church. God did not arbitrarily dictate social norms for his people. The Creator revealed certain principles and social patterns because he knew what would lead to lasting peace and happiness for his creatures. Following biblical principles on justice in society is the only way to lasting peace and social harmony for all human societies.

The biblical vision of the coming kingdom suggests the kind of social order God wills. And the church is supposed to be a model now (imperfect, to be sure) of what the final kingdom of perfect justice and peace will be like. That means that the closer any *secular* society comes to the biblical norms for just relationships among the people of God, the more peace, happiness and harmony that society will enjoy. Obviously, sinful persons and societies will never get beyond a dreadfully imperfect approximation. But social structures do exert a powerful influence on saint and sinner alike. Christians, therefore, should exercise political influence to implement change in society at large.

That the biblical authors did not hesitate to apply revealed norms to persons and societies outside the people of God supports this point. Amos announced divine punishment on the surrounding nations for their evil and injustice (Amos 1—2). Isaiah denounced Assyria for its pride and injustice (Is 10:12-19). The book of Daniel shows that God removed pagan kings like Nebuchadnezzar in the same way that he destroyed Israel's rulers when they failed to show mercy to the oppressed (Dan 4:27). God obliterated Sodom and Gomorrah no less than Israel and Judah because they neglected to aid the poor and feed the hungry (Ezek 16:49). As the Lord of the universe, Yahweh applies the same standards of social justice to all nations.

This last principle bears directly on the issues of this chapter. Some countries, like the United States, Russia, Canada and Australia, have a bountiful supply of natural resources within their national boundaries. Do they have an absolute right to use these resources as they please solely for the advantage of their own citizens? Not according to the Bible. If we believe Scripture, then we must conclude that the human right of all persons to earn a just living clearly supersedes the right of the developed nations to use resources for themselves. We are only stewards, not absolute owners. God is the absolute owner, and he insists that the earth's resources be shared.

Before sketching specific steps for applying these principles, I must register one disclaimer and one clarification.

We must constantly remember the large gulf between revealed principles and contemporary application. There are many valid ways to apply biblical principles. The application of biblical norms to socioeconomic questions today leaves room for creativity and honest disagreement among biblical Christians.[2] Objecting to *my application* of biblical ethics to contemporary society is not at all the same as rejecting biblical principles. Of course, not all applications are equally valid; but humility and tolerance of each other's views are imperative. We can and must help each other see where we are unfaithful to biblical revelation and biased by our economic self-interest. Scripture, as always, is the norm.

One clarification is also necessary. To argue that Christians should work politically to change those aspects of our economic structures that are unjust is not to call for a violent revolution that would forcibly impose a centralized, statist society. I believe that the way of Jesus is the way of nonviolent love, even for enemies. I therefore reject the use of lethal violence.[3] The exercise of political influence in a democratic society, of course, involves the use of nonlethal pressure (or force). When we legislate penalties for drunken driving or speeding, we use an appropriate kind of nonlethal "force." The same is true when we pass legislation that changes foreign policies toward poor nations, makes trade patterns more just, restricts the oppressive policies of multinational corporations or increases foreign economic aid. In a democratic society, of course, such changes can occur only if a majority freely agree or at least quietly acquiesce.

As we work to correct unjust economic structures, it is important constantly to promote decentralized decision making and control. Both Marxist totalitarianism and multinational corporations centralize power in the hands of a tiny group of individuals. Often, the choices of these powerful elites reflect their own self-interest, not what is good for the majority. It should be possible to work both for a decentralization of economic power and a more just economy built on the basic biblical affirmation that God is on the side of justice for the poor and oppressed.

What then are some practical steps we can take?

Who Will Be Helped?

We face a complex question: Given the present situation in the less developed countries, who would benefit from changes such as increased economic foreign aid or more just patterns of international trade?

Foreign aid and free trade would not necessarily benefit the poorest half of the developing countries one iota. North Americans and Europeans are not to blame for all the poverty in the world today. Sin is not just a White European phenomenon. Many of the LDCs are ruled by a few wealthy elite, many of whom are largely unconcerned about the suffering of the masses in their lands. They often own a large percentage of the best land, on which they grow cash crops for export to earn the foreign exchange they need to buy luxury goods from the developed world. Meanwhile, the poorest 30 to 70 per cent of the people face grinding poverty.

That is why more foreign aid and improved trading patterns for developing countries would not necessarily improve the lot of the truly poor. Such changes might simply enable the wealthy elite to strengthen their repressive regimes.

But that does not mean that North Americans and Europeans can wash their hands of the whole problem. In many cases the wealthy elite continue in power because they receive massive military aid and diplomatic support from the United States and other industrial nations.[4] The United States has trained large numbers of police who have then tortured thousands of people working for social justice in countries like Chile and Brazil.[5] Western-based multinational corporations work closely with repressive governments. Events in Brazil, Chile, El Salvador and the Philippines demonstrate that the United States will support dictatorships that use torture and do little for the poorest one-half as long as these regimes are friendly to U.S. investments and foreign policy objectives.

A Change in Foreign Policy
What can be done? Western citizens could demand a drastic reorientation of Western foreign policy. We could demand a foreign policy that unequivocally sides with the poor.

If we truly believe that all people are created equal, then our foreign policy must be redesigned to promote the interests of all people and not just the wealthy elite in developing countries or our own multinational corporations. We should use our economic and diplomatic power to push for change in Third World dictatorships, especially those like Brazil, Chile, the Philippines and Uruguay, which make use of torture. We should also vigorously condemn the repression, totalitarianism and violation of human rights perpetuated by the Soviet Union in places like Afghanistan and Poland.

We need to press for ethical controls on the operations of our multinational corporations. The task, of course, is difficult precisely because MNCs are large and international. Since, however, the United States and Britain are the countries of origin for 75 per cent of the MNCs, we have a particular responsibility to see that the impact of MNCs on poor nations is positive rather than negative.[6]

Unfortunately, U.S. foreign policy has usually supported the economic interests of U.S. MNCs rather than the poor in the developing nations. In May 1981, for instance, the United States was the only nation out of 119 to vote in the World Health Organization against a code to control the advertising and marketing of infant formula by MNCs in the Third World. In spite of worldwide documentation of the evil effects of the marketing activities of Nestlé's and other MNCs,[7] the Reagan administration voted no because it said the code might damage "free enterprise."[8]

A foreign policy which seeks biblical justice for the poor will have to be willing to place ethical controls on the operations of MNCs, even if that is not in the short-term economic interest of the MNC and its American shareholders. Both by political activity and by well-designed citizen boycotts like the Nestlé boycott, Christian citizens can help reduce the negative impact of MNCs on the poor of the earth.[9]

We should also insist that foreign aid go only to countries seriously committed to Basic Needs Development strategies (see below, pp. 199-201). Aid to countries whose governments care little about improving the condition of the poor will likely end up in the pockets of the rich. U.S. foreign policy ought to encourage justice rather than injustice. Only then will proposed changes in international trade and foreign aid programs actually improve the lot of the poorest billion.

Social Change and Conversion
A fundamental change in Western policy toward the developing nations is imperative. But it is not enough. In addition, the poor masses in developing nations must be encouraged to demand sweeping structural changes in their own lands. We should actively promote nonviolent movements working to change unjust repressive governments.

Such changes, however, can only happen if a fundamental transformation of values occurs. In a recent scholarly book on land tenure in India, Robert Frykenberg of the University of Wisconsin lamented the growing gulf between rich and poor. "No amount of aid, science, and/or technology," he concluded, "can alter the direction of current processes without the occurrence of a more fundamental 'awakening' or 'conversion' among significantly larger numbers of people. . . . Changes of a revolutionary character are required, changes which can only begin in the hearts and minds of individuals."[10]

At precisely this point the Christian church—and missionaries in particular—can play a crucial role. Two things are important: first, evangelism; and, second, the whole message of Scripture. Evangelism is central to social change. Nothing so transforms the self-identity, self-worth and initiative of a poor, oppressed person as a personal, living relationship with God in Christ. Discovering that the Creator of the world lives in each of them gives new worth and energy to people psychologically crippled by centuries of oppression.

The second important component is sharing the whole biblical perspective. Some religious world views tend to create a fatalistic attitude toward poverty. Hinduism, for instance, teaches that those in the lower castes (and they usually are also the poorest) are there because of sinful choices in prior incarnations. Only by patiently enduring their present lot can they hope for a better life in future incarnations. In addition, Eastern religions de-emphasize the importance of history and material reality, considering them illusions to be escaped.

Biblical faith, on the other hand, affirms the goodness of the created, material world and teaches that the Creator and Lord of history demands justice now for the poor of the earth. As missionaries share this total biblical message, they can make a profound contribution to the battle against hunger, poverty and injustice.[11] To be sure, missionaries cannot engage directly in political activity in foreign countries. But they can and must teach the whole Word for the whole person. Why have missionaries so often taught Romans but not Amos to new converts in poor lands? If it is true, as we argued in Part 2, that Scripture constantly asserts that God is on the side of the poor, then missionaries should make this biblical theme a central part of their teaching. If we accept our Lord's Great Commission to teach "all that I have commanded you," then we dare not omit or de-emphasize the biblical message of justice for the oppressed, even if it offends ruling elites in the countries concerned.

Cross-cultural missionaries need not engage directly in politics. But they must carefully and fully expound for new converts the explosive biblical message that God is on the side of the poor and oppressed. The poor will learn quickly how to apply biblical principles to their own oppressive societies. The result will be changed social structures in developing countries.

Thus far we have looked at two things: a fundamental change in Western foreign policy, and a mass movement of social change rooted in new religious values in the LDCs. American Christians should promote both. But what else needs to happen?

Basic Needs Development

The most obvious structural solution to the tragedy of world hunger is to foster rapid economic development in the Third World. Third World nations would then be able either to produce all their own food and basic necessities, or to trade for them on the world market.

Throughout the fifties and sixties and into the seventies, this was the main focus of people concerned about the condition of the LDCs. Many economists advocated and many Third World governments implemented economic programs that were designed to produce economic growth, which at that time was thought to be synonymous with economic development. As the GNP of a country grew, people expected the forthcoming benefits eventually to "trickle down" to the poor masses so that the entire society would benefit. The poor would obtain jobs in a growing economy, and poverty would vanish.

Over the years, however, it became evident that, even when the GNP increased, the conditions of the poor people did not automatically improve.[12] Instead, the gap between the wealthy and the poor often increased, and the poor remained hungry. In light of the experience of the last several decades, it is now widely recognized that this trickle-down approach to development benefits the middle and upper classes but does much less, if anything, to help the poor.[13] Mahbub ul Haq, an economist with the World Bank, speaks for the growing consensus: "Growth in the GNP often does not filter down. What is needed is a direct attack on mass poverty."[14]

In the past decade, therefore, a new approach to the development of the Third World has emerged. It is often called "growth with equity." Development certainly includes economic growth, but economic growth must happen in such a way that the benefits of growth are equitably distributed. In other words, the poor must participate in economic progress.

There are several variants of the growth-with-equity approach to development, but the one most popular and perhaps most consistent with Christian principles is referred to as Basic Needs Development. Basic Needs Development focuses on the situation of the poor. It holds that all people have in common certain basic needs and that the highest priority of any economic program is to meet those needs for all people. Denis Goulet, Christian author of many books on development and development ethics, outlines these three basic needs: (1) life sustenance, (2) self-esteem, and (3) freedom to choose one's own course of action.[15]

It is really no surprise that basic needs go beyond the purely physical items of food, clothing, shelter and health care needed for life sustenance. Physical goods, for instance, could be generously supplied by some foreign agent in a paternalistic fashion. But while short-term aid is necessary and appreciated in some situations of desperate need (for example, during drought or war), long-term reliance on handouts reduces self-esteem and motivation. Similarly, a totalitarian society that meets all physical needs is not God's will for us. Persons should be free to shape their lives and societies.

According to Paul Streeten, editor of the prestigious development journal *World Development,* basic needs include not just the need for material goods but also "the need for self-determination, self-reliance, political freedom and security, participation in making the decisions that affect workers and citizens, national and cultural identity, and a sense of purpose in life and work."[16] Goulet's categories of self-esteem and freedom move in the same direction.

Because of this new focus on Basic Needs Development, the watchword in recent years in many circles (although not, unfortunately, in the Reagan administration) has become self-reliant development.[17] Self-reliant development means basically that each country will to a significant degree be economically independent so that its people can provide for their own needs. According to McGinnis, self-reliant development is "a model of development that emphasizes meeting the basic needs of people in a country through strategies geared to the particular human and natural resources, values and traditions of the country, and through strategies maximizing the collective efforts of people within each country and among Third World countries."[18]

Self-reliant development does not mean sealing the borders, refusing to trade with other countries or isolating the country from the world. Instead, self-reliance means "being so self-confident as a nation as to base our development on our own cultural values. Self-reliance is a very comprehensive concept which cuts across all walks of life. It implies not only our reliance on our own industry or agriculture, or on our own domestic resources or technology. It is relying on our own thinking and our own value systems, without being defensive or apologetic."[19]

Such a concept of development is necessarily broad. It means that no specific development measures will be applicable in all places at all times. Rather, an appropriate Basic Needs Development strategy for any country must take into account that country's unique context.[20] Much of what must be done to implement this strategy, naturally, can only come from the people in their respective countries. Therefore much of the burden rests squarely on the shoulders of the people in the Third World. This is as it should be. Self-esteem and freedom do not arise from First World development experts or political figures' telling officials from LDCs exactly what to do and how to do it.

Still, people from the developed world have much they can do in addition to changing the basic direction of their foreign policy and promoting basic values that foster social change. First, we should make international trade more fair. Second, we need to adopt new attitudes toward economic growth and the use of natural resources. Third, we need a new food policy. And finally, we must be willing to help with direct aid which will help prevent starvation during emergencies and empower the poor to earn their own way.

Making International Trade More Fair

In chapter six we saw how injustice has become firmly embedded in the patterns of trade in the international economic order. Under colonialism, mother countries often discouraged industrial development in the colonies, encouraging instead the export of agricultural products and raw materials. Some of the effects of the colonial period are still with us today. Changes in the international economic order are therefore essential.

Since the colonial period, the developed nations have continued to manipulate international trade relations to their economic advantage. The most frequently used strategy has been the erection of tariffs and other trade restrictions that have successfully kept many goods manufactured in the LDCs from entering the markets of the developed countries. As a result of such policies, many LDCs have become overly dependent on one or just a few primary commodities. The prices of most of these commodities run through periods of wide fluctuations, and some of them have undergone a long-term decline relative to the prices of manufactured goods coming from the developed countries.

Three things need to be done in the short run. First, developed nations should drastically reduce or eliminate trade barriers on imports from the LDCs. Second, commodity prices need to be stabilized to avoid wild, short-term fluctuations. Third, we must deal with the problem that some commodities exported by Third World nations have experienced a long-term decline of relative prices.

First, *trade barriers.* The long-standing Western policy of increasing import duties in proportion to the amount of processing and manufacturing the product has undergone has hindered industrial growth in the Third World.

An ironic aspect of trade barriers is that economic theory suggests that both the LDCs and industrialized nations would be better off after their removal. Developed nations would benefit because we could buy many imported goods more cheaply than before. Indeed, Guy Erb, writing in the *Colombia Journal of World Business,* estimated that trade restrictions in 1971 cost U.S. consumers an extra $10 to $15 billion. That amounted to $200 to $300 for every U.S. family.[21] Of course the LDCs would be better off because they would increase both their production and income if they could increase exports. (Whether the poorest 50 per cent would be better off is another issue, and one which a U.S. foreign policy focused on justice would have to address.)

Still, it is not politically easy to remove such trade restrictions because the people employed in the businesses protected by them would suffer. Although the numbers would be relatively small when we consider the size of our total economy, some people would lose their jobs. But there is a remedy for this problem. It is called *adjustment assistance.* Adjustment assistance is a government program designed to facilitate the movement of unemployed workers into new areas of employment. It compensates workers for the period during which they are unemployed, and it helps them to relocate and find jobs with comparable pay. In the long term, economists expect that no jobs would be lost. As the LDCs returned to the United States to spend their new income, the businesses they patronized would need to hire the displaced workers to meet the new demand. The Brandt report emphasized that both a reduction in protective trade barriers and an improvement of the currently feeble programs of adjustment assistance are necessary.[22]

Some attempts have been made in the past few years to reduce trade barriers on products produced by LDCs. In 1976, for example, the United States took a significant step by granting tariff preferences for manufactured products from the LDCs. Seven and a half years later, however, the program remains limited in scope. Bread for the World noted recently that "only 25 percent of developing country imports into the United States are eligible products."[23]

The Caribbean Basin Initiative launched on February 24, 1982, by President Reagan includes a tariff reduction package. To this extent the initiative was a step in the right direction. Unfortunately, as the bills moved through Congress more and more exemptions to the tariff reductions were restored. Speaking of the bill, the *Chicago Tribune* editorialized: "Unfortunately, various special interests have made sure that the provision does not apply to the most important goods produced in the Caribbean—textiles, oil, shoes, leather goods, canned tuna. Sugar, though duty free, will still be restricted by tight import quotas. All this makes the bill much less valuable than it could be, if not quite pointless."[24]

Presently, knowing that developed countries are facing their own economic crises, people in the rich countries are demanding more protection from the "cheap imports" from the LDCs. Indeed, one of the major issues in the 1984 presidential election will be how much each candidate is willing to protect home industries troubled by foreign competition. By saying no to short-term selfishness, American voters can promote trading patterns that could reduce hunger abroad—and that would in the long run benefit American consumers.

We must call our fellow citizens to be more concerned about hungry people abroad than with economic convenience at home. In his book *Economic Development,* Theodore Morgan emphasizes that removing tariff barriers would be helpful to developing nations. But he concludes on a pessimistic note: "Experience to date suggests that domestic pressure in MDC's [more developed countries] from firms and worker organizations will make concessions as modest in the future as they have been in the past."[25] Those who believe that God is on the side of the poor, however, must defy such pessimism and vested interests, and try to effect the necessary political changes.

Merely removing restrictions on imports, however, does not

guarantee that the poor masses in the Third World will enjoy the benefits. If local governing elites seize the land of peasants so that they and multinational corporations can grow crops for export, only the rich benefit. If local governing elites suppress labor unions so that the workers who manufacture the goods for export receive low wages, only the rich benefit. How then can we remove our trade barriers in such a way that the poorest people will benefit?

In 1984 the U.S. Congress will review the Generalized System of Preferences (GSP) law which governs all U.S. trade incentives to other nations.[26] It is important that the GSP be designed not only to open American markets to Third World goods; the law must also promote justice within those countries so that the poorer 50 per cent benefit significantly from exports sent to us.

We could write two important provisions into the GSP to do this. The law could require that countries that export agricultural products under the GSP have a Stable Food Production Plan. Such a plan would be designed to make sure that production of food for export does not undercut the need to grow food for domestic consumption. A second set of provisions could demand that countries exporting goods to us under the GSP have fair labor practices and respect human rights. These stipulations would encourage labor unions and other movements which would enable the workers to benefit from the economic growth stimulated by our trade preferences.

Trade—fair trade—could reduce hunger and starvation abroad.

Second, *a mechanism must be found that will stabilize commodity prices.* From 1974 to 1975 the world price of copper dropped from $1.52 to 53¢ per pound.[27] Such fluctuation devastates the economies of LDCs which depend on them.

In 1975 the European Common Market took a small step to reduce such havoc. It established a stabilization fund (with only $450 million in funding, however) for twelve basic commodities exported to Europe by forty-six former colonies. The fund guarantees a minimum return on these twelve items.

In May 1976 a further step was taken. At the fourth meeting of the United Nations Conference on Trade and Development (UNCTAD IV), the concept of a $3 billion commodity plan was adopted. It was to cover nineteen different commodities which developing countries export. Prices "remunerative and just to producers and equitable to consumers" were to be set. A subsequent conference in 1977 was to establish a $3 billion fund to stabilize prices. But the United States refused to commit itself to participate.[28]

At the fifth UNCTAD meeting participants discussed more fully the idea of a common fund to stabilize a wide range of commodity prices. The main purpose of the common fund would be to establish a central financing facility that would monitor and regulate the movement of prices on a whole series of commodities. But although the principle of the common fund was approved even by the United States, final negotiations have been slow. By the time of the sixth UNCTAD meeting in July of 1983, no final agreement had been reached—and none is yet in sight. Both the Brandt commission and the UNCTAD VI conference recommend that these negotiations be completed with all due haste so that the operation of the fund can begin.[29]

This is not likely to happen soon, however. The 1981 summit in Cancun was supposed to take up the issue of the common fund, but the United States, although at one time it had approved the fund "in principle," gave no indication that it would support such a fund or even negotiate about it. Instead, the Reagan administration is promoting an extreme version of free market economics, and the common fund has no role to play in such a theory of international economics. If any progress is to be made in this area, the United States has to change its position.

Third, *the problem of long-term decline of relative prices of some commodities must be faced squarely.* In 1982 the International Monetary Fund reported that the gap between the purchasing power of raw commodities exported by developing nations and the price of imports of manufactured goods was the greatest in twenty-five years.[30] The suggestion that developed nations pay higher prices will probably not do much good. The only lasting solution is to assist economies severely affected by declining prices to move into the production of other goods.

But Third World countries cannot do this by themselves. They need economic aid from the developed countries to foster the development of their economies and to move their people, land and other resources into the production of other goods. As can be seen, this ties in closely with the reduction in trade barriers, which creates incentive to move into other areas of manufacturing. The proposed common fund also contains elements which speak to this need. Be-

sides investing in and regulating buffer stocks, the fund would
finance "investments which could help the production, processing,
and marketing of commodities."[31] LDCs suffering from a long-term
decline in the relative terms of trade could thus obtain loans from
the fund to finance investments in new areas.

We have discussed three short-term recommendations that could
increase the benefits poor nations get from international trade: reducing trade barriers; establishing a price stabilization scheme; and
increasing aid designed to facilitate movement toward production
of commodities whose prices are not in a long-term decline. The
goal, of course, is to aid the Third World move toward self-reliant
development.

What else can we do to help them reach that goal?

New Attitudes toward Growth and Resource Use
Economic growth has been a catchword in the developed world for
years. With hardly a second thought, almost everyone assumes that
economic growth is desirable. We usually equate a growing economy
with a healthy economy—one that provides jobs, opportunities for
advancement and a rising standard of living. As a result, economic
growth has been heavily promoted in the developed world and has
led to the incredibly disproportionate consumption of natural resources that I reviewed in chapter six.

Unfortunately, as we also saw in that chapter, the extremely high
levels of resource consumption in the developed world have caused
the carrying capacity of the earth to deteriorate. Sustained industrialization and population growth seriously threaten the stability of
the world environment. The atmosphere is being progressively
loaded down both with foreign substances and with excessive quantities of natural ones, which combine to damage the quality of air and
cause the earth's overall temperature to rise. Agricultural and industrial uses of water are eroding the world's water supplies both by
decreasing their availability and by contaminating large reservoirs.
Renewable resources like agricultural land, timber and fish are
being carelessly used up with little concern for sustaining or re-
plenishing them.[32]

Such deterioration of the earth's carrying capacity is cause for
concern. Among other things, it decreases prospects for the continued development of LDCs. The development of the Third World

is much more important just now than the continued growth of the developed world. What then must we do?

The obvious answer is that the developed world consume less and pollute less. This is essentially correct; but, as mentioned in chapter six, it is more easily said than done. As MIT economist Lester Thurow points out, given today's economic structures, environmental crusades that denigrate growth and advocate greater pollution control may well benefit the middle and upper classes at the expense of the poor. Under current structures an end to growth may lead to a rise in unemployment. Increased pollution control equipment may raise the prices of goods needed by the poor. In addition, we have no clear reason to suppose that simply lowering consumption will in any way help the Third World. On the other hand, a cleaner environment may well raise the standard of living of the wealthier classes who retain their jobs and have enough money to get out and enjoy the enhanced environment.[33]

Few economists doubt the validity of this analysis. But it would be wrong to conclude that it is useless or misguided to decrease the use of resources or end pollution. Rather, Thurow's warning illuminates the size and complexity of the obstacles that we must overcome.

The pervasive notion that increased consumption leads to greater happiness is at the heart of our dilemma. When we use the term *standard of living*, it is commonly thought to refer exclusively or primarily to the level of *material* consumption. By Christian definition, however, a person's standard of living is "high" when he or she lives in proper relationship with God, other people and the earth. Right relationships with others and the earth certainly include an adequate supply of material resources. But constantly increasing material affluence in no way guarantees an improved standard of living. Unfortunately, this Christian perspective disappeared long ago in the historical development of Western society.[34]

Ironically, even by a secular definition of happiness economic growth and rising affluence do not generate greater happiness. In a highly acclaimed but little implemented study, conservative economist Richard Easterlin has shown that a highly affluent society is no happier on the whole than a less affluent one (provided basic needs are largely met). The reason is that people tend to measure their happiness by how much they consume relative to their neighbors. As all try to get ahead, most tend to rise together; and people are continually frustrated in their efforts to achieve happiness. Easterlin concludes: "To the outside observer, economic growth appears to be producing an ever more affluent society, but to those involved in the process, affluence will always remain a distant, urgently sought, but never attained goal."[35] Growth occurs, the earth is used and abused —but no perceptible benefit results.

To Christians this should be no surprise. We should be the first to reject this rat race to surpass our neighbors. Knowing that material goods are not what brings ultimate happiness, we should be the first to experiment with simpler lifestyles. As we reduce our demand for dwindling resources, we witness to others that happiness is not found primarily in material possessions.

As we move in this direction, we need to be alert to Thurow's warnings. If, in our advanced state of technology, significant numbers of people consume less, there will be less need for production. Declining demand will signal a decline in the need for workers. So we need long-term structural changes if displaced workers are to find other jobs. Because of the monumental proportions of the changes needed, they must be slow and gradual. Therefore I offer suggestions both for the immediate future and for the more distant future.

In the short run, a simpler lifestyle lived by Christians will mean more money not being spent on consumption goods. If large numbers of people save rather than spend this income, severe unemployment will probably ensue. If, however, we donate the income we have saved to agencies doing development work in poor nations, a major reduction in employment is unlikely. Recipients of the aid will spend the money on goods they need to enjoy an adequate level of material well-being, and the dollars spent on these goods must eventually return to buy things from U.S. businesses. As we in the developed nations begin to consume less and share more, we also spur indigenous development in the Third World, thus making the distribution of goods and assets more just from a biblical perspective.

As we adopt this short-run approach, Christians all over the world ought to re-examine priorities. If by a miracle of God's grace we could significantly reduce the gap between rich and poor, the pressing need for massive redistribution would be largely gone. With distributional justice attained, we would have to ask ourselves the next question: Should we once again pursue the same sort of economic growth we once did? The obvious answer is no. As we saw earlier, the carrying capacity of the earth is ultimately threatened. Redistributing the earth's burden does not lessen the full load. Shifting a heavy load from one side of the wagon to a more even spread may ease excessive pressure on certain points, but the total poundage of the load will not diminish.

Christians must seek to change the demand for goods and services away from heavy resource usage and environment-damaging goods toward goods and services that make less demand on the earth's carrying capacity.[36] One suggestion is that people spend more of their time and money creating vibrant, active Christian churches. Another is to spend more money on the arts (drama, music and other creative arts), thus creating an incentive for more people to engage in these activities instead of in the production of more material goods. People could work fewer hours at their jobs, and in their new leisure time they could serve the community or spend more time with their families or in constructive hobbies.

In the long run, then, sweeping changes will come. It is hoped that, through increasingly faithful Christian witness, the Spirit will work in the hearts of others so that our society will abandon the heretical notion that happiness comes through ever-expanding material abundance. In the long run there must be the kinds of relationships between persons on the one hand and people and the earth on the other which are discussed in the pathbreaking book *Earthkeeping*, put out by a group of scholars under the auspices of the Calvin Center for Christian Scholarship. We do not have the right, *Earthkeeping* argues, to use and abuse God's creation for selfish purposes. God has put the whole earth, including its land, rivers, mountains, animals and plants, under our care. We are to be stewards of the creation. We should not, therefore, pursue economic and technological growth that unnecessarily damages creation. Instead, God commands us to live in harmony with himself, with people *and* with creation.[37]

The study offers thirty suggestions on how individuals and society ought to change to incorporate these ideas into their lives. I will mention only two of them, but I encourage readers to pick up the book and study the rest. First, say the writers of *Earthkeeping*, "*our lives as stewards must give testimony to the fact that the achievement of the central purposes of life is not directly proportional to the level of consumption.* Our lifestyles, as well as our educational institutions, must convince others that the lack of restraint in consumption and production typical of Western nations does not lead to increased happiness."[38]

What will this mean for production? How are we to decide what to produce and how to produce it? A second suggestion responds to these queries:

Stewards should exercise their managing and technological abilities, but the purpose of those dominating abilities is not only the welfare of the self; it is primarily the care and enhancement of other people and of the rest of creation. We are technological creatures; we are makers, and we have abilities to do things efficiently and well. These abilities enable us to have dominion, to exercise stewardship. Always, then, technology (which has so often been used for destructive dominion) should be the tool of stewardship. It should be genuinely "appropriate" technology. Practically, this means using all the devices and skills of science in order to understand the workings and the welfare of the earth's creatures and our fellow humans. But it also means a restraint on the use of those powers, if the integrity of a thing is wrongly interfered with.[39]

Exactly what this stewardship of technology may mean for the distant future is difficult to say. But only through obedience to biblical principles can we hope to solve the ominous problems of our day.

In the short run, however, we know it is necessary to consume fewer goods. It will also be necessary to re-examine priorities and redirect our individual and social goals to fruitful instead of harmful ends. We must look to the development of technology that is consistent with God's call to care for all persons and his creation.

A New Food Policy

In developing the outlines of a new food policy, we again face short-run and long-run considerations. In the short term the need is to make sure hungry people everywhere get enough to eat. In the long term the goal is to help the LDCs develop to the point where their peoples are capable of producing or trading for their own food needs. The short-term objective will require substantial food aid. The long run will also require aid, but it needs aid of the type that promotes Basic Needs Development.

In developing a viable food policy, it is important to distinguish between *physical* and *economic* availability of food.[40] Food is physically available if it is physically possible to produce enough food for everyone. Food is economically available if everyone can afford to buy the food that is being (or could be) produced.

When one deals only with *physical* availability of food, the future looks hopeful.[41] All regions except Africa have had per capita increases in food production in the past twenty years. Most specialists believe that if population growth continues to slow down, it is indeed possible in the foreseeable future to grow enough food for everyone. Temporary emergencies may, of course, arise in specific areas, and so emergency food aid and adequate grain reserves will still be essential. But in general there will be enough food for all.

Far more difficult, however, is the problem of the *economic* availability of food. People who have neither land on which to grow food nor jobs with which to produce income to buy food simply starve— even when the food supply is ample to feed everyone. One billion people will seek to enter the job market between 1970 and 2000. There simply are not enough jobs for all people. Many schemes for modernizing agriculture use high technology and consequently throw many rural people out of work. (In developing countries, as much as eighty per cent of the total population live in rural areas.) A successful long-term food policy must therefore focus on things like creating jobs and redistributing resources (including skills and land) so that people can grow or buy the food they need.

For now and the immediate future, as Lester Brown informs us, North America has virtually "monopolistic control of the world's *exportable* grain supplies."[42] The percentage of all international grain exports controlled by the United States and Canada is much higher than the percentage of oil exports controlled by the OPEC countries. In addition, Third World countries in recent years have become more dependent on imported grain.

In the short run (especially during emergencies like the devastating African famine in 1984), short-term food aid is imperative to prevent starvation. But food aid should be used to encourage recipients to make the tough political decisions called for by a Basic Needs Development strategy. Great care must be taken that food aid does not discourage grain production in the LDCs. To avoid creating such a dependency cycle, donators can tie the grain to food-for-work projects, where food is used to pay the workers. Projects could, for example, promote rural agricultural development, thereby contributing to the long-run solution.

A food program should be designed for humanitarian rather than political purposes. In 1974 fully one-half of all U.S. food aid went, for obvious political reasons, to the two tiny countries of South Vietnam and Cambodia. Subsequent legislation specified that only twenty-five per cent of total food aid could go to countries not on the internationally accepted list of MSA (most seriously affected) countries. In 1976 the lion's share of this unrestricted twenty-five per cent went to Chile and South Korea.[43] Both countries had repressive dictatorships—and both were among the richest of the developing countries. The political misuse of food aid could be largely avoided if food assistance went through multilateral channels and private charitable organizations rather than via bilateral agreements between the United States and individual developing nations.

The Reagan administration, however, has decided to make food aid serve short-term U.S. political concerns. Secretary of Agriculture John R. Block, for example, has said that food aid ought to be used as a weapon to force compliance with U.S. political and military objectives. President Reagan has indicated that he prefers that aid be given on a bilateral basis. These decisions signal a retreat from the aid policies that are necessary to help a hungry world.

The establishment of adequate grain reserves would also help reduce hunger and provide greater food security. Two kinds of reserves are needed: emergency grain reserves and market-stabilization reserves.[44] The emergency grain reserve would be used only to meet short-term food emergencies like those in Cambodia in the late seventies and in Africa in the early eighties. A market-stabilization reserve would receive grain supplies when supply was high and prices low, and it would place those grains on the market when supply fell and prices climbed. Such a reserve would help both farmers and consumers avoid wide fluctuations of price.

In 1975 the United Nations established a 500,000-ton International Emergency Food Reserve. Later the United States established a 4-million-ton Emergency Grain Reserve. However, both the United States Department of Agriculture and the United Nations

Food and Agricultural Organization (FAO) recommend a 10-million-ton reserve.[45]

In 1977 the United States established a farmer-owned grain reserve which by May 1982 contained 15 million tons of wheat and 37 million tons of feed grains.[46] The FAO recommends a reserve of 61 to 73 million tons. While the United States has done more than other producing nations to establish a market-stabilization fund, it could also take the lead in drawing other nations into an international market-stabilization reserve and increasing that reserve to the level recommended by the FAO.

As indicated above, the most difficult task of a viable food policy is to promote the *economic* availability of food. To do that, LDCs need programs and policies that do the following: maximize job opportunities in rural areas; protect the rights of agricultural workers; equip poor rural people with the tools (knowledge, credit, land, appropriate technology) to earn their own way; increase research on labor intensive and low-cost farming methods; develop small-scale industries (for example, for producing farm equipment and processing farm products) in rural areas. As we have already seen, developed nations can encourage such programs by their foreign policy and their trade relations with LDCs.

The right kind of foreign aid is also important.

Bombs vs. Bread: Foreign Aid and Military Expenditures

What about foreign aid? Many critics want to reduce or eliminate foreign aid. Conservatives have argued that it has failed to reduce anti-American hostility or to promote U.S. foreign policy and that it has often been wasted by corrupt, inefficient governments. Radicals have argued that the purpose was never the reduction of hunger, but rather the promotion of U.S. foreign policy objectives; that it never gets to the real problem, which is the powerlessness of the poor; and that in fact aid strengthens the power of oppressive Third World elites.[47]

Sometimes these problems and the news stories about waste and corruption tempt us to abandon foreign aid. But that would be a hasty response. Certainly changes are imperative. But wisely targeted economic foreign aid can make a difference.

In 1967 smallpox killed two million people in the world. By 1981 smallpox had totally disappeared. The reason? A massive program to eradicate this killer. Millions of dollars in U.S. foreign aid helped defeat this annual killer of two million people.[48]

Two questions are especially pertinent if we would provide aid wisely: What would make our aid more effective? and How much aid is needed?

1. A Focus on the Poorest. First of all, most economic foreign aid should be designed to enable the poorest people in the poorest nations to meet their own basic needs. Since most poor people are rural, the focus must be on integrated rural development. That will usually mean land reform; agricultural extension services including credit, improved seeds, fertilizer, pesticides; rural public works programs such as irrigation projects; agricultural research; introduction of appropriate technology; and the development of light industry located in rural areas to complement the agricultural development.

It is particularly important that basic, minimal health care, education and a secure food supply be available to the rural masses.[49] Only then will the population explosion slow down. A study by the World Bank concluded, "In all developing countries, policies which succeed in improving the conditions of life for the poor, and in providing education and employment opportunities for women, are likely to reduce fertility. An improvement in the welfare of the poor appears to be essential before fertility can fall to developed country levels."[50]

Such a conclusion should not surprise the Christian. If, as the Bible teaches, God is at work in history liberating the poor and oppressed, then we should expect that an effective development strategy would be one that brings justice to the poor masses. At the same time this approach to development focused on the poorest provides a decisive answer to "lifeboat" theorists. Foreign aid to promote rural development is not a foolish gesture which sustains millions now only to doom even more later. Rather, foreign aid which encourages agricultural production as well as (at the least) minimal education and health care among the rural masses is probably the only way to check the population explosion in time to avoid global disaster. Justice and effectiveness coincide.

Some genuine progress in targeting U.S. aid on the poor occurred in 1973 with the "New Directions" reforms. Projects funded by the U.S. Agency for International Development (AID), designed to benefit the poor, rose significantly. But even so, AID projects still too often bypassed the poorest people. In December 1982, Congress passed legislation that required that 40 per cent of AID's development assistance go to finance goods and services for those classified by the World Bank as "absolutely poor." The Reagan administration, however, strongly opposed the measure and succeeded in restricting it to the 1983 budget.[51] In subsequent years, concerned citizens should ensure that the per cent spent on the absolutely poor goes even higher.

2. *A Focus on Empowerment.* Development assistance should have a primary focus on empowering the powerless. Much poverty and hunger result from the fact that the poor have no economic or political power to change the oppressive structures which keep them poor. Tragically, a great deal of U.S. aid goes to some of the world's repressive governments. Obviously, empowering the poor will threaten some oppressive corrupt elites currently in power—in the local village, the state, the nation and the globe. But only if development assistance empowers the poor so that they can shape their own destiny will it foster justice rather than dependence.

Empowerment of the poor will often mean land reform and an end to the political corruption by which the powerful maintain oppressive systems. It would also mean an end to the violation of human rights and the promotion of unions and other organizations that enable the poor to exercise influence in shaping their societies.

In 1979 the Interreligious Task Force on U.S. Food Policy did a study of all nations that receive U.S. bilateral assistance. All sixty-six countries were needy, but only two had any long-standing governmental commitment to equitable development, human rights and agrarian reform.[52] We could alter the situation by offering development assistance only to countries that agree to a "Basic Human Needs Agreement"—that is, countries which agree to an overall development strategy to empower the absolutely poor via measures such as land reform, secure human rights, and so on. We could offer such countries trade preferences and reduced tariffs on their exports to us.[53] We could also forgive a portion of the crippling foreign debts of those developing nations that signed Basic Human Needs agreements.

3. *A Long-range Approach.* Short-term economic and political considerations have hindered the effectiveness of foreign aid. Too

much aid continues to go to nations because they are currently of geopolitical interest to the donor. Giving aid through multilateral channels such as the United Nations rather than via bilateral agreements between the United States and the developing country tends to reduce the influence of short-term political considerations.[54] Furthermore, the United States has "tied" a good portion of its aid, demanding that the money be used to purchase American goods and services. Since American prices are often higher than global market prices, the aid provides fewer goods and services than it could otherwise. The long-range goal of a global society free of widespread hunger and poverty, rather than immediate political or economic concerns, should govern the granting of aid.

4. *Ecological Sustainability.* Both the Brandt commission and the U.S. Presidential Commission on World Hunger warn against persisting in development which results in continuing deterioration of the world's resources of soil, water and forests. Western capital-intensive, energy-intensive farming, for instance, is not a model to promote in developing nations. Our aid should promote appropriate technology and a labor-intensive approach that is sensitive to preserving a sound global ecosystem.

5. *Separation from Military Assistance.* Including both economic aid and military assistance in the U.S. foreign aid budget confuses citizens. They should be separated so that the case for each can be made on its own merits. The Reagan administration has increased military assistance six times faster than development aid.[55] That emphasis needs to be reversed.

If we improve the way we give foreign aid, it can help reduce hunger, poverty and injustice. But how much aid is needed?

How Much Is Enough?

Between 1947 and 1952, the United States poured $23 billion ($47 billion in terms of 1975 dollars) into Western Europe under the Marshall Plan.[56] One has only to look at the material prosperity of Western Europe today to realize that it was the most successful aid program the world has ever seen. The plight of one billion poor people today is just as desperate as that of the people of war-ravaged Europe in the late 1940s. The developed world, led by committed Christians in those countries, could lead the fight for greater aid for the developing world.

Paul Streeten, one of the foremost proponents of Basic Needs Development, has estimated that in order to generate development programs to help meet the basic needs of people only in the poorest nations of the Third World, we will need about $20 billion annually from now until 2000. (Streeten noted in 1979 that developed countries were then contributing $14 billion in aid, but only $6 billion went to the poorest countries.)[57] The Brandt commission's estimate, based on a more comprehensive development program than that of Streeten, called for $40 to $54 billion in annual contributions. (The Brandt commission also reported a shortfall in 1980 of $21 to $35 billion.)[58]

One plank of the New International Economic Order promoted by the Third World is that developed nations contribute .7 per cent of their GNP in aid. A few nations have achieved this target (some Scandinavian countries and the Netherlands). Others, most notably the United States, have not committed themselves to this modest target, which is only one-third of what we did in the Marshall Plan when we were less than half as affluent. In fact, the U.S. contribution of .5 per cent in 1960 has now fallen to .2 per cent.[59] This trend must be reversed. Tragically, under the Reagan administration U.S. foreign aid has not even increased enough to keep up with inflation. Other rich nations have also been slow to increase their commitments.

At the most recent meeting of UNCTAD in June and July of 1983, the developing nations, suffering under a mountain of international debt, requested a substantial increase in new aid commitments. But, as the *Wall Street Journal* reports, "the industrial nations, reluctant to take actions that might hurt their own economies, wouldn't extend new funds. Instead, they asserted that the economic recovery, if left unhindered, would spread to the developing nations."[60]

The world faces a crucial choice. Steps to help the poor and hungry on the scale needed require enormous sums of money. Yet the governments of the world continue to prefer bombs to bread. World expenditures on armaments spiral upward each year. Do the people of the world want to spend as much on arms each year (about $600 billion in 1982) as the poorest half of humanity receives in total annual income? Do we want the annual budget of the World Health Organization to equal about five hours of world military spending?

Government budgets reflect fundamental priorities and values in the same way that the budgets of churches and families do. Bread for the World reported in 1982 that if Congress approved President Reagan's recommendations, military spending would jump in the next five years from 25 to 38 per cent of the federal budget. At the same time, antihunger programs (both at home and abroad) would decline from 3 to 2 per cent. Such priorities are not biblical. Nor, I believe, do they reflect the deepest values of the American people.

Ironically, such priorities are bad not just for the hungry, but also for our economy. Careful studies have demonstrated that spending tax money on the military is the *least efficient* way of producing jobs. Building military equipment requires high technology and therefore relatively few workers. One billion dollars spent on training nurses creates 85,000 new jobs; the same money spent for military equipment produces only 45,000 new jobs.[61]

To reverse priorities, we need legislation that would create an annual independent analysis of the defense budget. (Congressional committees estimate that $10 to $30 billion in waste and mismanagement could be cut from the defense budget without reducing U.S. military strength.) We can support the transfer amendments regularly introduced in Congress to transfer funds from military spending to antihunger programs at home and abroad. And we can urge our representatives to vote for legislation to finance the "conversion" of military industries to civilian production.

President Eisenhower was surely correct: "Every gun that is made, every warship launched, every rocket fired signifies, in the final sense, a theft from those who hunger and are not fed, those who are cold and are not clothed."[62]

James Cogswell, veteran director of the Office of World Service and World Hunger for the Presbyterian Church in the United States, has suggested that we begin to explore new sources of funding for Third World development.[63] We could develop a modest international income tax on a sliding scale. We could levy a modest tax on international trade, arms production and international travel. We could renegotiate the Law of the Sea and use the wealth of the oceans to help the poor. A World Development Fund in which decision making was more evenly shared by borrowers and lenders could manage these new resources.

Such proposals are visionary in the current political climate of selfish nationalism. But they are in keeping with God's special concern for the poor and the biblical principle of jubilee. In the long run, too, it is in the best interests of everyone to reduce poverty in the world. Increasing foreign aid both through larger contributions by affluent nations and through new sources of funding represents one battlefront in the total war on hunger that Christians must wage.

The tasks outlined in this chapter seem overwhelming. Only as individuals join with other concerned citizens can they effectively promote the necessary structural changes. Here are a few organizations working to change public policy.

Bread for the World

Bread for the World (BFW) is a Christian citizens' movement in the United States whose goal is to change governmental policy on all issues that affect hungry people. BFW has organized local chapters at the grassroots level in every congressional district across the country. A monthly newsletter keeps members up-to-date on current administrative and legislative activity. Members influence legislation by calling, writing or visiting government officials, especially their own congressional representatives.

Bread for the World is an explicitly Christian organization. Worship is a regular part of the meetings of local chapters. Art Simon, the director, is a devout Missouri Synod Lutheran. BFW makes a conscious effort to involve at every level, including the staff and board of directors, a large number of evangelicals, mainline church folk and Catholics. Many prominent evangelicals are active on the board of directors: Myron Augsburger, former president of Eastern Mennonite College; David McKenna, president of Asbury Theological Seminary; Lemuel Tucker, president of Voice of Calvary; and Senator Mark Hatfield.

Bread for the World practices what it preaches. Salaries are based primarily on need, not position. The salary of the executive director is less than that of the packager! Volunteers carry out most of BFW's local activities, and income comes largely from the $15 annual membership fee.

BFW has been very successful in affecting public policy. In 1981 it developed, helped introduce, and greatly facilitated the passage of the Hunger and Global Security bill. This bill was based on the belief that "a major world-wide effort to conquer hunger and poverty, far from being a gesture of charity to be offered or withheld according to temporary political whims, holds the key to both global and national security."[64] The bill declared "that the U.S. [will] make the elimination of hunger the primary focus of its relationships with the developing countries, beginning with the decade of the 1980's."[65] Its provisions increased funding for health programs in LDCs and reoriented the aid given to multilateral development banks so that it would reach the people most in need.

Founded in 1974, Bread for the World is a rapidly growing movement. Since 1976 membership has grown from 14,000 to over 43,000 in 1983. BFW offers Christian citizens an effective way to help shape the public policies which will mean life or death for millions of people in the next few decades. (See Appendix B for its address and the addresses of the organizations which follow.)

Evangelicals for Social Action

Evangelicals for Social Action (ESA) is an evangelical organization devoted to promoting justice, liberty and peace from a biblical perspective. ESA believes that prayer and radical dependence on the Holy Spirit must be central to any major contemporary movement to bring structural change in society. ESA also believes that a consistent biblical stance cuts across ideological stereotypes of left and right. Concerned to strengthen the family and oppose abortion on demand, ESA also believes a biblical position means working against racism and the nuclear arms race.

Reducing hunger and economic injustice is one of ESA's central concerns. It offers its members a regular newsletter, weekend discipleship workshops on hunger and justice, tracts for justice for church distribution, and fellowship in local chapters across the country. Organized in the late 1970s, ESA had over 5,000 members by 1984 and was growing rapidly.

Numerous other organizations attempt to change public policy. The following are among the more important.

The Interfaith Action for Economic Justice is a Washington-based religious lobby. It consists of the Washington staff of U.S. religious bodies. The staff analyzes issues, testifies before Congress and monitors legislation on all hunger-related matters. The task force mails a regular newsletter, an occasional newsletter called *Hunger,* and appeals for urgent communication with members of

Congress when food legislation is pending.

The Interfaith Centre on Corporate Responsibility examines the relation of nultinational corporations to world hunger. Although not a membership organization, the Interfaith Centre pro vides information on request.

Other citizen lobbies include Network, an organization staffed by Catholic sisters who publish a monthly newsletter, a quarterly and a hunger packet; and Friends Committee on National Legislation, which also issues a monthly newsletter.

The proposals suggested thus far envisage the reform of present economic structures. There are, of course, important fundamental questions that we have not discussed. Many Christians have sharply criticized capitalism,[66] and some have called for democratic socialism.[67] Others have articulately defended capitalism.[68] Examination of this growing debate, however, would carry us beyond both the space limitations of this chapter and the author's competence.[69]

It is increasingly clear, however, that it is time to re-examine economic orthodoxies of all ideological perspectives. We need economists immersed in biblical faith who will rethink economics as if poor people mattered. I have only an incomplete idea of what a modern version of the year of jubilee would look like. But at the heart of God's call for jubilee is a divine demand for regular, fundamental redistribution of the means for producing wealth so that people can earn their own way. We must discover new, concrete models for applying this biblical principle in our interdependent world. I hope and pray for a new generation of economists and political scientists who will devote their lives to formulating, developing and implementing a contemporary model of jubilee.

The Liberty Bell hanging in historic Philadelphia could become a powerful symbol for Western citizens working to share our resources with the poor of the world. The inscription on the Liberty Bell, "Proclaim liberty throughout the land," comes from the biblical passage on jubilee (Lev 25:10). These words promised to Hebrews enslaved in debt the freedom and the land necessary to earn a living. Today poverty enslaves hundreds of millions. The God of the Bible still demands institutionalized mechanisms which will enable everyone to earn a just living. The jubilee inscription on the Liberty Bell issues a ringing call for international economic justice.

Do Christians have the courage to demand and implement the structural changes needed to make that ancient inscription a contemporary reality?

Epilog

We live at one of the great turning points in history. The present division of the world's resources dare not continue. And it will not. Either courageous pioneers will persuade reluctant nations to share the good earth's bounty, or we will enter an era of catastrophic conflict.

Christians should be in the vanguard. The church of Jesus Christ is the most universal body in the world today. All we need to do is truly obey the One we rightly worship. But to obey will mean to follow. And he lives among the poor and oppressed, seeking justice for those in agony. In our time, following in his steps will mean simple personal lifestyles. It will mean transformed churches with a corporate lifestyle consistent with worship of the God of the poor. It will mean costly commitment to structural change in secular society.

Do Christians today have that kind of faith and courage? Will we pioneer new models of sharing for our interdependent world? Will we dare to become the vanguard in the struggle for structural change?

I must confess my fear that the majority of affluent "Christians" of all theological labels have bowed the knee to Mammon. If forced to choose between defending their luxuries and following Jesus among the oppressed, I am afraid they will imitate the rich young ruler.

But I am not pessimistic. God regularly accomplishes his will through faithful remnants.[1] Even in affluent nations, there are millions of Christians who love their Lord Jesus more than houses and lands. More and more Christians are coming to realize that their Lord calls them to feed the hungry and seek justice for the oppressed.

If at this moment in history a few million Christians in affluent nations dare to join hands with the poor around the world, we will decisively influence the course of world history. Together we must strive to be a biblical people ready to follow wherever Scripture leads. We must pray for the courage to bear any cross, suffer any loss and joyfully embrace any sacrifice that biblical faith requires in an Age of Hunger.

We know that our Lord Jesus is alive! We know that the decisive victory over sin and death has occurred. We know that the Sovereign of the universe wills an end to hunger, injustice and oppression. The resurrection of Jesus is our guarantee that, in spite of the massive evil that sometimes almost overwhelms us, the final victory will surely come.[2] Secure on that solid rock, we will plunge into this unjust world, changing now all we can and knowing that the Risen King will complete the victory at his glorious return.

Appendix A: Resource Materials

General Works on World Hunger

Barnet, Richard J. *The Lean Years: Politics in the Age of Scarcity*. New York: Simon and Schuster, 1980.

Bauer, P.T. *Equality, the Third World, and Economic Delusion*. Cambridge, Mass.: Harvard Univ. Press, 1981.

Benne, Robert. *The Ethic of Democratic Capitalism: A Moral Reassessment*. Philadelphia: Fortress Press, 1981.

Berger, Peter. *Pyramids of Sacrifice*. New York: Basic Books, 1975. A sociological analysis.

Birch, Bruce C., and Rasmussen, Larry L. *The Predicament of the Prosperous*. Philadelphia: Westminster Press, 1978.

Borgstrom, Georg. *The Food and People Dilemma*. Belmont, Calif.: Duxbury Press, 1973.

Brandt, Willy, et al. *North-South: A Program for Survival*. Cambridge, Mass.: MIT Press, 1980.

Brown, Lester R. *In the Human Interest*. New York: Norton, 1974.

Byron, William, ed. *The Causes of World Hunger*. New York: Paulist Press, 1982.

Cahill, Kevin M., ed. *Famine*. Maryknoll, N.Y.: Orbis Books, 1982.

Camara, Dom Helder. *Revolution through Peace*. New York: Harper & Row, 1971.

Chinweizu. *The West and the Rest of Us*. New York: Random House, 1975.

Connelly, Philip, and Perlman, Robert. *The Politics of Scarcity: Resource Conflicts in International Relations*. New York: Oxford Univ. Press, 1975.

Corson-Finnerty, Adam D. *World Citizen: Action for Global Justice*. Maryknoll, N.Y.: Orbis Books, 1982.

Davis, Shelton H. *Victims of the Miracle: Development and the Indians of Brazil*. Cambridge: At the University Press, 1977.

De Jesus, Carolina Maria. *Child of the Dark*. Trans. David St. Clair. New York: Signet Books, 1962. An explosive personal account of urban Brazilian poverty.

Eckholm, Erik P. *Down to Earth: Environment and Human Needs*. New York: Norton, 1982.

Ensminger, Douglas, and Bomani, Paul. *Conquest of World Hunger and Poverty*. Ames, Iowa: Iowa State Univ. Press, 1980.

Freudenberger, C. Dean, and Minus, Paul M.,Jr. *Christian Responsibility in a Hungry World*. Nashville: Abingdon Press, 1976.

Fryer, Jonathan. *Food for Thought: The Use and Abuse of Food Aid in the Fight against World Hunger*. Geneva, Switzerland: World Council of Churches, 1981.

George, Susan, and Paige, Nigel. *Food for Beginners*. New York: Norton, 1983.

Gheddo, Piero. *Why Is the Third World Poor?* Maryknoll, N.Y.: Orbis Books, 1973.

Gilder, George. *Wealth and Poverty.* New York: Basic Books, 1981.

Goudzwaard, Bob. *Aid for the Overdeveloped West.* Toronto: Wedge, 1975.

———. *Capitalism and Progress: A Diagnosis of Western Society.* Trans. Josina Van Nuis Zylstra. Grand Rapids, Mich.: Eerdmans, 1979.

Griffiths, Brian. *Morality and the Market Place: Christian Alternatives to Capitalism and Socialism.* London: Hodder and Stoughton, 1982.

Heilbroner, Robert L. *An Inquiry into the Human Prospect.* New York: Norton, 1974.

Jegen, Mary Evelyn, and Wilbur, Charles K., eds. *Growth with Equity.* New York: Paulist Press, 1979.

Lappé, Frances Moore, and Collins, Joseph. *Food First: Beyond the Myth of Scarcity.* Boston: Houghton Mifflin, 1977.

Lappé, Frances Moore; Collins, Joseph; and Kinley, David. *Aid as Obstacle: Twenty Questions about Our Foreign Aid and the Hungry.* San Francisco: Institute for Food and Development Policy, 1980.

Lewis, John P., and Kallab, Valeriana, eds. *U.S. Foreign Policy and the Third World: Agenda 1983.* New York: Praeger, 1983. This annual publication of the Overseas Development Council contains an invaluable collection of statistics and a useful summary of recent developments.

Lutz, Charles P., ed. *Farming the Lord's Land: Christian Perspectives on American Agriculture.* Minneapolis: Augsburg, 1980.

Mathiesen, J. *Basic Needs and the New International Economic Order.* Washington, D.C.: Overseas Development Council, 1981.

McGinnis, James B. *Bread and Justice: Toward a New International Economic Order.* New York: Paulist Press, 1979.

Millett, Richard. *Guardians of the Dynasty: A History of the U.S. Created Guardia Nacional De Nicaragua and the Somoza Family.* Maryknoll, N.Y.: Orbis Books, 1977.

Minear, Larry. *New Hope for the Hungry?* New York: Friendship Press, 1975.

Mische, Gerald, and Mische, Patricia. *Toward a Human World Order: Beyond the National Security Straitjacket.* New York: Paulist Press, 1977.

Mooneyham, W. Stanley. *What Do You Say to a Hungry World?* Waco, Tex.: Word Books, 1975.

Munoz, Heraldo, ed. *From Dependency to Development: Strategies to Overcome Underdevelopment and Inequality.* Boulder, Colo.: Westview Press, 1981.

Myrdal, Gunnar. *The Challenge of World Poverty.* New York: Random House, 1971. A classic.

Nelson, Jack A. *Hunger for Justice: The Politics of Food and Faith.* Maryknoll, N.Y.: Orbis Books, 1981.

Rich, William. *Smaller Families through Social and Economic Progress.* Washington: Overseas Development Council, 1973.

Rifkin, Jeremy. *Entropy.* New York: Viking Press, 1980.

Rodney, Walter. *How Europe Underdeveloped Africa.* London: Bogle-L'Ouverture, 1972.

Schiller, John A., ed. *The American Poor.* Minneapolis: Augsburg, 1982.

Schumacher, E. F. *Small Is Beautiful: Economics As If People Mattered.* New York: Harper & Row, 1973.

Schwartz-Nobel, Loretta. *Starving in the Shadow of Plenty.* New York: Putnam's, 1981.

Simon, Arthur. *Bread for the World.* Grand Rapids, Mich.: Eerdmans; New York: Paulist Press, 1975. Superb overview of public policy issues. Rev. ed. 1984.

Sivard, Ruth Leger. *World Military and Social Expenditures 1983.* Leesburg, Va.: World Priorities, 1983. An annual collection of useful data.

Skillen, James W. *International Politics and the Demand for Global Justice.* Sioux Center, Iowa: Dordt College Press, 1981.

Taylor, John V. *Enough Is Enough.* London: SCM Press, 1975. An excellent overview with considerable biblical analysis.

U.S., The Council on Environmental Quality and the Department of State, *Global 2000 Report to the President.* Vol. 1. Washington, D.C.: Government Printing Office, 1980.

Wilkinson, Loren, ed. *Earthkeeping: Christian Stewardship of Natural Resources.* Grand Rapids, Mich.: Eerdmans, 1980.

Wortman, Sterling, and Cummings, Ralph W., Jr. *To Feed This World: The Challenge and the Strategy.* Baltimore: Johns Hopkins Univ. Press, 1978.

Lifestyle

Beckmann, David M. and Donnelly, Elizabeth A. *The Overseas List: Opportunities for Living and Working in Developing Countries.* Minneapolis: Augsburg, 1979.

Eller, Vernard. *The Simple Life: The Christian Stance toward Possessions.* Grand Rapids, Mich.: Eerdmans, 1973. It is important to read Eller's warning against legalism, but the overall effect is to give aid and comfort to our carnal inclination to rationalize our sinful affluence.

Ewald, Ellen Buchman. *Recipes for a Small Planet.* New York: Ballantine Books, 1973. Recipes for delicious meatless dishes.

Foster, Richard J. *Freedom of Simplicity.* New York: Harper & Row, 1981.

Gish, Arthur G. *Beyond the Rat Race.* Scottdale, Pa.: Herald Press, 1973.

Kerr, Graham. *The Graham Kerr Step-by-Step Cookbook.* Elgin, Ill.: David C. Cook, 1982.

Lappé, Frances Moore. *Diet for a Small Planet.* Rev. ed. New York: Ballantine, 1975. "How to" book on simple, nutritious diet.

Longacre, Doris Janzen. *More-with-Less Cookbook.* Scottdale, Pa.: Herald Press, 1976. Commissioned by the Mennonite Central Committee; simple lifestyle recipes of Pennsylvania Dutch quality!

———. *Living More with Less.* Scottdale, Pa.: Herald Press, 1980.

Macmanus, Sheila. *Community Action Sourcebook: Empowerment of People.* New York: Paulist Press, 1982.

McGinnis, James, and McGinnis, Kathleen. *Parenting for Peace and Justice.* Maryknoll, N.Y.: Orbis Books, 1981.

Shannon-Thornberry, Milo. *Alternate Celebrations Catalogue.* Washington, D.C.: Alternatives, 1982.

Sider, Ronald J., ed. *Lifestyle in the Eighties: An Evangelical Commitment to Simple Lifestyle.* Philadelphia: Westminster, 1982.

———. *Living More Simply: Biblical Principles and Practical Models.* Downers Grove, Ill.: InterVarsity Press, 1980.

Vanderlip, D. George. *Discovering a Christian Lifestyle: Guidelines from the New Testament.* Valley Forge, Pa.: Judson Press, 1978.

Development

Batchelor, Peter. *People in Rural Development*. Exeter: Paternoster, 1981.

Dumont, René and Rosier, Bernard. *The Hungry Planet*. New York: Praeger, 1969. Still good on agricultural development.

Dunne, George H. *The Right to Development*. New York: Paulist Press, 1974.

Freire, Paulo. *Pedagogy of the Oppressed*. Trans. Myra B. Ramos. New York: Herder and Herder, 1970. A revolutionary educational philosophy.

Goulet, Denis. *A New Moral Order*. Maryknoll, N.Y.: Orbis Books, 1974.

Morgan, Theodore. *Economic Development: Concept and Strategy*. New York: Harper & Row, 1975.

Sider, Ronald J., ed. *Evangelicals and Development: Toward a Theology of Social Change*. Philadelphia: Westminster, 1982.

Sinclair, Maurice. *The Green Finger of God*. Exeter: Paternoster, 1980.

Sine, Tom, ed. *The Church in Response to Human Need*. Monrovia, Calif.: Missions Advanced Research Communication Center, 1983.

Stoesz, Edgar. *Beyond Good Intentions*. Akron, Pa.: Mennonite Central Committee, 1972. Practical discussion of development.

Theology, Biblical Studies and the Church

Armerding, Carl E., ed. *Evangelicals and Liberation*. Nutley, N.J.: Presbyterian and Reformed, 1977.

Banks, Robert J. *Paul's Idea of Community*. Grand Rapids, Mich.: Eerdmans, 1980.

Batey, Richard. *Jesus and the Poor: The Poverty Program of the First Christians*. New York: Harper & Row, 1972.

Boerma, Conrad. *The Rich, the Poor—and the Bible*. Philadelphia: Westminster, 1979.

Boesak, Allan. *Farewell to Innocence*. Maryknoll, N.Y.: Orbis Books, 1977.

Brueggemann, Walter. *The Land*. Philadelphia: Fortress Press, 1977.

Byron, William J. *Toward Stewardship: An Interim Ethic of Poverty, Pollution and Power*. New York: Paulist Press, 1975.

Cassidy, Richard J. *Jesus, Politics and Society: A Study of Luke's Gospel*. Maryknoll, N.Y.: Orbis Books, 1978.

Catherwood, Sir Frederick. *The Christian in Industrial Society*. London: Tyndale Press, 1964.

Cesaretti, C. A., and Cummins, Stephen, eds. *Let the Earth Bless the Lord: A Christian Perspective on Land Use*. New York: Seabury Press, 1981.

Cosby, Gordon. *Handbook for Mission Groups*. Waco, Tex.: Word Books, 1975.

Cone, James H. *God of the Oppressed*. New York: Seabury Press, 1975.

Dayton, Donald W. *Discovering an Evangelical Heritage*. New York: Harper & Row, 1976.

De Santa Ana, Julio. *Good News to the Poor: The Challenge of the Poor in the History of the Church*. Geneva, Switzerland: World Council of Churches, 1977.

Dickinson, Richard D. N. *To Set at Liberty the Oppressed*. Geneva, Switzerland: CCPD, 1975.

Escobar, Samuel, and Driver, John. *Christian Mission and Social Justice*. Scottdale, Pa.: Herald Press, 1978.

Gollwitzer, Helmut. *The Rich Christians and Poor Lazarus*. Trans. David Cairns. New

York: Macmillan, 1970.

Gremillion, John, ed. *The Gospel of Peace and Justice: Catholic Social Teaching since Pope John.* Maryknoll, N.Y.: Orbis Books, 1976.

Harper, Michael. *A New Way of Living.* Plainfield, N.J.: Logos International, 1973.

Hengel, Martin. *Poverty and Riches in the Early Church: Aspects of a Social History of Early Christianity.* Philadelphia: Fortress Press, 1974.

Johnson, Luke T. *Sharing Possessions.* Philadelphia: Fortress Press, 1981.

Kerans, Patrick. *Sinful Social Structures.* New York: Paulist Press, 1974.

Kirk, Andrew. *Liberation Theology: An Evangelical View from the Third World.* Atlanta: John Knox Press, 1979. A useful introduction to the voluminous, important literature on "liberation theology."

————. *Theology and the Third World Church.* Downers Grove, Ill.: InterVarsity Press, 1983.

————. *Theology Encounters Revolution.* Downers Grove, Ill.: InterVarsity Press, 1980.

Kraybill, Donald B. *The Upside Down Kingdom.* Scottdale, Pa.: Herald Press, 1978.

Lernoux, Penny. *Cry of the People.* Garden City, N.Y.: Doubleday, 1980.

Ludwig, Thomas E., Westphal, Merold, et al. *Inflation, Poortalk and the Gospel.* Valley Forge, Pa.: Judson Press, 1981.

Mott, Stephen C. *Biblical Ethics and Social Change.* New York: Oxford, 1982.

Perkins, John. *With Justice for All.* Glendale, Calif.: Regal, 1982.

Pilgrim, Walter E. *Good News to the Poor: Wealth and Poverty in Luke-Acts.* Minneapolis: Augsburg, 1981.

Pope John Paul, *"Laborem Exercens." National Catholic Reporter,* 25 September 1981, pp. 11ff.

Samuel, Vinay. *The Meaning and Cost of Discipleship.* Bombay: Bombay Urban Industrial League for Development, 1981.

Scott, Waldron. *Bring Forth Justice.* Grand Rapids, Mich.: Eerdmans, 1980.

Seccombe, David Peter. *Possessions and the Poor in Luke-Acts.* Studien zum Neuen Testament und seiner Umwelt, 1982.

Sider, Ronald J., ed. *Cry Justice: The Bible Speaks on Hunger and Poverty.* Downers Grove, Ill.: InterVarsity Press; New York: Paulist Press, 1980.

Sine, Tom. *The Mustard Seed Conspiracy.* Waco, Tex.: Word, 1981.

Taylor, Richard K. *Economics and the Gospel.* Philadelphia: United Church Press, 1973. Excellent book with special attention to the United States.

Wallis, James. *Agenda for Biblical People.* New York: Harper & Row, 1976.

————. *The Call to Conversion: Recovering the Gospel for These Times.* New York: Harper & Row, 1981.

Westphal, Carol. "Covenant Parenting for Peace and Justice." Office of Family Life, Reformed Church of America. (Write RCA Distribution Center, 18525 Torrence Avenue, Lansing, IL 60438.)

White, John. *The Golden Cow: Materialism in the Twentieth-Century Church.* Downers Grove, Ill.: InterVarsity Press, 1979.

Ziesler, J.A. *Christian Asceticism.* Grand Rapids, Mich.: Eerdmans, 1973.

Periodicals

The New Internationalist. 113 Atlantic Ave., Brooklyn, NY 11201. An influential development periodical with a radical analysis of the relationship of the developing and developed worlds.

The Other Side. Box 12236, Philadelphia, PA 19144. A journal of radical discipleship; frequent articles on hunger, justice.

Seeds. 222 East Lake Drive, Decatur, GA 30030. An excellent magazine on world hunger published by Southern Baptists.

Sojourners. 1321 Otis Street, N.E., Washington, D.C. 20017. A biblical magazine with regular articles on economic justice, discipleship and community.

Transformation: An International Dialogue on Evangelical Social Ethics. 312 W. Logan Street, Philadelphia, PA 19144. One of the best places to listen to all parts of the worldwide evangelical community.

U.N. Development Forum. A monthly tabloid *free* from Center for Economic and Social Information, United Nations, New York, NY 10017.

Numerous other religious journals regularly carry related items: *Christian Century, Christianity and Crisis, Christianity Today, Commonweal, Engage/Social Action, Worldview.*

Audiovisuals

A vast array of excellent audiovisuals are available. For lists write to almost any of the organizations listed in Appendix B. Especially helpful are the lists from Bread for the World, Mennonite Central Committee and World Hunger Education Service.

Appendix B: Organizations

Alternatives, Box 1707, 1124 Main St., Forest Park, GA 30051. Publishes a newsletter on simple living, an *Alternate Celebrations Catalog*, and so on.

American Enterprise Institute for Policy Research, 1150 17th St., N.W., Washington, D.C. 20036. An influential conservative think tank on a wide range of public policy issues, including hunger.

American Friends Service Committee, 1501 Cherry St., Philadelphia, PA 19102. An established Quaker relief, development and justice agency.

Amnesty International, 304 W. 58th St., New York, NY 10023. Amnesty's focus is human rights.

Bread for the World, 6411 Chillum Place, N.W., Washington, D.C. 20012. An effective Christian citizens' lobby.

Brethren House Ministries, 6301 56th Ave., N., St. Petersburg, FL 33709. Workshops, filmstrips and publications (for example, *Hunger Activities for Children* [1978] and *Hunger Activities for Teens* [1979]) on issues of hunger and lifestyle.

Canadian Hunger Foundation, 323 Chapel St., Ottawa, Ontario K1N 7Z2, Canada.

Catholic Relief Services, 1011 First Avenue, New York, NY 10022. The major Catholic relief and development agency.

Church World Service, 475 Riverside Drive, New York, NY 10027. The NCC's agency for relief, development and justice.

Cooperative League of the U.S.A., 59 E. Van Buren St., Chicago, IL 60605.

CROP, Box 968, Elkhart, IN 46514. Interdenominational fund raising for relief and development; CROP sponsors hunger banquets, hunger walks and so on.

Educational Concerns for Hunger Organizations, R. R. 2, Box 852, North Ft. Myers, FL 33903. A publication for agricultural missionaries and those interested in subsistence farming.

Environmental Defense Fund, 162 Old Town Road, East Setauket, NY 11733.

Evangelicals for Social Action, P.O. Box 76560, Washington, D.C. 20013. An evangelical organization focused on education and action for justice and peace.

Food and Agricultural Organization, 1776 F. Street, N.W., Washington, D.C. 20437. A United Nations agency.

Friends Committee on National Legislation, 245 Second St., N.E., Washington, D.C. 20002. Issues a monthly newsletter.

Institute for Food and Development Policy, 2588 Mission St., San Francisco, CA 94110.

Institute for Peace and Justice, 2913 Locust St., St. Louis, MO 63103. A wide range of educational tools, workshops and newsletter from a Catholic perspective.

Interfaith Action for Economic Justice, 100 Maryland Ave., N.E., Washington, D.C.

20002-5694. A coalition of Protestant, Catholic and Jewish Washington-based staff working to impact public policy on issues such as food, agriculture, health and human services, development, economic policy. Regular newsletter on legislative issues and a toll-free number for legislative update (800-424-7292).

Interfaith Centre on Corporate Responsibility, 475 Riverside Dr., New York, NY 10027.

Jubilee Fund, 300 W. Apsley, Philadelphia, PA 19144. A fund supporting indigenous, wholistic Third World projects which combine evangelism, social action, community and discipleship. An affiliate, Jubilee Handicrafts, markets Third World handicrafts.

Mennonite Central Committee, 21 S. 12th St., Akron, PA 17501. A large evangelical relief and development agency heavily involved in long-range development. The Washington office publishes an excellent newsletter, *Washington Memo.*

Network, 224 D St., S.E., Washington, D.C. 20005. A citizen lobby staffed by Catholic sisters who publish a monthly newsletter, a quarterly and a hunger packet.

World Concern, 19303 Fremont Avenue, N., Seattle, WA 98133.

The World Council of Churches, 475 Riverside Drive, New York, NY 10027. Books, pamphlets and newsletters on a wide range of hunger and development issues.

World Hunger Education Service, 1317 G St., N.W., Washington, D.C. 20005.

World Relief Commission, P.O. Box WRC, Wheaton, IL 60187. The official relief and development arm of the National Association of Evangelicals.

World Vision International, Box O, Pasadena, CA 91109. The largest evangelical relief and development agency.

Worldwatch Institute, 1776 Massachusetts Ave., Washington, D.C. 20036.

Notes

Introduction

[1]James P. Grant, *The State of the World's Children 1982-83* (Oxford: Oxford Univ. Press, 1983), p. 1. Stephen Coats, "Military Spending and World Hunger," Bread for the World (hereafter, BFW) Background Paper, no. 62 (August 1982):1. See also Willy Brandt, *North-South: A Program for Survival* (Cambridge, Mass.: MIT Press, 1980), p. 16.

Chapter 1: A Billion Hungry Neighbors

[1]"Iracema's Story," *Christian Century,* 12 November 1975, p. 1030.

[2]Robert L. Heilbroner, *The Great Ascent: The Struggle for Economic Development in Our Time* (New York: Harper & Row, 1963), pp. 33-36.

[3]Coats, "Military Spending and World Hunger," p. 1. See also National Research Council, *World Food and Nutrition Study: The Potential Contributions of Research* (Washington, D.C.: National Academy of Sciences, 1977), p. 34.

[4]Brandt, *North-South,* p. 18.

[5]John P. Lewis and Valeriana Kallab, eds., *U.S. Foreign Policy and the Third World: Agenda 1983* (New York: Praeger, 1983), p. 210.

[6]See *World Development Report 1981* (New York: Oxford Univ. Press [for the World Bank], 1981), pp. 135 and 137 for growth statistics.

[7]Arthur Simon, *Bread for the World* (Grand Rapids, Mich: Eerdmans; Paramus, N.J.: Paulist Press, 1975), pp. 64-65. The *New York Times* reported on 11 July 1976, p. 3, "According to [Brazilian] government statistics, wages for unskilled workers, after taking inflation into account, have fallen almost 40 per cent since the right-wing military government took power 12 years ago. Meanwhile the Gross National Product rose more than 150 per cent in the period. . . . There has been a radical distribution of income in favor of wealthier economic sectors." Also: "Brazil's agriculture expands fast, but mostly for benefit of well-to-do," *New York Times,* 16 August 1976, p. 2. For the statistic on malnutrition see the World Bank Country Study, *Brazil: Human Resources Special Report* (Washington, D.C.: The World Bank, 1979), p. 61 of Annex 3.

[8]"Trade with Justice," BFW Background Paper, no. 67 (August 1983):4.

[9]Theodore Morgan, *Economic Development: Concept and Strategy* (New York: Harper & Row, 1976), p. 205. See pp. 167-90 for an excellent overview of the effects of malnutrition. See also *World Development Report 1981,* pp. 182-83, for statistical references.

[10]Kathleen Newland, *Infant Mortality and the Health of Societies,* Worldwatch Paper, no.

47 (December 1981):15.

[11]The rumor at the World Bank is that the Brazilian government will not release the distributional data because it does not like the numbers.

[12]This data comes from the *World Development Report 1980*, pp. 111, 143, 157. Distribution data, population data and GNP data are used to come up with the average income figures for the respective classes.

[13]W. Stanley Mooneyham, *What Do You Say to a Hungry World?* (Waco, Tex.: Word Books, 1975), pp. 38-39.

[14]1974 Production Year Book of the FAO (Rome: FAO, 1975), pp. 25-26, 29-30.

[15]John W. Sewell et al., *The United States and World Development: Agenda 1977* (London: Praeger, 1977), p. 188. Calculations from the table on p. 188 show that the price of nitrogenous fertilizer rose by 230 per cent from 1972 to 1974. Phosphate rose by 127 per cent, potash by 40 per cent. The weighted average price rise was 150 per cent.

[16]John W. Sewell et al., *The United States and World Development: Agenda 1980* (New York: Praeger, 1980), p. 60; Sewell's emphasis.

[17]Lester R. Brown, *In the Human Interest* (New York: Norton, 1974), pp. 55-56.

[18]Larry Minear, *New Hope for the Hungry?* (New York: Friendship Press, 1975), p. 19.

[19]Grant, *State of the World's Children*, p. 1.

[20]Quoted in Brown, *In the Human Interest*, p. 102. See also World Health Organization, Ruth Rice Puffer and Carlo V. Serrano, *Patterns of Mortality in Childhood: Report of the Inter-American Investigation of Mortality in Childhood* (Pan-American Health Organization [regional office of WHO], Scientific Publication Series, no. 262), 1973, pp. 164-66.

[21]*Child of the Dark: The Diary of Carolina Maria de Jesus* (New York: Dutton, 1962), p. 42.

[22]Mooneyham, *Hungry World*, p. 48.

[23]Roger D. Hanson, ed., *U.S. Foreign Policy and the Third World: Agenda 1982* (New York: Praeger, 1982), pp. 155, 160.

[24]See the 1982 figures in World Health Organization, *Health Conditions in the Americas* (Pan-American Health Organization, Scientific Publication Series, no. 427).

[25]Ibid., p. 102.

[26]Mooneyham, *Hungry World*, p. 191.

[27]See Erik P. Eckholm, *Down to Earth: Environment and Human Needs* (New York: Norton, 1982), p. 37.

[28]Quoted in BFW *Newsletter*, July 1976. This issue has an excellent refutation of Hardin and Paddock's call for triage and lifeboat ethics.

[29]Donella H. Meadows et al., *The Limits to Growth*, 2d ed. (New York: Universe Books, 1974), p. 29.

[30]Ervin Laszlo et al., eds., *Goals for Mankind* (New York: Dutton, 1977); D. Gabor et al., eds., *Beyond the Age of Waste* (Elmsford, N.Y.: Pergamon Press, 1978); Wassily Leontief et al., *The Future of the World Economy: A United Nations Study* (New York: Oxford Univ. Press, 1977). This computer project, headed by U.S. economist (and Nobel Prize winner) Professor Wassily Leontief, concludes that there are adequate resources for continued economic growth in all nations for the foreseeable future.

[31]Robert L. Heilbroner, *An Inquiry into the Human Prospect* (New York: Norton, 1974), pp. 47-48.

[32]Ibid., p. 39.

[33]Ibid., pp. 42-43.

[34]Mooneyham, *Hungry World,* p. 50.

[35]Mark Hatfield, "World Hunger," *World Vision* 19 (February 1975):5.

[36]Quoted in Stephen Coats, "Hunger, Security and U.S. Foreign Policy," BFW Background Paper, no. 53 (May 1981).

[37]U.S., The Council on Environmental Quality and the Department of State, *Global 2000 Report to the President* (Washington, D.C.: Government Printing Office, 1980), 1:iv.

[38]*Philadelphia Inquirer,* 13 October 1974, p. 9b.

[39]Supplement to *Radar News,* January 1975, pp. 3-4.

[40]Compare Ronald J. Sider, "Where Have All the Liberals Gone?" *The Other Side* 12, no. 3 (May-June 1976):42-44.

Chapter 2: The Affluent Minority

[1]*Revolution through Peace* (New York: Harper & Row, 1971), p. 142.

[2]Ruth Leger Sivard, *World Military and Social Expenditures 1982* (Leesburg, Va.: World Priorities, 1982), p. 19.

[3]There are, however, several serious problems with using GNP as a standard for comparison:

a. GNP and GNP per capita say nothing about the distribution of income. A country with a certain GNP per capita that is evenly distributed may be much better off than a country with a much higher GNP per capita, but in which a small proportion of the population controls a disproportionately high share of the GNP.

b. Less developed economies are usually largely rural and may trade goods and services without using money. Although World Bank figures attempt to account for such contingencies, there is no doubt a wide margin of error in their statistics.

c. Since we are really interested in what each person can buy with his income, international comparisons can be quite difficult. Prices of similar goods and services are different in different countries. Haircuts, for example, may cost a lot in the United States, but they do not cost much in Kenya.

d. GNP figures may not be all that closely correlated with measures of welfare. If, for example, the government of Iran decides to produce a great stock of military equipment, the GNP may rise significantly, but it would be hard to argue that the people in Iran are better off.

[4]*Global 2000,* p. 13.

[5]James W. Howe et al., *The U.S. and World Development: Agenda for Action, 1975* (New York: Praeger, 1975), p. 166.

[6]*Newsweek,* 18 August 1975, p. 66. Irving B. Kravis et al., *A System of International Comparisons of Gross Product and Purchasing Power* (Baltimore: Johns Hopkins Univ. Press, 1975), esp. pp. 8-9.

[7]See chapter 6, pp. 25-32.

[8]Telephone conversation, 21 July 1983.

[9]At the same time we must remember that ruminants (cattle, sheep) unlike pigs can convert grass, hay and silage into protein. Marginal land unsuited for growing grain should certainly continue to be used to raise cattle.

[10]"Facts on Food," supplement to *Development Forum*, November 1974.

[11]Jean Mayer, "Heart Disease: Plans for Action," *U.S. Nutrition Policies in the Seventies* (San Francisco: W. H. Freeman and Co., 1973), p. 44.

[12]"How Much Is Enough?" *Consumer Reports* 38, no. 9 (1974):668.

[13]Quoted in Mooneyham, *Hungry World*, p. 184. For excellent suggestions toward more healthy eating patterns, see Doris Longacre, *More with Less Cookbook* (Scottdale, Pa.: Herald Press, 1976) and Frances Moore Lappé, *Diet for a Small Planet*, rev. ed. (New York: Ballantine, 1975).

[14]For the earlier figures, see Brown, *In the Human Interest*, p. 44. 1982 figures come from George Allen, agricultural economist, USDA; telephone conversation, 21 July 1983.

[15]Unpublished data from the National Health and Nutrition Examination Survey (1976-80) of the National Center for Health Statistics. 32% of all men and 36% of all women are 10% overweight. 16% of all men and 24% of all women are 20% overweight. (Telephone conversation, 9 August 1983, with Sidney Abraham, Chief, Nutrition Statistics Branch, National Center for Health Statistics.) See further "Overweight Adults in the United States," advance data, no. 51, 30 August 1979.

[16]According to the U.S. City Average Consumer Price Index for All Urban Consumers, All Items, of the U.S. Bureau of Labor, the consumer price index (based on 1967 as 100) was 146.9 in June 1974, and 298.1 in June 1983. Thus the inflation rate from 1974 to 1983 was 102.9%.

[17]"Middle Class? Not on $15,000 a Year," *Philadelphia Inquirer*, 28 October 1974, p. 9a.

[18]*Newsweek*, 21 September 1977, pp. 30-31. The 1977 dollar figures used in the article were $15,000, $18,000 and $25,000, which convert to the 1983 equivalents in the text since the per cent change in the CPI was 64%.

[19]*New York Times*, 12 July 1949. Quoted in Jules Henry, *Culture against Man* (New York: Random House, 1963), p. 19.

[20]Robert N. Bellah, *The Broken Covenant* (New York: Seabury Press, 1975), p. 133. See also Wilbur Schramm, Jack Lyle and Edwin B. Parker, *Television in the Lives of Our Children* (Stanford: Stanford Univ. Press, 1961).

[21]Richard K. Taylor, "The Imperative of Economic De-Development," *The Other Side* 10, no. 4 (July-August 1974):17. For the figures on advertising and education, see U.S. Bureau of the Census, *Statistical Abstract, 1982-83*, p. 566.

[22]Bellah, *Broken Covenant*, p. 134.

[23]*Newsweek*, 28 October 1974, p. 69; my emphasis.

[24]John V. Taylor, *Enough Is Enough* (London: SCM Press, 1975), p. 71.

[25]Vernard Eller, *The Mad Morality or the Ten Commandments Revisited* (New York: Abingdon, 1970), p. 70.

[26]Patrick Kerans, *Sinful Social Structures* (New York: Paulist Press, 1974), pp. 80-81.

[27]See the helpful comments on this in Art Gish, *Beyond the Rat Race* (Scottdale, Pa.: Herald Press, 1973), pp. 122-26.

[28]BFW *Newsletter*, May 1976, p. 1; Howe, *Agenda for Action, 1975*, p. 258.

[29]Paul A. Laudicina, *World Poverty and Development: A Survey of American Opinion* (Washington, D.C.: Overseas Development Council, 1973), p. 21.

[30]These statistics are obtained by adapting data on population and GNP per capita

found in *U.S. Statistical Abstracts 1982,* p. 421, and from foreign aid data found in
World Development Report 1982, pp. 140-41.

[31]Quoted in a supplement to the *UN Development Forum,* April 1976, p. 2.

[32]Aid as a percentage of GNP figure is taken from Lewis and Kallab, eds., *U.S. Foreign Policy and the Third World: Agenda 1983,* p. 273.

[33]*Economist,* 13 September 1980, pp. 27-28.

[34]Sivard, *World Military and Social Expenditures 1982,* p. 6.

[35]Sivard, *World Military and Social Expenditures 1981,* p. 6.

[36]Triage is any system used to allocate a scarce commodity, such as medical help or food, only to those whom it may help to survive and not to those who have no chance of surviving or who will survive without assistance.

[37]Garrett Hardin, "Lifeboat Ethics: The Case against Helping the Poor," *Psychology Today* 8, no. 4 (September 1974):38ff. See also William and Paul Paddock, *Famine 1975!* (Boston: Little, Brown and Co., 1967), reprinted in 1976 under the title *Time of Famines: America and the World Food Crisis.*

[38]Brown, *In the Human Interest,* pp. 113-14; my emphasis.

[39]Labor-intensive development uses people rather than machines (for example, dams can be built by five thousand people carrying ground and stones just as well as by two bulldozers and three earthmovers). Advocates of intermediate technology urge developing nations to move from, for example, the hoe to the ox-drawn plow rather than from the hoe to the huge tractor. See E. F. Schumacher, *Small Is Beautiful* (New York: Harper Torchbooks, 1973), esp. pp. 161-79.

[40]Howe, *Agenda for Action, 1975,* pp. 60-62.

[41]For short critiques of triage and lifeboat ethics, see Lester Brown, *The Politics and Responsibility of the North American Breadbasket,* Worldwatch Paper, no. 2 (October 1975), p. 36; and BFW *Newsletter,* July 1976.

[42]Robert H. Schuller, *Your Church Has Real Possibilities!* (Glendale, Calif.: Regal Books, 1974), p. 117.

Part Two: A Biblical Perspective on the Poor & Possessions

[1]Quoted in *Post-American* 1, no. 4 (Summer 1972), p. 1.

[2]Laudicina, *World Poverty and Development,* p. 21.

[3]Ronald J. Sider, ed., *Cry Justice: The Bible Speaks on Hunger and Poverty* (New York: Paulist Press; Downers Grove, Ill.: InterVarsity Press, 1980).

Chapter 3: God & the Poor

[1]See, for instance, Enzo Gatti, *Rich Church–Poor Church?* (Maryknoll, N.Y.: Orbis Books, 1974), p. 43. Liberation theology in general leans in this direction. For excellent evaluations of liberation theology, see J. Andrew Kirk, *Liberation Theology: An Evangelical View from the Third World* (Atlanta, Ga.: John Knox Press, 1980); and Harvie Conn's two excellent chapters (8 and 9) on liberation theology in Stanley N. Gundry and Alan F. Johnson, eds., *Tensions in Contemporary Theology* (Chicago: Moody Press, 1976).

[2]Ernst Bammel, "πτωχός," in Gerhard Kittell and Gerhard Friedrich, eds., *Theological Dictionary of the New Testament,* trans. Geoffrey W. Bromiley, 10 vols. (Grand Rapids, Mich.: Eerdmans, 1968), 6:888. Hereafter called *TDNT.*

[3]A. Gelin, *The Poor of Yahweh* (Collegeville, Minn.: Liturgical Press, 1964), pp. 19-20.

[4]See the helpful distinctions among those who are poor because of (1) sloth, (2) calamity, (3) exploitation, and (4) voluntary choice in R. C. Sproul, "Who Are the Poor?" *Tabletalk* 3, no. 6 (July 1979). See also the discussion of the "spiritual poor" below, n. 26.

[5]Unlike some liberation theologians who take the exodus merely as an inspirational device, I assert that in the exodus God was *both* liberating oppressed persons and *also* calling out a special people to be the recipients of his special revelation. Yahweh called forth a special people so that through them he could reveal his will and salvation for all people. But his will included, as he revealed even more clearly to his covenant people, that his people should follow him and be on the side of the poor and oppressed. The fact that Yahweh did not liberate all poor Egyptians at the exodus does not mean that he was not concerned for the poor everywhere any more than the fact that he did not give the Ten Commandments to everyone in the Near East means that he did not intend them to have universal application. Because God chose to reveal himself in history, he disclosed to particular people at particular points in time what he willed for all people everywhere.

[6]John Bright,*A History of Israel* (Philadelphia: Westminster Press, 1959), pp. 240-41.

[7]Ibid.

[8]Roland de Vaux, *Ancient Israel* (New York: McGraw Hill, 1965), 2:72-73.

[9]So also in the case of Judah; compare Ezek 20, Jer 11:9-10.

[10]Preaching the gospel and seeking justice for the poor are *distinct, equally important* dimensions of the total mission of the church; see my "Evangelism, Salvation and Social Justice: Definitions and Interrelationships," *International Review of Mission*, July 1975, pp. 251ff. (esp. p. 258), and my "Evangelism or Social Justice: Eliminating the Options," *Christianity Today*, 8 October 1976, pp. 26-29.

[11]This is not to deny that a "spiritual" usage of the term *the poor* emerged in the intertestamental period. But even then, the material, economic foundation was never absent. See my "An Evangelical Theology of Liberation," in Kenneth S. Kantzer and Stanley N. Gundry, eds., *Perspectives on Evangelical Theology* (Grand Rapids, Mich.: Baker, 1979), pp. 122-24.

[12]See also Rev 7:16.

[13]Richard Batey, *Jesus and the Poor* (New York: Harper & Row, 1972), p. 7.

[14]Martin Hengel, *Property and Riches in the Early Church: Aspects of a Social History of Early Christianity* (Philadelphia: Fortress Press, 1974), p. 38.

[15]Batey, *Jesus and the Poor,* p. 6.

[16]See also Psalm 107:35-41. See chapter 5, p. 115, for a discussion of the different versions of the beatitudes in Matthew 5 and Luke 6.

[17]One dare not overlook, of course, the biblical teaching that obedience brings prosperity. See chapter 5, pp. 113-15, for a discussion of this theme.

[18]Bright, *History of Israel,* p. 306. For a similar event, see Daniel 4 (esp. v. 27).

[19]See also Mic 2:1-3.

[20]Joachim Jeremias, *The Parables of Jesus* (London: SCM Press, 1954), pp. 128-30, and others have argued that Jesus' point was an entirely different one. But I am still inclined to follow the usual interpretation; see, for instance, *The Interpreter's Bible,* 8:288-92.

[21]Ibid., p. 290.

[22]Clark H. Pinnock, "An Evangelical Theology of Human Liberation," *Sojourners,* February 1976, p. 31.

[23]"The Bible and the Other Side," *The Other Side* 11, no. 5 (September-October 1975): 57.

[24]See J. A. Motyer, *The Day of the Lion: The Message of Amos* (Downers Grove, Ill.: Inter-Varsity Press, 1974), pp. 129-37, for a good exegesis of these verses. See also Mic 6:6-8; Jas 2:14-17.

[25]That is not to say that God is unconcerned with true worship. Nor does Amos 5:21-24 mean that God is saying, "I do not want you to defend my rights, real or imaginary; I want you to struggle and expend your energies in advancing the rights of the poor and oppressed" (Gatti, *Rich Church–Poor Church?* p. 17). Such a dichotomy ignores the central prophetic attack on idolatry. God wants both worship and justice. Tragically, some people today concentrate on one, some on the other. Few seek both simultaneously.

[26]G. E. Ladd, *A Theology of the New Testament* (Grand Rapids, Mich.: Eerdmans, 1974), p. 133. For this whole topic of whether Matthew 25, 1 John 3 and so on must be limited in their application to Christians, see the superb discussion of Stephen C. Mott, *Biblical Ethics and Social Change* (New York: Oxford Univ. Press, 1982), pp. 34-36.

[27]God does not desire the salvation of the poor more than the salvation of the rich. I disagree strongly with Gatti's assertion: "They [the poor and oppressed] are the ones that have the best right to that word [of salvation]; they are the privileged recipients of the Gospel" (*Rich Church–Poor Church?* p. 43). God desires all people —oppressors and oppressed alike—to be saved. No one has any "right" to hear God's Word. We all deserve death. It is only by contrast with the sinful perversity of Christians who prefer to preach in the suburbs rather than the slums that Jesus and Paul seem to be biased in favor of preaching to the poor.

[28]For a more elaborate development of these points, see my "An Evangelical Theology of Liberation," pp. 117-20.

[29]See chap. 6, pp. 84-89.

[30]See my several articles on the resurrection listed in n. 2 of the epilog.

Chapter 4: Economic Relationships among the People of God
[1]Also Ezek 47:14. See the discussion and the literature cited in Mott, *Biblical Ethics and Social Change,* pp. 65-66; and Stephen Charles Mott, "Egalitarian Aspects of the Biblical Theory of Justice," in the *American Society of Christian Ethics, Selected Papers 1978,* ed. Max Stackhouse (Newton, Mass.: American Society of Christian Ethics, 1978), pp. 8-26.

[2]See the excellent book edited by Loren Wilkinson, *Earthkeeping: Christian Stewardship of Natural Resources,* 2d ed. (Grand Rapids, Mich.: Eerdmans, 1980), esp. pp. 232-37.

[3]See in this connection the fine article by Paul G. Schrotenboer, "The Return of Jubilee," *International Reformed Bulletin,* Fall 1973, pp. 19ff. (esp. pp. 23-24).

[4]See also Eph 2:13-18. Marc H. Tanenbaum points out the significance of the day of atonement in "Holy Year 1975 and Its Origins in the Jewish Jubilee Year," *Jubilaeum*

(1974), p. 64.

[5]For the meaning of the word *liberty* in Lev 25:10, see Martin Noth, *Leviticus* (Philadelphia: Westminster, 1965), p. 187: "Derōr, a 'liberation' . . . is a feudal word from the Accadian (an)durāru = 'freeing from burdens.' "

[6]Roland de Vaux reflects the scholarly consensus that Leviticus 25 "was a Utopian law and it remained a dead letter" (*Ancient Israel*, 1:177). Tanenbaum ("Holy Year 1975," pp. 75-76), on the other hand, thinks it was practiced. The only other certain references to it are in Lev 27:16-25, Num 36:4 and Ezek 46:17. It would be exceedingly significant if one could show that Is 61:1-2 (which Jesus cited to outline his mission in Lk 4:18-19) also refers to the year of jubilee. De Vaux doubts that Is 61:1 refers to the jubilee (*Ancient Israel*, 1:176). The same word, however, is used in Is 61:1 and Lev 25:10. See John H. Yoder's argument in *Politics of Jesus* (Grand Rapids, Mich.: Eerdmans, 1972), pp. 64-77; see also Robert Sloan, *The Acceptable Year of the Lord* (Austin, Tex.: Scholar Press, 1977); and Donald W. Blosser, "Jesus and the Jubilee" (Ph.D. diss., Univ. of St. Andrews, 1979).

[7]De Vaux, *Ancient Israel*, 1:173-75.

[8]Leviticus 25 seems to provide for emancipation of slaves only every fiftieth year. But the purpose is the same: prevention of ever greater inequality among God's people.

[9]See Jeremiah 34 for a fascinating account of God's anger at Israel for their failure to obey this command.

[10]Some modern commentators think that Deuteronomy 15:1-11 provides for a one-year suspension of repayment of loans rather than an outright remission of them. See S. R. Driver, *Deuteronomy*, International Critical Commentary, 3d ed. (Edinburgh: T. and T. Clark, 1895), pp. 179-80. But Driver's argument is basically that remission would have been *impractical*. He admits that v. 9 seems to point toward remission of loans. So too Gerhard von Rad, *Deuteronomy* (Philadelphia: Westminster, 1966), p. 106.

[11]See de Vaux, *Ancient Israel*, 1:174-75, for discussion of the law's implementation. In the Hellenistic period, there is clear evidence that it was put into effect.

[12]See also de Vaux, *Ancient Israel*, 1:165.

[13]This is an extremely complicated problem which has been debated throughout church history. The long dispute among Lutherans over the "third use of the law" is one example of the perennial debate.

[14]De Vaux, *Ancient Israel*, 1:171.

[15]See, ibid., p. 170; and Taylor, *Enough Is Enough*, pp. 56-60.

[16]Driver, *Deuteronomy*, p. 178.

[17]For a highly fascinating, scholarly account of the entire history, see Benjamin Nelson, *The Idea of Usury: From Tribal Brotherhood to Universal Otherhood*, 2d ed. (Chicago: Univ. of Chicago Press, 1969).

[18]See the excellent discussion by Bob Goudzwaard, *Capitalism and Progress: A Diagnosis of Western Society* (Grand Rapids, Mich.: Eerdmans, 1979).

[19]See Mt 4:23; 24:14; Mk 1:14-15; Lk 4:43; 16:16; and my "Evangelism, Salvation and Social Justice," pp. 251-67. Also, my "Words and Deeds," *Journal of Theology for Southern Africa*, Fall 1979, pp. 31-50.

[20]For this common interpretation, see Batey, *Jesus and the Poor*, pp. 3, 9, 100, n. 8; J. A. Ziesler, *Christian Asceticism* (Grand Rapids, Mich.: Eerdmans, 1973), p. 45; *TDNT*,

3:796; *Interpreter's Bible,* 8:655, 690; Carl Henry, "Christian Perspective on Private Property," in *God and the Good,* ed. C. Orlebeke and L. Smedes (Grand Rapids, Mich.: Eerdmans, 1975), p. 98.

[21]See also Batey, *Jesus and the Poor,* p. 8.

[22]Taylor, *Economics and the Gospel,* p. 21.

[23]See D. Guthrie et al., ed., *The New Bible Commentary Revised* (Grand Rapids, Mich.: Eerdmans, 1970), p. 980; Batey, *Jesus and the Poor,* p. 38.

[24]*TDNT,* 3:796.

[25]The key verbs are *epipraskon* and *diemerizon* (Acts 2:45) and *epheron* (Acts 4:34). See *Interpreter's Bible,* 9:52; Batey, *Jesus and the Poor,* pp. 33, 103, n. 9.

[26]Ziesler, *Christian Asceticism,* p. 110.

[27]Batey, *Jesus and the Poor,* pp. 36, 96-97.

[28]See Keith F. Nickle, *The Collection: A Study of Paul's Strategy,* Studies in Biblical Theology, no. 48 (Naperville, Ill.: Allenson, 1966), p. 29; and *Interpreter's Bible,* 9:153.

[29]See Diane MacDonald, "The Shared Life of the Acts Community," *Post-American,* July 1975, p. 28.

[30]See *Interpreter's Bible,* 9:150-52, for a summary of the reasons for accepting the reliability of this account.

[31]See Nickle, *The Collection,* pp. 68-69.

[32]See *TDNT,* 3:804ff.

[33]In fact, Paul was probably at Jerusalem to deliver the gift mentioned in Acts 11:27-30. See *Interpreter's Bible,* 9:151.

[34]See *TDNT,* 3:807-8.

[35]See also the striking use of *koinōnos* in Philemon 17-20. As fellow Christians, the slave Onesimus, his master Philemon and Paul are all partners *(koinōnoi).* This common fellowship means that Paul can ask Philemon to charge Onesimus' debt to his own account. But Paul and Philemon are also partners in Christ. Furthermore, Philemon owes Paul his very soul. Therefore, Paul suggests there is no need for anyone to reimburse Philemon. Their fellowship in Christ cancels any debt that Onesimus might otherwise owe. See *TDNT,* 3:807.

[36](The italics are mine.) Not all translations are accurate. But the Greek word *isotēs* clearly means "equality." So Charles Hodge: "The word *isotēs* means here neither reciprocity nor equity, but equality, as the illustration in verse 15 shows." *An Exposition of the Second Epistle to the Corinthians* (Grand Rapids, Mich.: Eerdmans, n.d.), p. 205. So too C. K. Barrett, *The Second Epistle to the Corinthians* (New York: Harper & Row, 1973), pp. 226-27; and the Tyndale commentary by R. V. G. Tasker, *The Second Epistle of Paul to the Corinthians* (Grand Rapids, Mich.: Eerdmans, 1958), p. 117.

[37]Quoted in Hengel, *Property and Riches in the Early Church,* pp. 42-43.

[38]Ibid., pp. 42-44.

[39]Quoted ibid., p. 45.

[40]On December 5, 1975, the *Wall Street Journal* reported that since 1971 a professional archaeologist had been measuring the amount of food thrown away in Tucson, Arizona. He discovered that the average family discards $100 worth of food each year (and that does not count food fed to pets or ground up in the garbage disposal. Assuming a family size of five, 236 million North Americans discard $4.7 billion worth of food each year. Using the figures on per capita GNP (1973) in

Roger D. Hansen, *Agenda for Action, 1976* (New York: Praeger, 1976), p. 146, I estimated (in 1976) that 120 million African Christians earned $25 billion annually. (I assumed 74 million at $150 per year; 45 million at $300; and 1 million at $1,000.)

[41]C. H. Jacquet, Jr., ed., *Yearbook of American and Canadian Churches: 1974* (New York: National Council of Churches, 1974), p. 263.

[42]See Helmut Gollwitzer, *The Rich Christians and Poor Lazarus*, trans. David Cairns (New York: Macmillan, 1970), p. 5; and Arthur C. Cochrane, *Eating and Drinking with Jesus* (Philadelphia: Westminster Press, 1974).

Chapter 5: A Biblical Attitude toward Property & Wealth

[1]So, correctly, Carl F. H. Henry, "Christian Perspective on Private Property," p. 97; Hengel, *Property and Riches in the Early Church*, p. 15.

[2]See further Emil Brunner, *Justice and the Social Order*, trans. Mary Hottinger (London: Lutterworth Press, 1945), pp. 42ff., 133ff.; and E. Clinton Gardner, *Biblical Faith and Social Ethics* (New York: Harper & Row, 1960), pp. 285-91.

[3]Adam Smith, *The Wealth of Nations* (1776; reprint ed., New York: Modern Library, 1937).

[4]See, for example, Gary North, "Free Market Capitalism," in *Wealth and Poverty: Four Christian Views of Economics*, ed. Robert G. Clouse (Downers Grove, Ill.: Inter-Varsity Press, 1984).

[5]See Goudzwaard, *Capitalism and Progress*.

[6]Henry, "Christian Perspective on Private Property," p. 97.

[7]Hengel, *Property and Riches in the Early Church*, p. 12.

[8]See Tony Cramp, "Cutting the Cake," *Third Way*, 28 July 1977, pp. 3-6.

[9]Walther Eichrodt, "The Question of Property in the Light of the Old Testament," in *Biblical Authority for Today*, ed. Alan Richardson and W. Schweitzer (London: SCM Press, 1951), p. 261.

[10]Ibid., p. 271.

[11]See further Gardner, *Biblical Faith and Social Ethics*, pp. 276-77.

[12]*Interpreter's Bible*, 7:320; see also 1 Tim 6:17-19.

[13]A. W. Argyle, *Matthew*, The Cambridge Bible Commentary (Cambridge: Cambridge Univ. Press, 1963), p. 58. So too *Interpreter's Bible*, 7:318.

[14]Camara, *Revolution through Peace*, pp. 142-43.

[15]*TDNT*, 6:271. Taylor (*Enough Is Enough*, p. 45) suggests that the word connotes "excess" or "wanting more and more."

[16]For a discussion of church discipline, see my "Watching Over One Another in Love," *The Other Side* 11, no. 3 (May-June 1975):13-20, 58-60 (esp. p. 59).

[17]For a good discussion of this issue, see Ziesler, *Christian Asceticism.*

[18]See the biblical texts in Sider, *Cry Justice*, pp. 175-87 for the former and pp. 148-53 for the latter.

[19]See Gordon D. Fee, "The New Testament View of Wealth and Possessions," *New Oxford Review* (May 1981):9: "It is only as one is righteous—i.e., walks in accordance with God's law—that one is promised the blessing of abundance and family. But to be righteous meant especially that one cared for or pleaded the cause of the poor and the oppressed."

[20]Taylor, *Enough Is Enough*, chap. 3.

[21]See further the twenty references in Batey, *Jesus and the Poor,* p. 92.

[22]Ziesler, *Christian Asceticism,* p. 52. See further my "An Evangelical Theology of Liberation," pp. 122-25.

[23]See chap. 1, p. 28, on Heilbroner's predictions.

Chapter 6: Structural Evil & World Hunger

[1]"Edison High School—A History of Benign and Malevolent Neglect," *Oakes Newsletter* 5, no. 4 (14 December 1973): 1-4; and "Northeast High Took the Glory Away," *Sunday Bulletin,* 27 January 1974, sect. 1, p. 3.

[2]Rodney Stark et al., "Sounds of Silence," *Psychology Today,* April 1970, pp. 38-41, 60-67.

[3]Bright, *History of Israel,* p. 241, n. 84.

[4]Compare Is 3:13-17.

[5]This is not to deny that the degree of responsibility and guilt has some relationship to the degree of one's awareness, understanding and conscious choice. See my more extended comments in "Racism," *United Evangelical Action* 36 (Spring 1977):11-12. At the same time, it is important to remember that we regularly *choose* not to learn more about topics that we know would challenge and demand a change in our current thinking and living. For an excellent, extended treatment of systemic evil (including a discussion of the Pauline concept of the "principalities and powers"), see Mott, *Biblical Ethics and Social Change,* chap. 1.

[6]Mooneyham, *Hungry World,* pp. 128, 117.

[7]See especially Piero Gheddo, *Why Is the Third World Poor?* (Maryknoll, N.Y.: Orbis Books, 1973).

[8]See chap. 1, n. 1; and Brandt, *North-South,* p. 90.

[9]Mahbub ul Haq, *The Poverty Curtain* (New York: Columbia Univ. Press, 1976), p. 162. For more on the impact of colonialism on the Third World, see Walter Rodney, *How Europe Underdeveloped Africa* (London: Bogle-L'Ouverture Pub., 1972). Rodney explains how European nations found culturally sophisticated African nations and under colonial practices gradually stripped them of their cultural, social and economic vitality. In a shorter but succinct case study, Cristobal Kay points out the injustices that prevailed during the first years of European contact in South America ("Comparative Development of the European Manorial System and the Latin American Hacienda System," *Journal of Peasant Studies* 2, no. 2 [January 1975]). Of course there is danger here in siding too much with Marxist scholars who explain all history in terms of class struggle, but there is equal danger in denying the importance of history as a crucial explanatory factor. P. T. Bauer, for example, in *Equality, the Third World, and Economic Delusion* (Cambridge, Mass.: Harvard Univ. Press, 1981), disregards history and argues instead that current economic inequalities are almost totally due to differences in ingenuity, effort and resource distribution rather than to historical misuses of political and economic power. But Bauer's extremism on the one side is just as wrong as the Marxist's extremism on the other. For a balanced criticism of Bauer from a rather traditional economist, see Amartya Sen, "Just Desserts," a review of Bauer's book in the *New York Review of Books,* 4 March 1982. It is also interesting to note that David Beckmann, a Christian economist working at the World Bank and author of the recent *Where Faith and Economics Meet*

(Minneapolis, Minn.: Augsburg Press, 1981), attributes much of Third World poverty to colonial and other exploitative practices.

[10] Gunnar Myrdal, *Asian Drama: An Inquiry into the Poverty of Nations,* 3 vols. (New York: Twentieth Century Fund, 1968), 1:455. See pp. 447-62 for a more extended analysis.

[11] For two divergent views about the origin and validity of the mercantilist spirit, see William Cunningham, "Medieval and Modern Economic Ideas Contrasted," *Growth of English Industry and Commerce,* 3 vols. (London: John Murray, 1910), 1:457-72; and G. Schmoller, *The Mercantile System and Its Historical Significance* (New York: Macmillan, 1895).

[12] James B. McGinnis, *Bread and Justice* (New York: Paulist Press, 1979), pp. 29-31.

[13] June Kronholz, "Gabon's Been Working on Its New Railroad, But Pay Day Is Far Off," *Wall Street Journal,* 30 July 1981, pp. 1ff.

[14] Most of the concern seems to derive from a studied awareness of our own self-interest. It is virtually impossible to "sell" American voters on a government program of aid, for example, unless it can be supported by reference to national self-interest.

[15] Joan Robinson, *Aspects of Development and Underdevelopment* (Cambridge: At the University Press, 1979).

[16] For a balanced summary, see Gheddo, *Why Is the Third World Poor?* pp. 69-100.

[17] Figures for Ecuador, Guyana and Honduras are taken from *Economic and Social Progress in Latin America,* 1978 Report of the Inter-American Development Bank, Washington, D.C. Figures for Kenya, the Philippines and the U.S. are taken from *U.S. Statistical Abstracts,* 1979, pp. 437, 442-51, 874, 907.

[18] For a careful discussion of how U.S. tariff structures discriminate against the exports of poor countries, see Guy F. Erb, "U.S. Trade Policies toward Developing Areas," *Columbia Journal of World Business* 8, no. 3 (Fall 1973):59-67.

[19] James P. Grant, "Can the Churches Promote Development?" *Ecumenical Review* 26 (January 1974):26.

[20] McGinnis, *Bread and Justice,* p. 72.

[21] "Brazil vs. the US," *New York Times,* 7 January 1968; "Brazil Agrees to Accept Terms," *Wall Street Journal,* 20 February 1968.

[22] Theodore Morgan, *Economic Development: Concept and Strategy* (New York: Harper & Row, 1975), p. 316.

[23] Quoted in McGinnis, *Bread and Justice,* p. 72.

[24] See, for example, W. Arthur Lewis, *The Evolution of the International Economic Order* (Princeton, N.J.: Princeton Univ. Press, 1978), pp. 23-24.

[25] Gheddo, *Why Is the Third World Poor?* p. 83.

[26] *New Internationalist,* August 1975, p. 1.

[27] *World Development Report 1982,* p. 28.

[28] See the chart showing the trend over the last 30 years, ibid., pp. 26-30. For a summary of other views, see John Spraos, "The Statistical Debate on the Net Barter Terms of Trade between Primary Commodities and Manufacturers," *Economic Journal* 90 (March 1980):107-28.

[29] Donald Hay, "The International Socio-Economic Political Order and Our Lifestyles," in *Lifestyle in the Eighties: An Evangelical Commitment to Simple Lifestyle,* ed.

Ronald Sider (Philadelphia: Westminster Press, 1982), p. 104.

[30]Hans W. Singer, *International Development: Growth and Change* (New York: McGraw Hill, 1964), p. 165.

[31]"Appointments in Santiago (I): Rough Sledding Ahead," *Journal of Commerce*, 27 March 1972, editorial.

[32]See United Nations, *A Study of the Problems of Raw Materials and Development* (A/9556, pt. 2), 1 May 1974; and *Newsweek*, 15 September 1975, pp. 38-40.

[33]Grant, "Can the Churches Promote Development?" p. 26.

[34]See, for example, W. M. Corden, *The NIEO Proposals: A Cool Look*, Thames Essay, no. 21 (London: Trade Policy Research Centre, 1979); and Herbert G. Grubel, "The Case against the New International Economic Order," *The Contemporary International Economy*, ed. John Adams (New York: St. Martin's Press, 1979). Grubel argues that while the NIEO may be politically appealing to small, poor countries, it would be economically harmful to them. He does not believe that either the developed, wealthy countries or multinational corporations possess any inordinate market power. His suggestion is that instead of setting up some huge bureaucratic system, the poor countries ought to encourage, with their own internal pricing policies or collective action in the UN, a more competitive international economic environment.

[35]Hay, "The International Socio-Economic Political Order," pp. 116-22, and Donald Hay, "North and South: The Economic Debate," in *The Year 2000*, ed. John R. W. Stott (Downers Grove, Ill.: InterVarsity Press, 1984).

[36]It is interesting to note that, in 1975, then-Secretary of State Henry Kissinger proposed nine new international agencies to aid the poorer nations. Further, he promised to give poor nations preferential import tariffs for their goods. But in reporting the substance behind the proposals, *Newsweek* noted that "Kissinger's expectations, . . . *in fact his hope*, . . . is that negotiations will stretch out over months and perhaps years" (*Newsweek*, 15 September 1975, p. 45; my emphasis).

[37]For a summary of the details of the nearly finalized treaty, see S. P. Jagota, "Developments in the UN Conference on the Law of the Sea," *Third World Quarterly* 3, no. 2 (April 1981):286-319. See also "Sea-Law Conference Begins Final Phase," *UN Chronicle* 18 (May 1981); and *Newsweek*, 23 March 1981.

[38]Willy Brandt, *North-South: A Program for Survival*. For a review of the report and its initial impact, see Miguel S. Wionczek, "The Brandt Report," *Third World Quarterly* 3, no. 1 (January 1981):104-18; or John P. Lewis, "Shaking Loose from a Difficult Year," *OECD Observer*, no. 107 (November 1980):6-13.

[39]"End of Dialogue?" *Third World Quarterly* 4, no. 2 (April 1982):xii. For a further evaluation of Cancun, see *Cancun: A Candid Evaluation*, produced by the Roundtable Secretariat of the North-South Roundtable, 1717 Massachusetts Ave., N.W., Washington, D.C. 20036.

[40]Mooneyham, *Hungry World*, pp. 117-18.

[41]*Newsweek*, 10 December 1979, p. 98.

[42]Brown, *In the Human Interest*, p. 92.

[43]This is a study commissioned by President Carter in 1977. Its purpose was to develop an integrated study of long-range environmental change, with a view to policy and program adjustment in light of significant findings.

[44]*Global 2000,* 1:iii.

[45]Here the report is consistent with a similar report done by Interfutures. This report is summarized in "Are There Physical Limits to Growth?" *OECD Observer,* no. 100 (September 1979).

[46]*Global 2000,* 1:36.

[47]E. F. Schumacher, "Implication of the Limits to Growth Debate—Small Is Beautiful," *Anticipation,* no. 13 (December 1972):14.

[48]Lester C.Thurow in his book *The Zero-Sum Society* (New York: Basic Books, 1980) argues that an end to growth will disproportionately hurt the people of the United States that can least afford it. He further argues that under the present structures of society and the economy, it is unrealistic to argue for immediately ending growth because the system could not bear the stress of major structural change.

[49]Georg Borgstrom, *The Hungry Planet* (New York: Collier-Macmillan, 1967), esp. chap. 1; and "Present Food Production and the World Food Crisis," mimeographed paper presented 2 September 1974.

[50]Borgstrom, "Present Food Production," p. 3.

[51]Simon, *Bread for the World,* pp. 19-20.

[52]Borgstrom, "Present Food Production," p. 12.

[53]For a summary of this entire process, see part 3 of Frances Moore Lappé and Joseph Collins, *Food First* (Boston: Houghton Mifflin, 1977).

[54]Quoted ibid., p. 77.

[55]Borgstrom, "Present Food Production," p. 12.

[56]Grant, "Can the Churches Promote Development?" p. 24.

[57]Beverly Keene, "Export-Cropping in Central America," BFW Background Paper, no. 43 (January 1980):1.

[58]*World Development Report 1980,* p. 157. These figures (1977) seem to be the most recent available—see Lewis and Kallab, eds., *U.S. Foreign Policy and the Third World: Agenda 1983,* p. 228.

[59]The data for this section on Central American exports comes from Keene, "Export-Cropping in Central America."

[60]Data for the following is in Ricki Ross, "Land and Hunger: Philippines," BFW Background Paper, no. 55 (July 1981).

[61]Michael P. Todaro, *Economic Development in the Third World* (New York: Longman, 1977), p. 326.

[62]Joseph La Palombara and Stephen Blank, *Multinational Corporations and Developing Countries,* report no. 767 (New York: The Conference Board, 1979), p. 5.

[63]Todaro, *Economic Development,* pp. 328-29.

[64]Richard J. Barnet, "Multinationals and Development," *New Catholic World* 222, no. 1325 (September-October 1978):222. See also Richard J. Barnet, and Ronald Müller, *Global Reach: The Power of the Multinational Corporations* (New York: Simon & Schuster, 1974).

[65]Streeten and Lall (as noted in Hay, "International Socio-Economic Political Order," p. 113) found in their sampling of MNC investments in LDCs that only 12 per cent of new capital investment represented an inflow of funds from outside the LDCs.

[66]Hay, "International Socio-Economic Political Order," p. 84.

[67]Barnet, "Multinationals and Development," p. 225.

⁶⁸Ibid., p. 224; also mentioned by Hay, "International Socio-Economic Political Order," p. 113.

⁶⁹Ivan Illich ("Outwitting the 'Developed' Countries," in *The Political Economy of Development and Underdevelopment*, ed. Charles K. Wilber [New York: Random House, 1979], pp. 436-44) is a development ethicist who is particularly galled by the proliferation of soft drinks in the LDCs.

⁷⁰Grant, *The State of the World's Children 1982-83*, pp. 3-4. On the Nestlé boycott, see chap. 9, n. 9.

⁷¹H. W. Walter, "Marketing in Developing Countries," *Columbia Journal of World Business* (Winter 1974), quoted in Lappé and Collins, *Food First*, p. 309.

⁷²Todaro, *Economic Development*, p. 330; Todaro's emphases.

⁷³Hay, "International Socio-Economic Political Order," p. 123.

⁷⁴*Markings* (New York: Knopf, 1964), p. xxi.

⁷⁵*Philadelphia Inquirer*, 10 April 1975, pp. 1-2.

⁷⁶See "Bananas," *New Internationalist*, August 1975, p. 2.

⁷⁷"Action," *New Internationalist*, August 1975, p. 32.

⁷⁸Carl Oglesby and Richard Schaull, *Containment and Change* (New York: Macmillan, 1967), p. 104; and Stephen Schlesinger and Stephen Kinzer, *Bitter Fruit: The Untold Story of the American Coup in Guatemala* (Garden City, N.Y.: Doubleday, 1982).

⁷⁹See, for instance, Ronald J. Sider, "Love, Freedom, Justice? Nicaragua," *Report from the Capitol*, March 1983, pp. 10-12. For a superb historical overview of the way the United States has frequently interfered and supported repressive dictatorship in Nicaragua, see the book by evangelical historian Richard Millett, *Guardians of the Dynasty: A History of the U.S. Created Guardia Nacional De Nicaragua and the Somoza Family* (Maryknoll, N.Y.: Orbis Books, 1977).

⁸⁰See, for instance, Schlesinger and Kinzer, *Bitter Fruit*.

⁸¹"America's World Role: Should We Feel Guilty?" *Philadelphia Inquirer*, 18 July 1974, p. 7a.

⁸²See the helpful comments on this in Patrick Kerans, *Sinful Social Structures* (New York: Paulist Press, 1974), pp. 47-51.

Chapter 7: The Graduated Tithe & Other Less Modest Proposals

¹Ronald J. Sider, ed., *The Chicago Declaration* (Carol Stream, Ill.: Creation House, 1974), p. 2.

²J. D. Douglas, ed., *Let the Earth Hear His Voice: International Congress on World Evangelization, Lausanne, Switzerland* (Minneapolis: World Wide Pub., 1975), p. 6, sect. 9.

³"Creation, Technology, and Human Survival," Plenary Address, WCC's Fifth Assembly, 1 December 1975. This is a recent rendition of Elizabeth Seton's statement "Live simply that others may simply live."

⁴*New York Times*, 14 June 1973.

⁵This sermon was one of the series of sermons which constituted the standard doctrines of the early Methodists. See *The Works of John Wesley*, 14 vols. (1872; reprint ed., Grand Rapids, Mich.: Zondervan, n.d.), 5:361-77.

⁶Ibid., pp. 365-68.

⁷J. Wesley Bready, *England: Before and After Wesley* (London: Hodder and Stoughton, n.d.), p. 238.

[8]See Donella H. Meadows et al., *Limits to Growth*, p. 165.

[9]The U.S. Bureau of Labor Statistics reported that on April 30, 1975, the Federal Employment and Training Administration defined the (nonfarm) poverty level (and therefore the cut-off level for its programs) as $2,590 for a one-person family plus $820 for each additional person. See also BFW *Newsletter*, March 1976, p. 1.

[10]Michael Harper, *A New Way of Living* (Plainfield, N.J.: Logos International, 1973), p. 93. The early leader of the church, W. Graham Pulkingham, has written two books about Church of the Redeemer: *Gathered for Power* (New York: Morehouse-Barlow, 1972) and *They Left Their Nets* (New York: Morehouse-Barlow, 1973).

[11]Doris Longacre, *Living More with Less* (Scottdale, Pa.: Herald Press, 1980). See also the personal testimonies in Ronald J. Sider, ed., *Living More Simply: Biblical Principles and Practical Models* (Downers Grove, Ill.: InterVarsity Press, 1980), pp. 59-159.

[12]See Gene M. Daffern, "One Man Can Make a Difference," *These Times*, September 1982, pp. 6-11.

[13]See his moving testimony, "From Galloping Gourmet to Serving the Poor," in *Lifestyles in the Eighties*, pp. 174-82. For his new program, write to International Quality of Life Center, 505 Broadway, Tacoma, WA 98402.

[14]Ginny Hearn and Walter Hearn, "The Price Is Right," *Right On*, May 1973, pp. 1, 11.

[15]See my suggestions on this in "Living More Simply for Evangelism and Justice," in *Lifestyle in the Eighties*, pp. 32-35.

[16]These are included ibid., pp. 35-36.

[17]Lester R. Brown with Erik P. Eckholm, *By Bread Alone* (New York: Praeger, 1974), p. 198.

[18]The figure for grain used in making alcoholic beverages is from the U.S. Department of Agriculture. One ton of grain will feed five persons in India for a year.

[19]See Ron W. Jones, Julia Cheever and Ferry Ficklin, *Finding Community* (Palo Alto, Calif.: James E. Freel and Associates, 1971), pp. 48-50. Or visit the local welfare office!

[20]C. Dean Freudenberger and Paul M. Minus, Jr., *Christian Responsibility in a Hungry World* (Nashville: Abingdon, 1976), pp. 86-87.

[21]I owe much to John F. Alexander in the development of these criteria.

[22]Criteria *a, c, d* and *f* are adapted from Edward R. Dayton, "Where to Go from Here," Fuller Seminary's *Theology News and Notes*, October 1975, p. 19.

[23]Quoted from a fund-raising piece by Jubilee Fund (see Appendix); my emphasis.

[24]*Christianity Today*, 10 May 1974, pp. 32-33.

[25]Howe, *Agenda for Action, 1975*, p. 69.

[26]Minear, *New Hope for the Hungry*, p. 79.

Chapter 8: Watching Over One Another in Love

[1]Dave Jackson and Neta Jackson, *Living Together in a World Falling Apart* (Carol Stream, Ill.: Creation House, 1974), p. 15.

[2]See above, chap. 4, pp. 86-98.

[3]See my "Spare the Rod and Spoil the Church," *Eternity*, October 1976.

[4]From John Wesley's account (1743) of the origin of the class meetings *(The Works*

of John Wesley, 8:269).

⁵Peter Berger, *A Rumor of Angels* (Garden City, N.Y.: Anchor Books, 1970), p. 34 (also pp. 6-37). See also Peter Berger and Thomas Luckman, *The Social Construction of Reality* (Garden City, N.Y.: Doubleday, 1966).

⁶Berger, *A Rumor of Angels,* p. 17. See further pp. 41ff. for Berger's rejection of the common idea that the sociology of knowledge leads inexorably to thoroughgoing relativism.

⁷See Floyd Filson, "The Significance of the Early House Churches," *Journal of Biblical Literature* 58 (1939):105-12. See also the brief overview in John W. Miller's (mimeographed) "House Church Handbook." For a copy, write to John Miller, Conrad Grebel College, University of Waterloo, Waterloo, Ont., Canada.

⁸Personal conversation with John Poole. For further information or cassette tapes, write to Living Word Community, 142 N. 17th St., Philadelphia, PA 19143.

⁹I have relied largely on Gordon Cosby's *Handbook for Mission Groups* (Waco, Tex.: Word Books, 1975) for this discussion. See also Elizabeth O'Connor's several books about or for Church of the Savior, including: *Call to Commitment* (New York: Harper & Row, 1963); *Journey Inward, Journey Outward* (New York: Harper & Row, 1968). For further information, write to: Church of the Savior, 2025 Massachusetts Ave., N.W., Washington, D.C. 20036.

¹⁰Cosby, *Handbook for Mission Groups,* p. 63.

¹¹Ibid., p. 140.

¹²For further information about Dunamis, write to Dunamis Vocations Church, 2025 Massachusetts Ave., N.W., Washington, D.C. 20036. [(202) 387-1234]

¹³Howard A. Snyder, *The Problem of Wineskins: Church Structure in a Technological Age* (Downers Grove, Ill.: InterVarsity Press, 1975), pp. 140-42. See also his more recent *Liberating the Church: The Ecology of Church and Kingdom* (Downers Grove, Ill.: InterVarsity Press, 1983).

¹⁴For a discussion of Reba Place, see Jackson and Jackson, *Living Together in a World Falling Apart,* esp. pp. 36-39, 230-33. For the names and addresses of 24 communities, see their pp. 287-97.

¹⁵Ibid., p. 183.

¹⁶Ibid., p. 65.

¹⁷For a good historical perspective on Christian communes and an excellent bibliography, see Donald G. Bloesch, *Wellsprings of Renewal: Promise in Christian Communal Life* (Grand Rapids, Mich.: Eerdmans, 1974). For a handbook by a Catholic charismatic, see Stephen B. Clark, *Building Christian Communities* (Notre Dame, Ind.: Ave Maria Press, 1972).

Chapter 9: Structural Change

¹From an article in *Our Hope* 10, no. 2 (August 1903):76-77.

²See, for example, Clouse, ed., *Wealth and Poverty: Four Christian Views.*

³See most recently my *Nuclear Holocaust and Christian Hope* (Downers Grove, Ill.: InterVarsity Press, 1982), coauthored with Richard K. Taylor, and earlier my *Christ and Violence* (Scottdale, Pa.: Herald Press, 1978).

⁴See, for instance, Oglesby and Shaull, *Containment and Change,* pp. 72-111, and the books on Nicaragua and Guatemala also cited in chapter 6, notes 78 and 79.

[5]See Amnesty International, *Report on Torture* (New York: Farrar, Straus, and Giroux, 1975), especially the special report on Chile on pp. 243ff. See also Fred B. Morris, "Sustained by Faith under Brazilian Torture," *Christian Century,* 22 January 1975, pp. 56-60; *Latin America and Empire Report* 10, no. 1 (January 1976); and BFW Background Papers, no. 54 (June 1981) on El Salvador and no. 60 (June 1982) on "Military Aid, the World's Poor and U.S. Security."

[6]U.S. firms have 55 per cent of the assets of MNCs and British firms 20 per cent. Hay, "The International Socio-Economic Order," p. 111.

[7]See, most recently, Grant, *The State of the World's Children, 1982-83,* pp. 3-4.

[8]"The Breast vs. the Bottle," *Newsweek,* 1 June 1981, p. 54.

[9]This is not to argue that the total impact of MNCs is negative. For information on the Nestlé boycott and analyses of its impact, write to the Interfaith Centre on Corporate Responsibility (475 Riverside Drive, New York, NY 10027) and Infant Formula Action Coalition (INFACT), 1701 University Ave., S.E., Minneapolis, MN 55414.

[10]Robert E. Frykenberg, ed., *Land Tenure and Peasant in South Asia: An Anthology of Recent Research* (Madison, Wis.: Land Tenure Center, 1976), p. 14.

[11]See the interesting Indian case study, Saral K. Chatterji, *Religious Values and Economic Development: A Case Study,* Social Research Series, no. 5 (Bangalore: Christian Institute for the Study of Religion and Society, 1967).

[12]See, for example, page 6 in chapter 1 and corresponding notes 7 and 8.

[13]See, for example, Norman Faramelli, "Trade Barriers to Development in Poor Nations," in *The Causes of World Hunger,* ed. William Byron (New York: Paulist Press, 1982), chap. 9.

[14]Quoted in Ernest Loevinsohn, "Getting Aid to the Poor," BFW Background Paper, no. 59 (April 1982):2.

[15]See Denis Goulet, *The Cruel Choice* (New York: Atheneum, 1971), pp. 123-52.

[16]Paul Streeten, "A Basic-Needs Approach to Economic Development," in *Directions in Economic Development,* ed. Kenneth P. Jameson and Charles K. Wilber (Notre Dame, Ind.: Univ. of Notre Dame Press, 1979), p. 74.

[17]The actions of the Reagan administration make it clear that their primary concerns are the interest of U.S. businesses and military objectives, not the concept of Basic Needs Development. In fact, a report circulates that anyone at the U.S. Agency for International Development who mentions the concept of Basic Needs Development (popular in the Carter years) is in danger of losing his job.

[18]McGinnis, *Bread and Justice,* p. 261. Of course, to the extent that a nation's traditional values hinder development, Christians will want to share biblical values in a nonpaternalistic but forthright fashion.

[19]Mahbub ul Haq, as quoted ibid., p. 262. See also the discussion of self-reliance in Jack A. Nelson, *Hunger for Justice: The Politics of Food and Faith* (New York: Orbis Books, 1980), esp. pp. 159-80.

[20]Examples of successful Basic Needs Programs are the health program in the state of Kerala, India, as discussed by Streeten, "A Basic-Needs Approach," pp. 109-14; the village of Patti Kalyana's comprehensive program as reported in McGinnis, *Bread and Justice,* pp. 265-77; and the Sarvodaya Shramadana Movement in Sri Landa as discussed in *World Development Report 1980,* p. 75.

²¹Guy F. Erb, "U.S. Trade Policies toward Developing Areas," *Columbia Journal of World Business,* no. 3 (Fall 1973):60.

²²Brandt, *North-South,* p. 186. For some alternatives to trade adjustment assistance, see chapter 11 by George R. Neumann in *International Trade and Finance: Readings,* ed. Robert E. Baldwin and David J. Richardson, 2d ed. (Boston, Mass.: Little, Brown & Co., 1981).

²³"Hunger and Global Security," BFW Background Paper, no. 48 (February 1981):4.

²⁴*Chicago Tribune,* 6 July 1983, p. 16. I am not arguing here that the Caribbean Basin Initiative is a good program in its entirety. Other portions of the initiative, in particular the tax incentive to U.S. business, promote exactly the sort of economic structures that created many of the problems for countries of this region in the first place. For a careful assessment, see BFW Background Paper, no. 61 (July 1982) by John P. Olinger. Bread for the World did succeed in including in this legislation a Stable Food Production plan that is designed to ensure that increased production of sugar and beef for export does not harm the nutritional health of people in the region or increase concentration of land ownership (see BFW *Newsletter,* August 1983, p. 3).

²⁵Morgan, *Economic Development,* p. 320.

²⁶See the helpful analysis and recommendations in Olinger, "Trade with Justice."

²⁷*Time,* 22 December 1975, p. 22.

²⁸BFW *Newsletter,* June 1976.

²⁹Brandt, *North-South,* p. 150.

³⁰Olinger, "Trade with Justice," p. 3.

³¹Brandt, *North-South,* p. 150.

³²See the *Global 2000* study, which presents in detail the reasons the carrying capacity of the earth is under severe strain.

³³Thurow, *Zero-Sum Society,* pp. 103-7.

³⁴Bob Goudzwaard in *Capitalism and Progress* carefully traces the development of the corrupted notion of progress from its inception in the Enlightenment to the present.

³⁵Richard A. Easterlin, "Does Money Buy Happiness?" *The Public Interest,* no. 3 (Winter 1973):10. See also Martin Bolt and David G. Myers, "Why Do the Rich Feel So Poor?" in *The Human Connection* (Downers Grove, Ill.: InterVarsity Press, 1984).

³⁶See the emphasis on increasing personal services in Robert L. Stivers, *The Sustainable Society: Ethics and Economic Growth* (Philadelphia: Westminster, 1976). For a different view, see Simon Webley, "Can Christians Support Economic Growth as a Policy Objective?" *Christian Graduate,* March 1977, pp. 1-5. Roland Hoksbergen disagrees with Webley: "The Morality of Economic Growth," *Reformed Journal* 32, no. 12 (December 1982):10-13.

³⁷Wilkinson, ed., *Earthkeeping.*

³⁸Ibid., p. 273; their emphasis.

³⁹Ibid., p. 275; their emphasis.

⁴⁰I have benefited here from an unpublished BFW document prepared by Lorette Picciano-Hanson called "An Approach to World Food Security."

⁴¹Ibid.

⁴²Brown, *Politics and Responsibility of the North American Breadbasket,* p. 6; my emphasis.

[43]*Hunger*, June 1976, p. 3. *Hunger* is an occasional newsletter published by Interfaith Action for Economic Justice, 100 Maryland Ave., Washington, D.C. 20002.

[44]See the excellent discussion in Jayne Millar-Wood, "Food Insecurity: The Inadequacy and Unreliability of Reserves," *The Causes of World Hunger*, ed. William Byron (New York: Paulist Press, 1982), pp. 121-37.

[45]Ibid., p. 129.

[46]Ibid., p. 130.

[47]See, for instance, Frances Moore Lappé, *Aid as Obstacle: Twenty Questions about Our Foreign Aid and the Hungry* (San Francisco: Institute for Food and Development Policy, 1980). See also James A. Cogswell's excellent summary of both views in his "Crisis of Confidence in U.S. Aid to Poor Nations," in *The Causes of World Hunger*, ed. William Byron (New York: Paulist Press, 1982), pp. 141-45.

[48]Ernest Loevinsohn, "Making Foreign Aid More Effective," BFW Background Paper, no. 49 (March 1981).

[49]See above, chap. 1.

[50]Timothy King, ed., *Population Policies and Economic Development*, published for the World Bank (Baltimore: Johns Hopkins Univ. Press, 1974), p. 54. See also William Rich, *Smaller Families through Social and Economic Progress*, monograph, no. 7 (Washington, D.C.: Overseas Development Council, 1973), esp. p. 76.

[51]See the fascinating story of BFW's success on this legislation in BFW *Newsletter*, January 1983, pp. 1-2.

[52]James A. Cogswell, "Crisis of Confidence in U.S. Aid to Poor Nations," in *The Causes of World Hunger*, ed. William Byron (New York: Paulist Press, 1982), p. 155.

[53]Ibid., p. 154.

[54]As its dealings with Israel demonstrate, however, the UN is not free of inappropriate "politicizing" of issues.

[55]BFW *Newsletter*, July 1983.

[56]Simon, *Bread for the World*, p. 113.

[57]Streeten, "A Basic Needs Approach to Economic Development," p. 103.

[58]Brandt, *North-South*, p. 228.

[59]See table 10, p. 42.

[60]Michael J. Strauss, "Industrial Nations at UNCTAD Session Refuse to Grant Fresh Aid to Developing Nations," *Wall Street Journal*, 5 July 1983, p. 27.

[61]The data for this and the preceding paragraph comes from Stephen Coats, "Military Spending and World Hunger."

[62]Quoted in Simon, *Bread for the World*, p. 170.

[63]Cogswell, "Crisis of Confidence," p. 158.

[64]Cited from the report of the Presidential Commission on World Hunger in "Hunger and Global Security," p. 1.

[65]Ibid.

[66]For example, Donald A. Hay, *A Christian Critique of Capitalism*, Grove Booklet on Ethics, no. 5 (Bramcote, Nottingham: Grove Books, 1975); and Goudzwaard, *Capitalism and Progress*.

[67]Many liberation theologians advocate some form of socialism. See for instance Jose Miguez-Bonino, *Christians and Marxists* (Grand Rapids, Mich.: Eerdmans, 1976), and John Eagleson, ed., *Christians and Socialism: Documentation of the Christians for*

Socialism Movement in Latin America (Maryknoll, N.Y.: Orbis Books, 1975).

[68]Robert Benne, *The Ethic of Democratic Capitalism: A Moral Reassessment* (Philadelphia: Fortress Press, 1981); Michael Novak, *The Spirit of Democratic Capitalism* (New York: Simon and Schuster, 1982); and Michael Novak, "The Economic System: The Evangelical Basis of a Social Market Economy," *The Review of Politics* 43, no. 3 (July 1981):355-80.

[69]My own "layman's hunch" is that the right direction to grope for new solutions lies in some modification of the market economy and private "ownership." It is clear, I think, that collective agriculture is a disaster. Even more important, centralizing the ownership of property and the means of production in the state leads to such centralized power that totalitarianism is almost guaranteed. At the same time, "capitalist" MNCs have also centralized power to such a degree that political democracy is fundamentally threatened and workers have little participation in the decisions that affect their lives.

The jubilee and other biblical material point in the direction of decentralized ownership (or better stewardship under God, the only absolute owner). Farmers should normally own their own land. Smaller business enterprises should be encouraged. Industrial workers should be able to participate in the decisions affecting their own lives. (This can happen in a variety of ways: management-employee committees, cooperatives, and so on.) In order for persons to be co-creators of history with God in responsible freedom, decentralized stewardship of the earth's resources, not highly centralized state or MNC ownership, is necessary.

Epilog

[1]Robert Bellah says that "the quality of a culture may be changed when two percent of its people have a new vision" ("Civil Religion," *Psychology Today,* January 1976, p. 64).

[2]See my "A Case for Easter," *HIS,* April 1972, pp. 27-31. For a more extensive discussion, see also my "The Historian, the Miraculous and Post-Newtonian Man," *Scottish Journal of Theology* 25 (1972):309-19; "The Pauline Conception of the Resurrection Body in 1 Cor 15:35-54," *New Testament Studies* 21 (1975):428-39; "St. Paul's Understanding of the Nature and Significance of the Resurrection in 1 Cor 15:1-19," *Novum Testamentum* 19 (1977):1-18; and "Jesus' Resurrection and the Search for Peace and Justice," *Christian Century,* 3 November 1982, pp. 1103-8.

Topical
Index

Biblical Index

Evangelicals for Social Action (ESA) can help readers implement the concerns of this book. ESA is a national organization of committed Christians working to witness to the lordship of Jesus Christ in public life. Rejecting ideologies of left and right, ESA starts with biblical principles in an attempt to develop a thoroughly Christ-centered approach to a wide range of issues—the family, the nuclear arms race, abortion, hunger and economic justice.

With a national membership and local chapters around the country, ESA helps individuals solve large, complex problems by enabling them to link arms with others who share a biblical approach.

For more information on ESA, write me at Evangelicals for Social Action, P.O. Box 76560, Washington, D.C. 20013. Or call: (703) 237-7464.

Ronald J. Sider
President
Evangelicals for Social Action